Casenote™ *Legal Briefs*

COMMUNITY PROPERTY

Keyed to Courses Using

Bird's
California Community Property

Ninth Edition

Law & Business

AUSTIN   BOSTON   CHICAGO   NEW YORK   THE NETHERLANDS

© 2009 Aspen Publishers, Inc. All Rights Reserved.
a Wolters Kluwer business
http://lawschool.aspenpublishers.com

To contact Customer Care, e-mail customer.care@aspenpublishers.com, call 1-800-234-1660, fax 1-800-901-9075, or mail correspondence to:

Aspen Publishers
Attn: Order Department
P.O. Box 990
Frederick, MD 21705

Printed in the United States of America.

1 2 3 4 5 6 7 8 9 0

ISBN 978-0-7355-8590-4

About Wolters Kluwer Law & Business

Wolters Kluwer Law & Business is a leading provider of research information and workflow solutions in key specialty areas. The strengths of the individual brands of Aspen Publishers, CCH, Kluwer Law International and Loislaw are aligned within Wolters Kluwer Law & Business to provide comprehensive, in-depth solutions and expert-authored content for the legal, professional and education markets.

CCH was founded in 1913 and has served more than four generations of business professionals and their clients. The CCH products in the Wolters Kluwer Law & Business group are highly regarded electronic and print resources for legal, securities, antitrust and trade regulation, government contracting, banking, pension, payroll, employment and labor, and health-care reimbursement and compliance professionals.

Aspen Publishers is a leading information provider for attorneys, business professionals and law students. Written by preeminent authorities, Aspen products offer analytical and practical information in a range of specialty practice areas from securities law and intellectual property to mergers and acquisitions and pension/benefits. Aspen's trusted legal education resources provide professors and students with high-quality, up-to-date and effective resources for successful instruction and study in all areas of the law.

Kluwer Law International supplies the global business community with comprehensive English-language international legal information. Legal practitioners, corporate counsel and business executives around the world rely on the Kluwer Law International journals, loose-leafs, books and electronic products for authoritative information in many areas of international legal practice.

Loislaw is a premier provider of digitized legal content to small law firm practitioners of various specializations. Loislaw provides attorneys with the ability to quickly and efficiently find the necessary legal information they need, when and where they need it, by facilitating access to primary law as well as state-specific law, records, forms and treatises.

Wolters Kluwer Law & Business, a unit of Wolters Kluwer, is headquartered in New York and Riverwoods, Illinois. Wolters Kluwer is a leading multinational publisher and information services company.

Format for the Casenote Legal Brief

Nature of Case: This section identifies the form of action (e.g., breach of contract, negligence, battery), the type of proceeding (e.g., demurrer, appeal from trial court's jury instructions) or the relief sought (e.g., damages, injunction, criminal sanctions).

Party ID: Quick identification of the relationship between the parties.

Palsgraf v. Long Island R.R. Co.

Injured bystander (P) v. Railroad company (D)

N.Y. Ct. App., 248 N.Y. 339, 162 N.E. 99 (1928).

Fact Summary: This is included to refresh your memory and can be used as a quick reminder of the facts.

NATURE OF CASE: Appeal from judgment affirming verdict for plaintiff seeking damages for personal injury.

FACT SUMMARY: Helen Palsgraf (P) was injured on R.R.'s (D) train platform when R.R.'s (D) guard helped a passenger aboard a moving train, causing his package to fall on the tracks. The package contained fireworks which exploded, creating a shock that tipped a scale onto Palsgraf (P).

Rule of Law: Summarizes the general principle of law that the case illustrates. It may be used for instant recall of the court's holding and for classroom discussion or home review.

🏛 RULE OF LAW
The risk reasonably to be perceived defines the duty to be obeyed.

FACTS: Helen Palsgraf (P) purchased a ticket to Rockaway Beach from R.R. (D) and was waiting on the train platform. As she waited, two men ran to catch a train that was pulling out from the platform. The first man jumped aboard, but the second man, who appeared as if he might fall, was helped aboard by the guard on the train who had kept the door open so they could jump aboard. A guard on the platform also helped by pushing him onto the train. The man was carrying a package wrapped in newspaper. In the process, the man dropped his package, which fell on the tracks. The package contained fireworks and exploded. The shock of the explosion was apparently of great enough strength to tip over some scales at the other end of the platform, which fell on Palsgraf (P) and injured her. A jury awarded her damages, and R.R. (D) appealed.

Facts: This section contains all relevant facts of the case, including the contentions of the parties and the lower court holdings. It is written in a logical order to give the student a clear understanding of the case. The plaintiff and defendant are identified by their proper names throughout and are always labeled with a (P) or (D).

ISSUE: Does the risk reasonably to be perceived define the duty to be obeyed?

HOLDING AND DECISION: (Cardozo, C.J.) Yes. The risk reasonably to be perceived defines the duty to be obeyed. If there is no foreseeable hazard to the injured party as the result of a seemingly innocent act, the act does not become a tort because it happened to be a wrong as to another. If the wrong was not willful, the plaintiff must show that the act as to her had such great and apparent possibilities of danger as to entitle her to protection. Negligence in the abstract is not enough upon which to base liability. Negligence is a relative concept, evolving out of the common law doctrine of trespass on the case. To establish liability, the defendant must owe a legal duty of reasonable care to the injured party. A cause of action in tort will lie where harm, though unintended, could have been averted or avoided by observance of such a duty. The scope of the duty is limited by the range of danger that a reasonable person could foresee. In this case, there was nothing to suggest from the appearance of the parcel or otherwise that the parcel contained fireworks. The guard could not reasonably have had any warning of a threat to Palsgraf (P), and R.R. (D) therefore cannot be held liable. Judgment is reversed in favor of R.R. (D).

DISSENT: (Andrews, J.) The concept that there is no negligence unless R.R. (D) owes a legal duty to take care as to Palsgraf (P) herself is too narrow. Everyone owes to the world at large the duty of refraining from those acts that may unreasonably threaten the safety of others. If the guard's action was negligent as to those nearby, it was also negligent as to those outside what might be termed the "danger zone." For Palsgraf (P) to recover, R.R.'s (D) negligence must have been the proximate cause of her injury, a question of fact for the jury.

Concurrence/Dissent: All concurrences and dissents are briefed whenever they are included by the casebook editor.

▶ ANALYSIS

The majority defined the limit of the defendant's liability in terms of the danger that a reasonable person in defendant's situation would have perceived. The dissent argued that the limitation should not be placed on liability, but rather on damages. Judge Andrews suggested that only injuries that would not have happened but for R.R.'s (D) negligence should be compensable. Both the majority and dissent recognized the policy-driven need to limit liability for negligent acts, seeking, in the words of Judge Andrews, to define a framework "that will be practical and in keeping with the general understanding of mankind." The Restatement (Second) of Torts has accepted Judge Cardozo's view.

Analysis: This last paragraph gives you a broad understanding of where the case "fits in" with other cases in the section of the book and with the entire course. It is a hornbook-style discussion indicating whether the case is a majority or minority opinion and comparing the principal case with other cases in the casebook. It may also provide analysis from restatements, uniform codes, and law review articles. The analysis will prove to be invaluable to classroom discussion.

■—■

Quicknotes

FORESEEABILITY A reasonable expectation that change is the probable result of certain acts or omissions.

NEGLIGENCE Conduct falling below the standard of care that a reasonable person would demonstrate under similar conditions.

PROXIMATE CAUSE The natural sequence of events without which an injury would not have been sustained.

■—■

Issue: The issue is a concise question that brings out the essence of the opinion as it relates to the section of the casebook in which the case appears. Both substantive and procedural issues are included if relevant to the decision.

Holding and Decision: This section offers a clear and in-depth discussion of the rule of the case and the court's rationale. It is written in easy-to-understand language and answers the issue presented by applying the law to the facts of the case. When relevant, it includes a thorough discussion of the exceptions to the case as listed by the court, any major cites to the other cases on point, and the names of the judges who wrote the decisions.

Quicknotes: Conveniently defines legal terms found in the case and summarizes the nature of any statutes, codes, or rules referred to in the text.

Aspen Publishers is proud to offer *Casenote Legal Briefs*—continuing thirty years of publishing America's best-selling legal briefs.

Casenote Legal Briefs are designed to help you save time when briefing assigned cases. Organized under convenient headings, they show you how to abstract the basic facts and holdings from the text of the actual opinions handed down by the courts. Used as part of a rigorous study regimen, they can help you spend more time analyzing and critiquing points of law than on copying bits and pieces of judicial opinions into your notebook or outline.

Casenote Legal Briefs should never be used as a substitute for assigned casebook readings. They work best when read as a follow-up to reviewing the underlying opinions themselves. Students who try to avoid reading and digesting the judicial opinions in their casebooks or online sources will end up shortchanging themselves in the long run. The ability to absorb, critique, and restate the dynamic and complex elements of case law decisions is crucial to your success in law school and beyond. It cannot be developed vicariously.

Casenote Legal Briefs represents but one of the many offerings in Aspen's Study Aid Timeline, which includes:

- *Casenote Legal Briefs*
- *Emanuel Law Outlines*
- *Examples & Explanations* Series
- *Introduction to Law* Series
- Emanuel *Law in a Flash* Flashcards
- Emanuel *CrunchTime* Series

Each of these series is designed to provide you with easy-to-understand explanations of complex points of law. Each volume offers guidance on the principles of legal analysis and, consulted regularly, will hone your ability to spot relevant issues. We have titles that will help you prepare for class, prepare for your exams, and enhance your general comprehension of the law along the way.

To find out more about Aspen Study Aid publications, visit us online at *http://lawschool.aspenpublishers.com* or email us at *legaledu@wolterskluwer.com*. We'll be happy to assist you.

Free access to Briefs online!

Download cases from this Casenote Legal Brief. Simply fill out this form for full access to this useful feature provided by Loislaw. Learn more about Loislaw services on the inside front cover of this book or visit *www.loislawschool.com*.

Name	Phone ( )

Address	Apt. No.

City	State	ZIP Code

Law School	Year (check one) ☐ 1st ☐ 2nd ☐ 3rd

Cut out the UPC found on the lower left-hand corner of the back cover of this book. Staple the UPC inside this box. Only the original UPC from the book cover will be accepted. No photocopies or store stickers are allowed.

Attach UPC inside this box.

Email (Print legibly or you may not get access!)

Title of this book (course subject)

Used with which casebook (provide author's name)

Mail the completed form to:

Aspen Publishers, Inc.
Legal Education Division
Casenote Online Access
130 Turner Street, Building 3, 4th Floor
Waltham, MA 02453-8901

I understand that online access is granted solely to the purchaser of this book for the academic year in which it was purchased. Any other usage is not authorized and will result in immediate termination of access. Sharing of codes is strictly prohibited.

Signature _____

Upon receipt of this completed form, you will be emailed codes with which to access the briefs for this Casenote Legal Brief. Online briefs are not available for all titles. For a full list of Casenote Legal Brief titles, please visit *http://lawschool.aspenpublishers.com*.

Make a photocopy of this form and your UPC for your records.

For detailed information on the use of the information you provide on this form, please see the PRIVACY POLICY at www.aspenpublishers.com.

A. Decide on a Format and Stick to It

Structure is essential to a good brief. It enables you to arrange systematically the related parts that are scattered throughout most cases, thus making manageable and understandable what might otherwise seem to be an endless and unfathomable sea of information. There are, of course, an unlimited number of formats that can be utilized. However, it is best to find one that suits your needs and stick to it. Consistency breeds both efficiency and the security that when called upon you will know where to look in your brief for the information you are asked to give.

Any format, as long as it presents the essential elements of a case in an organized fashion, can be used. Experience, however, has led *Casenotes* to develop and utilize the following format because of its logical flow and universal applicability.

NATURE OF CASE: This is a brief statement of the legal character and procedural status of the case (e.g., "Appeal of a burglary conviction").

There are many different alternatives open to a litigant dissatisfied with a court ruling. The key to determining which one has been used is to discover *who is asking this court for what.*

This first entry in the brief should be kept as *short as possible.* Use the court's terminology if you understand it. But since jurisdictions vary as to the titles of pleadings, the best entry is the one that addresses who wants what in this proceeding, not the one that sounds most like the court's language.

RULE OF LAW: A statement of the general principle of law that the case illustrates (e.g., "An acceptance that varies any term of the offer is considered a rejection and counteroffer").

Determining the rule of law of a case is a procedure similar to determining the issue of the case. Avoid being fooled by red herrings; there may be a few rules of law mentioned in the case excerpt, but usually only one is *the* rule with which the casebook editor is concerned. The techniques used to locate the issue, described below, may also be utilized to find the rule of law. Generally, your best guide is simply the chapter heading. It is a clue to the point the casebook editor seeks to make and should be kept in mind when reading every case in the respective section.

FACTS: A synopsis of only the essential facts of the case, i.e., those bearing upon or leading up to the issue.

The facts entry should be a short statement of the events and transactions that led one party to initiate legal proceedings against another in the first place. While some cases conveniently state the salient facts at the beginning of the decision, in other instances they will have to be culled from hiding places throughout the text, even from concurring and dissenting opinions. Some of the "facts" will often be in dispute and should be so noted. Conflicting evidence may be briefly pointed up. "Hard" facts must be included. Both must be *relevant* in order to be listed in the facts entry. It is impossible to tell what is relevant until the entire case is read, as the ultimate determination of the rights and liabilities of the parties may turn on something buried deep in the opinion.

Generally, the facts entry should not be longer than three to five *short* sentences.

It is often helpful to identify the role played by a party in a given context. For example, in a construction contract case the identification of a party as the "contractor" or "builder" alleviates the need to tell that that party was the one who was supposed to have built the house.

It is always helpful, and a good general practice, to identify the "plaintiff" and the "defendant." This may seem elementary and uncomplicated, but, especially in view of the creative editing practiced by some casebook editors, it is sometimes a difficult or even impossible task. Bear in mind that the *party presently* seeking something from this court may not be the plaintiff, and that sometimes only the cross-claim of a defendant is treated in the excerpt. Confusing or misaligning the parties can ruin your analysis and understanding of the case.

ISSUE: A statement of the general legal question answered by or illustrated in the case. For clarity, the issue is best put in the form of a question capable of a "yes" or "no" answer. In reality, the issue is simply the Rule of Law put in the form of a question (e.g., "May an offer be accepted by performance?").

The major problem presented in discerning what is *the* issue in the case is that an opinion usually purports to raise and answer several questions. However, except for rare cases, only one such question is really the issue in the case. Collateral issues not necessary to the resolution of the matter in controversy are handled by the court by language known as *"obiter dictum"* or merely *"dictum."* While dicta may be included later in the brief, they have no place under the issue heading.

To find the issue, ask *who wants what* and then go on to ask *why did that party succeed or fail in getting it.* Once this is determined, the "why" should be turned into a question.

The complexity of the issues in the cases will vary, but in all cases a single-sentence question should sum up the issue. *In a few cases,* there will be two, or even more rarely, three issues of equal importance to the resolution of the case. Each should be expressed in a single-sentence question.

Since many issues are resolved by a court in coming to a final disposition of a case, the casebook editor will reproduce the portion of the opinion containing the issue or issues most relevant to the area of law under scrutiny. A noted law professor gave this advice: "Close the book; look at the title on the cover." Chances are, if it is Property, you need not concern yourself with whether, for example, the federal government's treatment of the plaintiff's land really raises a federal question sufficient to support jurisdiction on this ground in federal court.

The same rule applies to chapter headings designating sub-areas within the subjects. They tip you off as to what the text is designed to teach. The cases are arranged in a casebook to show a progression or development of the law, so that the preceding cases may also help.

It is also most important to remember to *read the notes and questions* at the end of a case to determine what the editors wanted you to have gleaned from it.

HOLDING AND DECISION: This section should succinctly explain the rationale of the court in arriving at its decision. In capsulizing the "reasoning" of the court, it should always include an application of the general rule or rules of law to the specific facts of the case. Hidden justifications come to light in this entry; the reasons for the state of the law, the public policies, the biases and prejudices, those considerations that influence the justices' thinking and, ultimately, the outcome of the case. At the end, there should be a short indication of the disposition or procedural resolution of the case (e.g., "Decision of the trial court for Mr. Smith (P) reversed").

The foregoing format is designed to help you "digest" the reams of case material with which you will be faced in your law school career. Once mastered by practice, it will place at your fingertips the information the authors of your casebooks have sought to impart to you in case-by-case illustration and analysis.

B. Be as Economical as Possible in Briefing Cases

Once armed with a format that encourages succinctness, it is as important to be economical with regard to the time spent on the actual reading of the case as it is to be economical in the writing of the brief itself. This does not mean "skimming" a case. Rather, it means reading the case with an "eye" trained to recognize into which "section" of your brief a particular passage or line fits and having a system for quickly and precisely marking the case so that the passages fitting any one particular part of

the brief can be easily identified and brought together in a concise and accurate manner when the brief is actually written.

It is of no use to simply repeat everything in the opinion of the court; record only enough information to trigger your recollection of what the court said. Nevertheless, an accurate statement of the "law of the case," i.e., the legal principle applied to the facts, is absolutely essential to class preparation and to learning the law under the case method.

To that end, it is important to develop a "shorthand" that you can use to make margin notations. These notations will tell you at a glance in which section of the brief you will be placing that particular passage or portion of the opinion.

Some students prefer to underline all the salient portions of the opinion (with a pencil or colored underliner marker), making marginal notations as they go along. Others prefer the color-coded method of underlining, utilizing different colors of markers to underline the salient portions of the case, each separate color being used to represent a different section of the brief. For example, blue underlining could be used for passages relating to the rule of law, yellow for those relating to the issue, and green for those relating to the holding and decision, etc. While it has its advocates, the color-coded method can be confusing and time-consuming (all that time spent on changing colored markers). Furthermore, it can interfere with the continuity and concentration many students deem essential to the reading of a case for maximum comprehension. In the end, however, it is a matter of personal preference and style. Just remember, whatever method you use, underlining must be used sparingly or its value is lost.

If you take the marginal notation route, an efficient and easy method is to go along underlining the key portions of the case and placing in the margin alongside them the following "markers" to indicate where a particular passage or line "belongs" in the brief you will write:

N   (NATURE OF CASE)
RL   (RULE OF LAW)
I   (ISSUE)
HL   (HOLDING AND DECISION, relates to
        the RULE OF LAW behind the decision)
HR   (HOLDING AND DECISION, gives the
        RATIONALE or reasoning behind the
        decision)
HA   (HOLDING AND DECISION, APPLIES
        the general principle(s) of law to the facts
        of the case to arrive at the decision)

Remember that a particular passage may well contain information necessary to more than one part of your brief, in which case you simply note that in the margin. If you are using the color-coded underlining method instead of margin notation, simply make asterisks or checks in the margin next to the passage in question in the colors that indicate the additional sections of the brief where it might be utilized.

The economy of utilizing "shorthand" in marking cases for briefing can be maintained in the actual brief writing process itself by utilizing "law student shorthand" within the brief. There are many commonly used words and phrases for which abbreviations can be substituted in your briefs (and in your class notes also). You can develop abbreviations that are personal to you and which will save you a lot of time. A reference list of briefing abbreviations can be found on page xii of this book.

C. Use Both the Briefing Process and the Brief as a Learning Tool

Now that you have a format and the tools for briefing cases efficiently, the most important thing is to make the time spent in briefing profitable to you and to make the most advantageous use of the briefs you create. Of course, the briefs are invaluable for classroom reference when you are called upon to explain or analyze a particular case. However, they are also useful in reviewing for exams. A quick glance at the fact summary should bring the case to mind, and a rereading of the rule of law should enable you to go over the underlying legal concept in your mind, how it was applied in that particular case, and how it might apply in other factual settings.

As to the value to be derived from engaging in the briefing process itself, there is an immediate benefit that arises from being forced to sift through the essential facts and reasoning from the court's opinion and to succinctly express them in your own words in your brief. The process ensures that you understand the case and the point that it illustrates, and that means you will be ready to absorb further analysis and information brought forth in class. It also ensures you will have something to say when called upon in class. The briefing process helps develop a mental agility for getting to the *gist* of a case and for identifying, expounding on, and applying the legal concepts and issues found there. The briefing process is the mental process on which you must rely in taking law school examinations; it is also the mental process upon which a lawyer relies in serving his clients and in making his living.

acceptance	acp	offer	O
affirmed	aff	offeree	OE
answer	ans	offeror	OR
assumption of risk	a/r	ordinance	ord
attorney	atty	pain and suffering	p/s
beyond a reasonable doubt	b/r/d	parol evidence	p/e
bona fide purchaser	BFP	plaintiff	P
breach of contract	br/k	prima facie	p/f
cause of action	c/a	probable cause	p/c
common law	c/l	proximate cause	px/c
Constitution	Con	real property	r/p
constitutional	con	reasonable doubt	r/d
contract	K	reasonable man	r/m
contributory negligence	c/n	rebuttable presumption	rb/p
cross	x	remanded	rem
cross-complaint	x/c	res ipsa loquitur	RIL
cross-examination	x/ex	respondeat superior	r/s
cruel and unusual punishment	c/u/p	Restatement	RS
defendant	D	reversed	rev
dismissed	dis	Rule Against Perpetuities	RAP
double jeopardy	d/j	search and seizure	s/s
due process	d/p	search warrant	s/w
equal protection	e/p	self-defense	s/d
equity	eq	specific performance	s/p
evidence	ev	statute of limitations	S/L
exclude	exc	statute of frauds	S/F
exclusionary rule	exc/r	statute	S
felony	f/n	summary judgment	s/j
freedom of speech	f/s	tenancy in common	t/c
good faith	g/f	tenancy at will	t/w
habeas corpus	h/c	tenant	t
hearsay	hr	third party	TP
husband	H	third party beneficiary	TPB
in loco parentis	ILP	transferred intent	TI
injunction	inj	unconscionable	uncon
inter vivos	I/v	unconstitutional	unconst
joint tenancy	j/t	undue influence	u/e
judgment	judgt	Uniform Commercial Code	UCC
jurisdiction	jur	unilateral	uni
last clear chance	LCC	vendee	VE
long-arm statute	LAS	vendor	VR
majority view	maj	versus	v
meeting of minds	MOM	void for vagueness	VFV
minority view	min	weight of the evidence	w/e
Miranda warnings	Mir/w	weight of authority	w/a
Miranda rule	Mir/r	wife	W
negligence	neg	with	w/
notice	ntc	within	w/i
nuisance	nus	without prejudice	w/o/p
obligation	ob	without	w/o
obscene	obs	wrongful death	wr/d

Table of Cases

CHAPTER 1

Development of the California Community Property System

Quick Reference Rules of Law

Maynard v. Hill

125 U.S. 190 (1888).

NATURE OF CASE: Appeal of divorce action.

FACT SUMMARY: [Facts not stated in casebook excerpt.]

🏛 RULE OF LAW
(1) Ignorance of the law does not affect its validity.
(2) The rights of the parties in a marriage are not based on their contractual agreement but depend on the law of the state.

FACTS: [Facts not stated in casebook excerpt.]

ISSUE:
(1) Does an individual's lack of knowledge of the law of divorce invalidate a divorce decree as it applies to him?
(2) Are the rights of the parties in a marriage based on their contractual agreement or on the law of the state?

HOLDING AND DECISION: [Judge not stated in casebook excerpt.]
(1) No. Ignorance of the law does not affect its validity. (2) The rights of the parties in a marriage are based on the law of the state. (1) The fact that no cause existed for the divorce and that it was obtained without the knowledge of the wife (D), cannot invalidate the law of divorce or the legislation underlying the law. Moreover, the husband's (P) bad conduct towards his wife and children can have no impact on the ability of congress to pass the law.
(2) Although the federal constitution prohibits the impairment of contracts by states, marriage is not a contract within the meaning of the prohibition. This provision of the Constitution applies to contracts involving property and does not restrict the right of state legislatures to pass laws regarding divorce. Marriage is more than a contract because it is a relationship which cannot be changed by the parties themselves, but rather the law holds the parties to various obligations and liabilities. The maintenance of marriage is of great public interest because it is the foundation of the family and society. Thus, although a marriage is declared to be a contract, as distinguished from a religious sacrament, for certain purposes such as consent to enter into, the marriage relation itself is not synonymous with the word contract as used in common law or statues. Marriage is, therefore, more than a contract because it is an institution founded upon consent of the parties, but regulated by public authority upon principles of public policy.

▶ ANALYSIS

California recognizes that it is the Legislature who has complete control over the regulation of marriages.

■══■

George v. Ransom

Creditor (P) v. Debtor's wife (D)

Cal. Sup. Ct., 15 Cal. 332, 76 Am. Dec. 490 (1860).

NATURE OF CASE: Appeal from denial of wife's separate funds in payment for husband's debt.

FACT SUMMARY: George (P), a creditor of Ransom's (D) husband, sought her separate funds in payment for her husband's debt.

🏛 RULE OF LAW

The creditor of the husband cannot subject the proceeds or dividends of the separate estate of his wife to his claim.

FACTS: George (P) was a creditor of Ransom's (D) husband. George (P) sought to subject dividends of certain stock purchased by Ransom (D) with her separate funds to payment for her husband's debt. His claim was denied, and he appealed.

ISSUE: Can a creditor of the husband subject the proceeds or dividends of the separate estate of the wife to his claim?

HOLDING AND DECISION: (Baldwin, J.) No. A creditor of the husband cannot subject the proceeds or dividends of the separate estate of the wife to his claim. Any legislative act which allows the fruits of the property of the wife to be taken from her and given to the husband or his creditors is unconstitutional. To hold otherwise would be to give the wife no more than the barren right to hold property while giving to the husband her beneficial right to enjoy. The purpose for safeguards over separate property are in part to protect the wife against the husband's improvidence, but this would fail if the wife's estate were only a reversionary interest of no use to her unless she survives her husband. Under common law, separate property of the wife is an estate in use and in title held by her for her exclusive benefit and advantage. To separate title and use would be to destroy the substance of the right of separate property. Affirmed.

▶ ANALYSIS

The court referred to the common law definition of separate property as it applied to the wife because the framers of the California constitution were schooled in and were primarily familiar with the common law which was the basis in adapting Spanish community property doctrines to their needs. Separate property is all property, real and personal, owned or claimed by a spouse before marriage; acquired afterward by gift, devise, bequest, or descent; or acquired after separation. The acquisition of property is timed at the point at which the right to an item of property is perfected. The practical effect of the decision above is that separate property rules apply not only to that property in its original or transmuted form, but also to income and profits it produces.

■■■

Quicknotes

SEPARATE PROPERTY Property owned by one spouse prior to marriage, or any income derived therefrom, and any property received by one spouse pursuant to a gift, devise, bequest or descent.

■■■

Stewart v. Stewart

Wife (P) v. Husband (D)

Cal. Sup. Ct., 199 Cal. 318, 249 P. 197 (1926).

NATURE OF CASE: Appeal from an action to quiet title.

FACT SUMMARY: Wife (P), who was happily married to husband (D), sought to quiet her title to an undivided half interest in community real property, record title to which was in her name.

RULE OF LAW
The wife does not have an undivided one-half valid present vested interest in the community property during the continuance of the marriage relation.

FACTS: Wife (P) brought an action against husband (D) to quiet her title to an undivided half interest in real property, record title to which was in her name. The property was community property, and wife (P) alleged that the parties remained happily married. Wife (P) argued that changes in the Civil Code of 1917 created in the wife a vested interest in an undivided one-half of the community property immediately upon acquisition of such property by the spouses or either of them and continues thereafter during the existence of the marriage relation. The trial court quieted wife's (P) title, and husband (D) appealed.

ISSUE: Does the wife have a present vested interest in the community property during the continuance of the marriage relation?

HOLDING AND DECISION: (Richard, J.) No. The wife does not have a present vested interest in the community property during the continuance of the marriage relation. Rather than give the wife a present vested interest, the amendments to the civil code were designed to give the wife added safeguards and protection against the fraudulent acts of the husband in the exercise of his control and dominion over the community property. Under the amendments a husband can convey community real property to one who has no knowledge of the marriage relation, but the wife can avoid such an instrument within one year from its recordation. This provision is entirely inconsistent with the existence of a present and vested ownership in the wife of an undivided one-half interest of such property. The effect of a wife's interest in the community property during the continuation of the marriage relation, while less than a vested interest, is "a much more definite and precise interest than is that of an ordinary heir." The wife through her contribution toward and acquisition and conservation of community property has been given rights to safeguard her interest and access to appropriate judicial remedies both before and after the time when her interest ripens and vests through death of or divorce from the husband. Here, wife (P) alleges that she and

husband (D) remain happily married. At no time did husband (D) deal with or dispose of community property fraudulently. In fact, husband (D) could not have done so since legal title was in wife's (P) name alone. The trial court was thus in error. Reversed.

ANALYSIS

Agreement cannot be found among the community property states concerning the nature of the interests of the spouses. In fact, it appears that a specific determination of the nature of the spouses' respective interests is not necessary in order to solve most community property issues. The interest of the spouses in community property was defined in California Civil Code § 5105, which read, "The respective interests of the husband and wife in community property during continuance of the marriage relation are present, existing and equal interests under the management and control of the husband. . . . This section shall be construed as defining the respective interests and rights of husband and wife in community property." This was amended in 1975 to provide, with certain exceptions, that husband and wife have equal management and control of the community with equal power of disposition as either spouse has of his or her separate property.

Quicknotes

COMMUNITY PROPERTY In community property jurisdictions, refers to all money or property acquired during the term of the marriage in which each spouse has an undivided one-half interest.

QUIET TITLE Equitable action to resolve conflicting claims to an interest in real property.

VESTED INTEREST A present right to property although the right to the possession of such property may not be enjoyed until a future date.

Marriage of Noghrey

Wife (P) v. Husband (D)

Cal. Ct. App., 169 Cal. App. 3d 326 (1985).

NATURE OF CASE: Appeal from decision finding a valid premarital agreement.

FACT SUMMARY: In Farima Noghrey's (P) petition for divorce against her husband Kambiz (D), Kambiz (D) contended that the antenuptial agreement at issue in this case encouraged and promoted divorce and, hence, was contrary to public policy of the State of California and unenforceable.

🏛 RULE OF LAW
Contracts which facilitate divorce or separation by providing for a settlement only in the event of such an occurrence are void as against public policy.

FACTS: Kambiz (D) and Farima Noghrey (P) were married for 7½ months when Farima (P) filed for divorce. Farima's (P) divorce petition alleged the existence of an antenuptial agreement setting forth the property rights of the parties. Farima (P) testified that she signed the document because a husband has to give some protection to a new wife in case of divorce. She explained that it was difficult for an Iranian woman to remarry after a divorce because she is no longer a virgin. In return for the premarital agreement, Farima (P) gave Kambiz (D) assurances that she was a virgin and was medically examined for that purpose. Kambiz (D) testified that he did not wish to sign the agreement but was coerced into doing so by Farima's (P) mother. Kambiz (D) also contended that the agreement encouraged and promoted divorce and, hence, was contrary to public policy of the State of California and unenforceable. The trial court found the premarital agreement valid, and Kambiz (D) appealed.

ISSUE: Are contracts which facilitate divorce or separation by providing for a settlement only in the event of such an occurrence void as against public policy?

HOLDING AND DECISION: (Foley, J.) Yes. Contracts which facilitate divorce or separation by providing for a settlement only in the event of such an occurrence are void as against public policy. An antenuptial agreement in which the terms encourage or promote divorce is against public policy and is unenforceable. The agreement at issue is not the type that seeks to define the character of property acquired after marriage nor does it seek to ensure the separate character of property acquired prior to marriage types of antenuptial agreements which are generally valid. The agreement here constitutes a promise by a husband (D) to give the wife (P) a very substantial amount of money and property, but only upon the occurrence of a divorce. Here, the wife (P) is encouraged by the very terms of the agreement to seek dissolution, and with all deliberate speed, lest the husband (D) suffer an untimely demise, nullifying the contract and the wife's right to the money and the property. The prospect of receiving a house and a minimum of $500,000 by obtaining the no-fault divorce available in California would menace the marriage of the best intentioned spouse. Reversed.

▶ ANALYSIS

A major aspect of the California community property system is the fact that the system's operation may be modified or limited by an agreement between the spouses. The system is subject to antenuptial and postnuptial contractual modification. Under the system of contractual modification, the spouses themselves can decide how their property will be classified—in effect, they can contract themselves out of the community property system.

■═■

Quicknotes

ANTENUPTIAL AGREEMENT An agreement entered into by two individuals, in contemplation of their impending marriage, in order to determine their rights and interests in property upon dissolution or death.

NO-FAULT DIVORCE A basis for terminating a marriage without the need for demonstrating misconduct on the part of either spouse.

■═■

Marriage of Bonds
Wife (P) v. Husband (D)
Cal. Sup. Ct., 24 Cal. 4th 1, 5 P.3d 815 (2000).

NATURE OF CASE: Appeal of judgment invalidating a premarital agreement.

FACT SUMMARY: In her divorce proceeding, Sun (P) argued that the premarital agreement was invalid because she entered into it involuntarily.

🏛 RULE OF LAW
Premarital agreements, where the less sophisticated party does not have independent counsel and has not waived counsel, should not be subject to strict scrutiny for voluntariness because the parties were not in a fiduciary relationship to one another.

FACTS: Sun (P) and Barry (D) entered into a written premarital agreement in which each of them waived any interest in the earnings and acquisitions of the other party during the marriage. Barry (D) testified that prior to getting married, Sun (P) agreed their earnings and acquisitions should be separate, she planned to pursue a career and she had no objection to the agreement. Sun's (P) native language was Swedish and she testified that prior to the marriage, her English skills were limited and that she often did not understand Barry (D). She further testified that they did not discuss money or property prior to their marriage and that she did not learn of the premarital agreement until she was outside of Barry's (D) lawyer's office on the day it was to be signed. She was informed on that day that Barry (D) would not marry her, the following day, unless she signed the agreement. She believed that Barry (D) wanted to retain ownership of property he owned before the marriage and was unaware that the agreement would affect her future. Barry's (D) attorney testified that he had met with Sun (P) two weeks prior to the signing of the agreement, that he discussed with her the drafting of an agreement to keep earnings and acquisitions separate and advised her that it might be in her best interest to obtain independent counsel. The couple was married the day after the agreement was signed in a small, informal ceremony in Las Vegas. The court of appeal found that a premarital agreement in which one party is not represented by independent counsel should be subject to strict scrutiny for voluntariness and that the trial court erred in finding the agreement to be voluntary. Barry (D) appealed.

ISSUE:
(1) Should a premarital agreement in which one party is not represented by independent counsel be subjected to strict scrutiny for voluntariness?
(2) Was the premarital agreement entered into voluntarily?

HOLDING AND DECISION: (George, C.J.)
(1) No. A premarital agreement in which one party is not represented by independent counsel should not be subjected to strict scrutiny for voluntariness.
(2) Yes. Sun (P) voluntarily entered into the premarital agreement. (1) Contrary to the court of appeal's assertion, premarital agreements should not be interpreted and enforced under the same standards applicable to marital settlement agreements. This is because unequal marriage settlements must be shown by the advantaged party not to have been the product of undue influence to be valid, but unequal prenuptial agreements must be shown by the party seeking to invalidate that it was entered into involuntarily or if no disclosure, that the terms were unconscionable when executed. Persons who enter into premarital agreements thus are not in a confidential relationship which gives rises to a fiduciary duty, as found with spouses. A confidential relationship may arise between friends, however a mere lack of independent advice is not sufficient to raise a presumption of undue influence or of constructive fraud, even when the consideration appears inadequate, unless some other incapacity is present, then it must be shown that no oppression took place. Since no fiduciary relationship is present between the parties to a premarital agreement, the agreement in which one party is not represented by independent counsel is not required to be subjected to strict scrutiny for voluntariness. (2) A premarital agreement is unenforceable if the party seeking to avoid the agreement can establish that the agreement was involuntary. Evidence of lack of capacity, duress, fraud, undue influence and coercion go towards a finding of involuntariness. Substantial evidence supports the trial court's finding that Sun (P) voluntarily entered into the agreement without being subject to fraud, coercion, or undue influence, and with full understanding of the agreement. The parties did not stand in a confidential relationship. Sun (P) was not threatened or forced to sign the agreement. She did not show any reluctance to signing it. The fact that the wedding was to be the day after the agreement was signed is immaterial because the wedding arrangements were informal and therefore it would have caused little embarrassment if the wedding had been postponed. Sun (P) was not surprised by the agreement because she had been aware of Barry's (D) intentions to protect his property and earnings. Sun (P) also had a reasonable

Continued on next page.

opportunity to obtain counsel. As evidenced by Barry (D) and his attorney's testimony, Sun (P) was aware of her rights and how the agreement adversely affected them because they explained the terms prior to Sun (P) signing them. Sun (P) thus did not carry her burden in demonstrating that the agreement was involuntary. Reversed.

▶ *ANALYSIS*

As in *Maynard v. Hill*, 125 U.S. 190 (1888), this court emphasizes that marriage is a regulated institution of social value and there are limitations on the ability of persons to contract with respect to it.

Quicknotes

FIDUCIARY Person holding a legal obligation to act for the benefit of another.

PRENUPTIAL AGREEMENT An agreement entered into by two individuals in contemplation of marriage, determining their rights and interests in property upon dissolution or death.

VOLUNTARY ACT An act that is undertaken pursuant to an individual's free will and without the influence of another.

Marriage of Burkle

Wife (P) v. Husband (D)

Cal. Ct. App., 139 Cal. App. 4th 712 (2006).

NATURE OF CASE: Appeal of trial court judgment.

FACT SUMMARY: Janet Burkle (P) and her husband, Ronald (D), executed a post-marital agreement that provided Ms. Burkle (P) with the financial security she sought. Ms. Burkle (P) acknowledged that neither of them obtained an unfair advantage as a result of the agreement, but claimed that the presumption of undue influence arose anyway, and that the burden of proving no undue influence fell on her husband. The trial court ruled in favor of Ronald Burkle (D).

> 🏛 **RULE OF LAW**
> (1) In order to raise a presumption that a transaction between spouses was induced by undue influence, the "advantage" of one spouse over the other must have been "unfair."
> (2) Where a trial court's conclusion that a presumption of undue influence was rebutted is supported by substantial evidence, it must be affirmed.

FACTS: Janet Burkle (P) abandoned her intent to divorce her husband, Ronald (D), in August 1997 when they reconciled and executed a post-marital agreement. Among other things, the agreement provided Ms. Burkle (P) with $1 million per year, which would be considered separate property upon receipt, $30 million as her share of the community assets, and a residence valued at up to $3 million as of June 1997. Ms. Burkle (P) waived rights to spousal support. The agreement purported to resolve financial issues between them—Ms. Burkle (P) wanted financial security, and Mr. Burkle (D) wanted the financial freedom to make risky investments. Despite signing the agreement with the advice of a team of attorneys, Ms. Burkle (P) argued that the post-marital agreement was void and unenforceable in her petition for dissolution of marriage on June 13, 2003. Ms. Burkle (P) acknowledged that neither of them obtained an unfair advantage as a result of the agreement, but claimed that the presumption of undue influence arose anyway, and that the burden of proving no undue influence fell on her husband. The trial court found that a presumption of undue influence cannot logically be applied in a case where benefits are obtained by both spouses, both are represented by attorneys, and both expressly acknowledge that neither has obtained an unfair advantage as a result of the agreement.

ISSUE:
(1) In order to raise a presumption that a transaction between spouses was induced by undue influence, must the "advantage" of one spouse over the other have been "unfair"?
(2) Where a trial court's conclusion that a presumption of undue influence was rebutted is supported by substantial evidence, must it be affirmed?

HOLDING AND DECISION: (Boland, J.)
(1) Yes. In order to raise a presumption that a transaction between spouses was induced by undue influence, the "advantage" of one spouse over the other must have been "unfair." No presumption of undue influence arises by the entry into an agreement by spouses. The relevant statute and case law prohibit a spouse from taking "any unfair advantage of the other," and treats the fiduciary duties of spouses like those of business partners, which run to each other. It would therefore be just as irrational to presume undue influence in a contract between spouses where there was not unfair advantage as it would between business partners. The trial court found that the agreement in this case provided mutual advantages, and provided Ms. Burkle (P) with the advantage she was bargaining for, which was financial security.
(2) Yes. Where a trial court's conclusion that a presumption of undue influence was rebutted is supported by substantial evidence, it must be affirmed. Even if a presumption of undue influence arose in this case, the trial court's conclusion must be affirmed because it is supported by substantial evidence. Both Burkles testified and evidence supported the trial court's conclusion that the transaction was entered freely and voluntarily, with full knowledge of the facts, and with a complete understanding of its legal effect. Affirmed.

▶ **ANALYSIS**

Under California law, the division of separate and community property occurs after the couple legally separate, a date Janet and Ron Burkle continue to dispute. Janet claims they separated in 2002, a decade after the date Ronald claims marked their separation. In the post-marital agreement, the Burkles resolved their different opinions about their separation date by agreeing to value the community property as of June 1997, about the time Janet Burkle filed for divorce the first time, and the agreement assessed the community property at about $60 million. This provided Janet with the financial security she sought at the time, because by fixing the value of the community property, Ronald's risky investments could not affect her

Continued on next page.

stake. As it turned out, Ronald's net worth sky-rocketed in the years following their execution of the agreement. If the community property had included money made by Ronald Burkle in the years following the 1997 agreement, Janet Burkle might be entitled to a substantially larger share of her husband's wealth, depending upon the date of separation.

■══■

Quicknotes

FIDUCIARY DUTY A legal obligation to act for the benefit of another, including subordinating one's personal interests to that of the other person.

SPOUSAL SUPPORT Payments made by one spouse to another in discharge of the spouse's duty pursuant to law, or in accordance with a written divorce or separation decree, in order to provide maintenance for the other spouse.

UNDUE INFLUENCE Improper persuasion that deprives an individual of freedom of choice.

■══■

Estate of Bibb

Son of deceased (P) v. Stepmother (D)

Cal. Ct. App., 87 Cal. App. 4th 461 (2001).

NATURE OF CASE: Appeal from judgment denying petition to establish an estate's ownership of certain property.

FACT SUMMARY: After his father died, Dozier (P) moved to have some of the property his stepmother (D) claimed she owned deemed property of his father's estate.

🏛 **RULE OF LAW**
(1) A grant deed signed by a husband transferring his separate property interest in real property to himself and his wife as joint tenants satisfies the express declaration requirement of the Family Code.
(2) An unsigned computer printout, entitled "DMV Vehicle Registration Information," reflecting that an automobile, which was previously registered in the husband's name alone, was reregistered in the names of the husband or the wife, does not satisfy the requirements for a valid transmutation under the Family Code.

FACTS: Everett had one child, Dozier (P), from his first marriage. During his first marriage, Everett purchased a lot and constructed an apartment building on it. Many years after his first wife died, Everett purchased a Rolls Royce and registered it in his name alone. After remarrying, the automobile was reregistered in the names of Everett or Evelyn (D), who was his second wife. In order to qualify for a loan to make repairs on the apartment building, Everett had to rely on his wife's (D) good credit and signed a grant deed conveying the real property from himself to himself and Evelyn (D), "his wife as joint tenants." Evelyn (D) signed the note secured by a deed of trust on the property. Shortly thereafter, Everett died intestate. Evelyn (D) reregistered the Rolls in her name alone and took title to the other property in her name alone. Dozier (P) filed a petition to establish the estate's ownership of the lot, apartment building and Rolls, contending that the property had not been validly transmuted from Everett's separate property under the Code. The trial court denied his petition and Dozier (P) appealed.

ISSUE:
(1) Did the grant deed signed by Everett transferring his separate property interest in real property to himself and Evelyn (D) as joint tenants satisfy the express declaration requirement of the Family Code?
(2) Did the unsigned computer printout, entitled "DMV Vehicle Registration Information" which reflected that the Rolls, which was previously registered in the Everett's name alone, was reregistered in the names of

Everett or Evelyn (D), satisfy the requirements for a valid transmutation under the Family Code?

HOLDING AND DECISION: (Walker, J.)
(1) Yes. A grant deed signed by a husband transferring his separate property interest in real property to himself and his wife (D) as joint tenants satisfies the express declaration requirement of the Family Code.
(2) No. An unsigned computer printout, entitled "DMV Vehicle Registration Information," reflecting that an automobile, which was previously registered in the husband's name alone, was reregistered in the names of the husband or the wife (D), does not satisfy the requirements for a valid transmutation under the Family Code.
(1) The Family Code provides that, "A trans-mutation of real or personal property is not valid unless made in writing by an express declaration that is made, joined in, consented to, or accepted by the spouse whose interest in the property is adversely affected." In order to have a valid transmutation under the Code, there must be a writing which satisfies the statute of frauds and an expression of intent to transfer the property interest. The writing must contain on its face a clear and unambiguous expression of intent to transfer an interest in the property, independent of extrinsic evidence. In this case, the grant deed that Everett signed is a writing that was made, joined in, consented to, or accepted by the spouse whose interest in the property is adversely affected. The deed, independent of extrinsic evidence, also contains a clear and unambiguous expression of intent to transfer an interest in the property. The deed was drafted in the statutory form required for expressing intent to transfer an interest in real property. "Grant" is the operative word for transferring interests in real property and, therefore, Everett's use of the word to convey the real property into a joint tenancy satisfied the express declaration requirement of the Code. The lot and apartment building thus was validly transmuted into property held in joint tenancy, became Evelyn's (D) separate property upon Everett's death, and was properly excluded from the probate estate. (2) Although the Vehicle Code creates a presumption that a vehicle registered in the names of two or more persons as co-owners, in the alternative by use of the word or, is held in joint tenancy, the Family Code can be viewed as effectively creating a presumption that transactions between spouses are not transmutations, rebuttable by evidence that the transaction was documented with a writing containing the requisite language. The

Continued on next page.

general form of title presumption created by the Vehicle Code should not be used to negate the requirement of the Family Code which assures that a spouse's separate property entitlements are not undermined. There is nothing on the face of the DMV printout evidencing that the change in the form of title was made, joined in, consented to, or accepted by Everett, the spouse whose interest in the property was adversely affected. The document also does not contain a clear and unambiguous expression of his intent to transfer his interest in the property, as is required by the Family Code. The Rolls Royce was, therefore, not validly transmuted from Everett's separate property, and the trial court erred in excluding it from the probate estate. Reversed with respect to the Rolls Royce. Affirmed in all other respects.

▶ ANALYSIS

Subsequent legislation in California allows a spouse in their will to revoke his prior consent to transmutate the property.

■═■

Quicknotes

INTESTACY To die without leaving a valid testamentary instrument.

INTESTATE ESTATE The property of an individual who dies without executing a valid will.

JOINT TENANCY An interest in property whereby a single interest is owned by two or more persons and created by a single instrument; joint tenants possess equal interests in the use of the entire property and the last survivor is entitled to absolute ownership.

STATUTE OF FRAUDS A statute that requires specified types of contracts to be in writing in order to be binding.

TRANSMUTATION The conversion of the separate property of one spouse into separate property of the other spouse or into community property, or the conversion of community property into the separate property of one spouse, by either an agreement or transfer made in a writing signed by the spouse whose interest is adversely affected and without the payment of consideration.

■═■

Marriage of Steinberger

Parties not identified.

Cal. Ct. App., 91 Cal. App. 4th 1449 (2001).

NATURE OF CASE: Appeal of judgment in a marital dissolution action.

FACT SUMMARY: James gave Buff a diamond ring in celebration of their fifth wedding anniversary. When the couple filed for divorce, Buff claimed that it was her separate property.

🏛 RULE OF LAW
When a gift is given to one spouse from the other and its value is substantial, taking into account the circumstances of the marriage, the property will not be considered that gifted spouse's separate property if there is not a written expressed declaration transmuting the property from community to separate.

FACTS: Five years after getting married, Buff and James bought a loose diamond with community funds. James subsequently put the diamond in a setting and presented the ring to Buff after their fifth anniversary with a card referring to their five years together and congratulating her on her promotion. Buff considered it a gift but James considered it as both a gift and an investment that they could both enjoy. Buff and James later filed for divorce. The trial court determined that the ring was unilaterally given to Buff as a fifth wedding anniversary gift and it was, therefore, Buff's separate property. James appealed.

ISSUE: Was the ring Buff's separate property?

HOLDING AND DECISION: (Cottle, J.) No. The ring was not Buff's separate property because it was substantial in value, taking into account the circumstances of the marriage. Since there was no written expressed declaration transmuting the property from community to separate, the property was not Buff's separate property. The Family Code's requirement that a valid transmutation of property requires an express declaration in writing that is made by the spouse whose interest in the property is adversely affected, does not apply to a gift between the spouses of jewelry that is not substantial in value taking into account the circumstances of the marriage. In this case, however, Buff did not argue that the evidence was insufficient to support the trial court's finding that the ring was substantial in value, therefore a writing was required to effectively transmute the property from community to separate, and the card presented to Buff was not a sufficient writing. Reversed as to the trial court's holding that the diamond ring was Buff's separate property and remanded.

▶ ANALYSIS

As the court's opinion in this case points out, in enacting the Family Code, the Legislature made a policy decision balancing the competing concerns of the practical informality of interspousal transfers and the extensive litigation regarding fraud in such transfers.

■══■

Quicknotes

COMMUNITY PROPERTY In community property jurisdictions refers to all money or property acquired during the term of the marriage in which each spouse has an undivided one-half interest.

SEPARATE PROPERTY Property owned by one spouse prior to marriage, or any income derived therefrom, and any property received by one spouse pursuant to a gift, devise, bequest or descent.

TRANSMUTATION The conversion of the separate property of one spouse into separate property of the other spouse or into community property, or the conversion of community property into the separate property of one spouse, by either an agreement or transfer made in a writing signed by the spouse whose interest is adversely affected and without the payment of consideration.

■══■

Property: Community or Separate

Quick Reference Rules of Law

Wilson v. Wilson

Wife (P) v. Husband (D)

Cal. Dist. Ct. App., 76 Cal. App. 2d 119, 172 P.2d 568 (1946).

NATURE OF CASE: Appeal from an interlocutory decree of divorce.

FACT SUMMARY: Husband (D) argued that the house which the parties occupied was his separate property, but the trial court, applying a presumption (that property acquired after marriage is community) on the basis of conflicting evidence, determined that the house was community property.

🏛 RULE OF LAW
Notwithstanding controverting testimony, a presumption alone will support a finding in accordance with it.

FACTS: The parties married in New York on January 15, 1931, and, shortly thereafter, established their domicile in San Francisco. They separated in 1940, and wife (P) brought this action for divorce in 1942, charging husband (D) with desertion and extreme cruelty. The trial court determined that the parties' San Francisco residence was community property and awarded wife (P) a one-half interest in it plus the exclusive right of occupancy. Husband (D) appealed, contending that he paid for the $20,000 house with accumulations of dividends from property acquired before marriage. He testified that his sole community income was $6,000 a year, while wife (P) testified that their living expenses were over $3,500 monthly. On that basis, he argued that the house must have been purchased with separate funds. However, husband (D) also testified that he estimated living expenses between $300 and $800 monthly. Also, wife (P), an artist, sold some of her works for substantial sums. The trial court applied the presumption that property acquired after marriage is community.

ISSUE: Notwithstanding controverting testimony, can a presumption alone support a finding in accordance with it?

HOLDING AND DECISION: (Peters, J.) Yes. Notwithstanding controverting testimony, a presumption alone will support a finding in accordance with it. First, the trial court was entitled to disbelieve husband's (D) testimony as to the support of the funds while believing his testimony as to their living costs. The record contained some evidence, although weak, from which it could be inferred that community funds were used to purchase the house. Such evidence, even without the presumption, was sufficient to support the court's finding. However, the presumption also supports the trial court's finding. Coupled with the presumption is the rule that the burden is on the party claiming the property is separate to establish that. While the presumption is rebuttable, whether husband's (D) evidence was sufficient to overcome it was a question

for the trial court. A presumption may outweigh the evidence adduced against it. Here, the trial court was justified in disregarding husband's (D) testimony and finding in accordance with the presumption. Further, the simple fact that the house was purchased after marriage was sufficient to raise the presumption. Wife (P) was under no duty to show that the funds used in the purchase were acquired after. To uphold husband's (D) contention that the rule is so limited would be to greatly limit the presumption and to take the burden of the party asserting the property to be separate. Affirmed.

▶ ANALYSIS

The presumption that all property acquired after marriage is community is found in Civil Code § 5110. To show that the property was in fact acquired during the marriage, there must be affirmative proof. Even where the marriage has been a lengthy one, there is no presumption that any certain piece of property was acquired after marriage. One concession is made though; the longer the marriage, less proof will ordinarily be accepted to show that certain wealth was acquired during marriage. Note that where the property in question is of a kind more likely to be acquired by married persons than by single persons, the court may consider such evidence in determining the sufficiency of the basis for the presumption.

Quicknotes

BURDEN OF PROOF The duty of a party to introduce evidence to support a fact that is in dispute in an action.

COMMUNITY PROPERTY In community property jurisdictions refers to all money or property acquired during the term of the marriage in which each spouse has an undivided one-half interest.

INTERLOCUTORY Intervening; temporary; refers to an issue that is determined during the course of a proceeding and which does not constitute a final judgment on the merits.

PRESUMPTION A rule of law requiring the court to presume certain facts to be true based on the existence of other facts, thereby shifting the burden of proof to the party against whom the presumption is asserted to rebut.

Marriage of Ettefagh

Wife (P) v. Husband (D)

Cal. Ct. App., 150 Cal. App. 4th 1578 (2007).

NATURE OF CASE: Appeal from judgment of dissolution.

FACT SUMMARY: Various interests in four parcels of land were conveyed to a man during his marriage, and his wife claimed they were community property when she filed for divorce. The trial court found they were the husband's separate property, because there was not evidence supporting the wife's claim that the funds used to purchase the properties came from her husband.

🏛 **RULE OF LAW**
The presumption under the California Family Code that property acquired by either spouse during marriage is community property may be rebutted by a preponderance of the evidence.

FACTS: Various interests in four parcels of land were conveyed to a Vahid Ettefagh (D) during his marriage to Semrin Ettefagh (P). Vahid (D) testified that none of his own funds were used for the purchase of the properties, and that his father and sister conveyed to him interests in the properties, which they purchased using their own funds. Semrin (P) claimed they were community property when she filed for divorce. The trial court found that the properties were presumed to be community assets under Section 760 of California's Family Code because they were acquired during the marriage. But the trial court also found that Vahid (D) rebutted that presumption through his testimony, and that of his father, that Vahid (D) did not use his own funds to purchase the property. The trial court found that there was no evidence supporting the Semrin (P) claim that the funds used to purchase the properties came from her husband. The trial court rejected Semrin's (P) argument that the community property presumption can only be overcome by clear and convincing evidence.

ISSUE: May the presumption under the California Family Code that property acquired by either spouse during marriage is community property be rebutted by a preponderance of the evidence?

HOLDING AND DECISION: (Simons, J.) Yes. The presumption under the California Family Code that property acquired by either spouse during marriage is community property may be rebutted by a preponderance of the evidence. The state's Evidence Code provides that the preponderance of the evidence standard is the "default standard of proof" in civil actions in California, and nothing in the state's constitutional, statutory, or case law (which is inconclusive on the issue) requires a higher standard of proof than preponderance of the evidence. It is also the appropriate standard because it equally distributes the risk that the court will apply the standard erroneously. Any other standard expresses a preference for one side's interest. Here, only money was at stake, and both spouses shared the risk of losing a one-half interest in the property if the trial court erred in classifying the property. Because the case law is inconclusive, and the nature of the parties' interests at risk is purely economic and relatively equal, the preponderance of the evidence standard is appropriate. Affirmed.

▶ ANALYSIS

While the court correctly determines that case law is inconclusive on the issue of what standard should be applied, dicta in other cases, has suggested that a clear and convincing standard should be applied.

■═■

Quicknotes

CLEAR AND CONVINCING EVIDENCE An evidentiary standard requiring a demonstration that the fact sought to be proven is reasonably certain.

COMMUNITY PROPERTY In community property jurisdictions refers to all money or property acquired during the term of the marriage in which each spouse has an undivided one-half interest.

DICTUM Statement by a judge in a legal opinion that is not necessary for the resolution of the action.

PREPONDERANCE OF THE EVIDENCE A standard of proof requiring the trier of fact to determine whether the fact sought to be established is more probable than not.

PRESUMPTION A rule of law requiring the court to presume certain facts to be true based on the existence of other facts, thereby shifting the burden of proof to the party against whom the presumption is asserted to rebut.

SEPARATE PROPERTY Property owned by one spouse prior to marriage, or any income derived therefrom, and any property received by one spouse pursuant to a gift, devise, bequest or descent.

■═■

Estate of Clark

Cal. Dist. Ct. App., 94 Cal. App. 453, 271 P. 542 (1928).

NATURE OF CASE: Action to declare that property received in a will contest was community property.

FACT SUMMARY: Clark contested his deceased son's will and the matter was settled through a compromise.

🏛 RULE OF LAW
Property acquired by compromise is separate property if the right compromised was separate property.

FACTS: Clark's son died. Clark would have been the sole heir if his son had died intestate. However, a will existed under which Clark would take nothing. Clark married and then filed a will contest. The will was declared invalid and Clark was awarded his son's estate. The heirs under the will appealed and a compromise was reached whereby the estate was split between Clark and the heirs. The appellate court then found the will to be valid and admitted it to probate. Clark died and his wife (P) claimed the one-half interest was community property and demanded her half. The court found that the compromise funds were Clark's separate property and denied her claim. Mrs. Clark (P) appealed on the basis that Clark's interest in his son's estate was spurious since the appellate court had found the will to be valid. As such, it was a mere nuisance suit and should be declared a community asset.

ISSUE: Is the compromise of a vested separate property right separate property?

HOLDING AND DECISION: (Crail, J.) Yes. If the property had come to Clark by will or intestacy, it would have been his separate property. If, after the contest, he had given one-half of his interest to the heirs it would have been his separate property. Clark had a vested right in his son's estate once the son had died. He had an immediate right to contest the will. This right was his separate property. The compromise of a right which is a separate property interest yields separate property. Any funds obtained through the compromise were Clark's separate property. The will was only declared valid after the compromise when Clark withdrew his objection. The claim was not spurious. Affirmed.

▶ ANALYSIS

The California Supreme Court very early construed the definition of community property to include "property taken in exchange for, or in the investment of, or as the price of the property so originally owned or acquired." 12 Cal. 247. Note that when Clark's son died, Clark at that instant obtained a property right that vested. Before his son's death, all he had was a mere expectancy in an inheritance. The right vested before his remarriage and was, therefore, his separate property. The property involved in the litigation came to Clark in exchange or payment for his separate property and, so, remained separate property. A mere expectancy is not a property right. In the case above, Clark's will contest was not only made in good faith, his contest was an assertion of a statutory right amounting to property.

Quicknotes

COMMUNITY PROPERTY In community property jurisdictions refers to all money or property acquired during the term of the marriage in which each spouse has an undivided one-half interest.

INTESTATE To die without leaving a valid testamentary instrument.

VESTED INTEREST A present right to property, although the right to the possession of such property may not be enjoyed until a future date.

Downer v. Bramet

Former wife of Bramet (P) v. Husband (D)

Cal. Ct. App., 152 Cal. App. 3d 837 (1984).

NATURE OF CASE: Appeal from judgment of nonsuit.

FACT SUMMARY: In Downer's (P) suit against Bramet (D), her former husband, Downer (P) claimed a community property interest in the sale of a one-third interest in a ranch conveyed to Bramet (D) by his employer after the parties separated.

🏛 RULE OF LAW
Earnings of property attributable to or acquired as a result of labor, skill, and effort of a spouse during marriage are community property.

FACTS: When Downer (P) and Bramet (D) separated in 1971, a marital settlement was executed. The agreement provided that all income and earnings of the former husband or former wife after December 1972 should be the separate property of the acquirer and that each party released any claim to such earnings or after-acquired property. The agreement also stated that if one party was possessed of any community property not set forth in the agreement that party would pay the other party one-half of the fair market value of the property. In August 1972, Bramet's (D) employer deeded the W-4 Ranch in Oregon to Bramet (D) and two other employees. Bramet (D) did not mention his interest in the ranch at the time he executed the settlement agreement. When the ranch was sold for $1,350,000 in 1980, Downer (P) brought suit after learning of the conveyance of the ranch to Bramet (D). Bramet's (D) employer testified at trial that the ranch had been a gift to Bramet (D). Downer (P) claimed a community property interest in one-third of the sale value of the ranch. The trial court granted a nonsuit in the action, and Downer (D) appealed.

ISSUE: Are earnings or property attributable to or acquired as a result of the labor, skill, and effort of a spouse during marriage community property?

HOLDING AND DECISION: (Kaufman, J.) Yes. Earnings or property attributable to or acquired as a result of the labor, skill, and effort of a spouse during marriage are community property. Here, even though the transfer of the ranch to Bramet (D) was legally a gift, there is substantial evidence that the gift was made by Bramet's (D) employer in recognition of Bramet's (D) devoted and skillful services during his employment. So the extent it was and to the extent the efforts and services were rendered during the marriage, the ranch interest of Bramet (D) and the proceeds of the sale were community property. Reversed and remanded.

▶ ANALYSIS

Under the Spanish-American community property scheme, a spouse, who in violation of marital obligations separated from the other spouse, lost any claim to have new acquisitions during the period of separation classified as community property. Under some circumstances, that spouse forfeited any claim to share in accumulation as of the time of separation. The innocent spouse continued to benefit from new acquisitions of the guilty spouse.

Quicknotes

COMMUNITY PROPERTY In community property jurisdictions refers to all money or property acquired during the term of the marriage in which each spouse has an undivided one-half interest.

MARITAL ASSET An asset that is acquired by spouses during their marriage and that is subject to division by the court upon dissolution.

SEPARATE PROPERTY Property owned by one spouse prior to marriage, or any income derived therefrom, and any property received by one spouse pursuant to a gift, devise, bequest or descent.

Marriage of Manfer

Wife (P) v. Husband (D)

Cal. Ct. App., 144 Cal. App. 4th 925 (2006).

NATURE OF CASE: Appeal from an interlocutory order.

FACT SUMMARY: The trial court found that the private conduct of a husband and wife demonstrated a complete and final break in their marriage in June 2004, but then applied the "outsider's viewpoint" standard to defer the date of separation to March 25, 2005, which is the date on which the couple made public their separation from each other. The wife appealed.

🏛 **RULE OF LAW**
To determine the date of separation of a married couple, the test is whether one or both of the parties perceived the rift in their relationship as final, as shown by their words and actions.

FACTS: In June 2004, Samuel Manfer (D) moved out of the family residence and into an apartment. Maureen (P) decided the marriage was over and both parties decided to hide their decision to dissolve the marriage from family and friends until after the holidays at the end of the year. They continued to have some social contact to keep up appearances, but did not have sex, commingle their funds, or support one another. In early 2005, Maureen (P) and Samuel (D) told their daughters and friends that they had separated. The trial court found that even though there was a preponderance of evidence that the private conduct of a husband and wife demonstrated a complete and final break in their marriage in June 2004, the "outsider's viewpoint" of the marriage was that they were not separated until March 25, 2005, which is the date on which the couple made public their separation from each other.

ISSUE: To determine the date of separation of a married couple, is the test whether one or both of the parties perceived the rift in their relationship as final, as shown by their words and actions?

HOLDING AND DECISION: (Ikola, J.) Yes. To determine the date of separation of a married couple, the test is whether one or both of the parties perceived the rift in their relationship as final, as shown by their words and actions. The date-of-separation test does not ask what the public thinks, but whether at least one of the parties intended to end the marriage and whether there was objective conduct showing the finality of the marital relationship. The public-perception standard that the trial court used was contrary to the established "subjective intent" legal standard as set forth in case law. Under the proper standard, the trial court's determination that March 15, 2005, was the date of separation is erroneous.

Because there were no factual findings of equivocation, ambivalence, or uncertainty on the part of either party, as a matter of law, the trial court could not defer the date of separation to coincide with public perception. Reversed.

▶ **ANALYSIS**

Accurate establishment of the date of separation is important because of its effect on the division of community property. Public perception might provide an easier route toward establishing the date of separation, since it is a fairly objective test. But subjective intent, as shown through objective behavior, is the rule in California.

■■■

Quicknotes

INTERLOCUTORY ORDER An order entered by the court determining an issue that does not resolve the disposition of the case, but is essential to a proper adjudication of the action.

OBJECTIVE STANDARD A standard that is not personal to an individual, but is dependent on some external source.

SEPARATION When a husband and wife cease to cohabitate.

SUBJECTIVE STANDARD A standard that is based on the personal belief of an individual.

■■■

Horsman v. Maden

Executor of deceased's estate (P) v. Deceased's estranged wife (D)

Cal. Dist. Ct. App., 48 Cal. App. 2d 635, 120 P.2d 92 (1941).

NATURE OF CASE: Appeal by executors of a will.

FACT SUMMARY: The Executors of the estate of Mr. Maden (P) disagreed with Mrs. Maden (D) as to whether Mr. Maden transferred community property to Mrs. Maden (D) during the marriage, thereby transforming the property that was transferred from community property into the separate property of Mrs. Maden (D), not community property.

🏛 RULE OF LAW
When determining the intent of the donor, "[d]eclarations, by an alleged donor made either before or after the transfer of the property, are admissible and such declarations need not have been made in the presence of the adverse party."

FACTS: Mr. and Mrs. Maden were married in 1914. During the marriage, real property as well as stocks and bonds were acquired as community property. The couple kept their securities in a joint safe deposit box. In addition, Mr. and Mrs. Maden kept funds in joint bank accounts. During 1933 the couple began to have marital difficulties. Mrs. Maden (D) removed the securities from the joint safe deposit box and placed them in a safe deposit box of her own. The parties separated and a dispute arose between the parties over support of Mrs. Maden (D). In October 1934 Mr. Maden met his wife (D) at the bank, where he endorsed the securities and permitted Mrs. Maden (D) to retain them. In 1935 Mr. Maden also executed and delivered to Mrs. Maden (D) a deed to their home, title of which had previously been in both of their names. Mr. Maden told his wife (D) not to record the deed; however, in 1937, Mrs. Maden (D) did record the deed. The parties never divorced. Shortly before Mr. Maden died, he made a will declaring all of the said property to be community property and disposing of the property as community property. There was "no recital in any of the transfers stating that the property was transferred to Mrs. Maden (D) as her separate property." The plaintiffs brought an action against the defendant to quiet title to certain real and personal property and to obtain an accounting with respect to the property disposed of by Mrs. Maden (D). The action was tried by a court without a jury and at the close of plaintiff's presentation, the court granted the defendant's motion for a nonsuit and entered a judgment of dismissal.

ISSUE: When determining the intention of the donor, may the declarations of the alleged donor, made either before or after the transfer, be admitted into evidence?

HOLDING AND DECISION: (Spence, J.) Yes. When determining the intention of the donor, declarations by an alleged donor, made either before or after the transfer of the property, are admissible. In addition, such declarations do not need to be made in the presence of the adverse party. This is a situation in which the property in question was admittedly acquired with community funds and in which it is claimed by the defendant that the property became the defendant's separate property because of executed gifts by the deceased. Although there is a presumption that property acquired by the defendant by a written instrument becomes her separate property, Civ. Code, § 164, this presumption is not conclusive between the parties, but disputable. A court may consider property to be community property regardless of whether the record title stands in the name of the husband or of the wife or in both of their names. And where it is claimed that an instrument in writing, executed by the husband to the wife, constituted a gift to the wife and changed the status of community property to that of separate property of the wife, the question of the intention of the husband in executing such instrument becomes "the all-important and controlling question." Here, the trial court erred in excluding evidence of such declarations and the error was prejudicial to the plaintiffs. The cases cited by the defendant are distinguishable because each of the instruments in the cited cases "expressly recited that the property was conveyed to the wife as her separate property." Reversed and remanded.

⟩ ANALYSIS

Property acquired during the marriage is community property regardless of whose names the property stands in. (citing *Salveter v. Salveter*, 206 Cal. 657, 275 P. 801 (1929); *Jansen v. Jansen*, 127 Cal. App. 294, 15 P.2d 777 (1932)). Moreover, the intent of the donor spouse in executing such an instrument becomes "the all-important and controlling question" (citing *Ruiz v. Dow*, 113 Cal. 490, 45 P. 867, 869; see also *Fanning v. Green*, 156 Cal. 279, 104 P. 308 (1909); *In re Estate of Bruggemeyer*, 115 Cal. App. 525, 2 P.2d 534 (1931)). In order for courts to determine the intent of the donor, evidence of the donor's declarations must be admitted.

■═■

Quicknotes

COMMUNITY PROPERTY In community property jurisdictions refers to all money or property acquired during the term of the marriage in which each spouse has an undivided one-half interest.

Continued on next page.

QUIET TITLE   Equitable action to resolve conflicting claims to an interest in real property.

RECORD AN INSTRUMENT   The recording of a document in the public record.

RECORD TITLE   Title to real property that is recorded in the public land records.

SEPARATE PROPERTY   Property owned by one spouse prior to marriage, or any income derived therefrom, and any property received by one spouse pursuant to a gift, devise, bequest or descent.

Marriage of Ashodian

Cal. Ct. App., 96 Cal. App. 3d 43 (1979).

NATURE OF CASE: Appeal from a portion of an interlocutory judgment of dissolution.

FACT SUMMARY: The court found certain real and personal property to be the separate property of Mrs. Ashodian, based on the presumption in effect prior to 1975 that property acquired by a married woman by an instrument in writing is her separate property.

🏛 RULE OF LAW
A separate property presumption applies to property acquired by a married woman prior to 1975 by an instrument in writing, but it is rebuttable (as to all except bona fide purchasers) by clear and convincing evidence.

FACTS: The record showed that Mrs. Ashodian had used money she earned during marriage and prior to 1975 as a real estate broker to purchase property in her own name, Mr. Ashodian having told her he did not understand the business and did not want to be bothered with it. Mr. Ashodian did, however, at Mrs. Ashodian's request sign grant deeds to two of the properties to aid in their transfer. Other than that, they never discussed these matters. The court, in entering an interlocutory judgment of dissolution of their marriage, concluded that these properties were the separate property of Mrs. Ashodian inasmuch as Mr. Ashodian had failed to introduce evidence sufficient to rebut the statutory presumption in effect prior to 1975 that property acquired by a married woman by an instrument in writing is her separate property.

ISSUE: Is there a rebuttable presumption that property acquired prior to 1975 by a married woman by an instrument in writing is her separate property?

HOLDING AND DECISION: (Stephens, J.) Yes. Prior to 1975, there was a rebuttable presumption that property acquired by a married woman by an instrument in writing was her separate property. That presumption still exists as to property acquired before 1975, but there is no similar presumption as to property acquired after that date. The reason is that in 1975 the statutes were amended to give the wife joint management and control of community property. Therefore, the presumption was no longer needed to protect a married woman's title to property in her own name (as it was when the husband had exclusive management and control of his wife's community property by statute). The presumption, which still exists as to pre-1975 acquisitions, can be overcome only by clear and convincing evidence. There was no such showing in this case. Affirmed.

▶ ANALYSIS

There is some historical basis for the suggestion that a non-statutory presumption of separate property may exist as to post-1975 acquisitions. Prior to the first enactment of a statutory presumption in 1889, there were cases that required such a presumption if a married man conveyed property to his wife or used community funds to buy property in his wife's name.

Quicknotes

COMMUNITY PROPERTY In community property jurisdictions refers to all money or property acquired during the term of the marriage in which each spouse has an undivided one-half interest.

INTERLOCUTORY JUDGMENT An order entered by the court determining an issue that does not resolve the disposition of the case, but is essential to a proper adjudication of the action.

SEPARATE PROPERTY Property owned by one spouse prior to marriage, or any income derived therefrom, and any property received by one spouse pursuant to a gift, devise, bequest or descent.

Estate of Levine

Cal. Ct. App., 125 Cal. App. 3d 701 (1981).

NATURE OF CASE: Petition to have a home declared community property.

FACT SUMMARY: Estelle Levine claimed her husband had never told her he intended the house they held as joint tenants to be community property.

🏛 RULE OF LAW
The presumption that the character of property held by spouses is as set forth in the deed thereto can be rebutted by showing an agreement or common understanding between spouses to the contrary but not simply showing the hidden intent of one spouse, undisclosed to the other spouse at the time of the conveyance.

FACTS: When Phillip Levine died, his son sought to have the probate court declare that the home he and Estelle Levine had held in joint tenancy was actually community property, half of which would go to his children. Evidence was offered to the effect that the Levines, who separately had grown children and had survived the loss of a spouse, married late in life and bought a residence which they held as joint tenants. There was evidence indicating that Phillip Levine had told others he intended to hold the home in joint tenancy for convenience only but wanted it to be considered community property so that he could leave his half to his children. Estelle Levine testified that he had never told her of these intentions. The court denied the petition to declare the residence to be community property.

ISSUE: Can the hidden intent of one spouse, undisclosed to the other, be used to rebut the presumption that the character of property they held is as set forth in the deed?

HOLDING AND DECISION: (Hastings, J.) No. For the purposes of determining the character of real property upon the death of a spouse, there is a rebuttable presumption that the character of the property is as set forth in the deed. It can be rebutted by showing that the character of the property was changed or affected by an agreement or common understanding between the spouses. It cannot, however, be overcome by testimony disclosing the hidden intention of one spouse undisclosed to the other spouse at the time of the conveyance. The statutory presumption that a single-family residence acquired during marriage and held in joint tenancy is presumed to be community property is of no help either, since it applies only in marriage dissolution or separation cases. Affirmed.

▶ *ANALYSIS*

This case illustrates one of the possible pitfalls of attempting to avoid probate by holding property as joint tenants. Property held in joint tenancy passes, upon the death of one tenant, to the other tenant by operation of law and without the necessity of probate administration. This is one of the reasons over 85% of the real property held by married people in California is held in joint tenancy.

■▬■

Quicknotes

COMMUNITY PROPERTY In community property jurisdictions refers to all money or property acquired during the term of the marriage in which each spouse has an undivided one-half interest.

JOINT TENANCY An interest in property whereby a single interest is owned by two or more persons and created by a single instrument; joint tenants possess equal interests in the use of the entire property and the last survivor is entitled to absolute ownership.

REAL PROPERTY Land, an interest in land, or anything attached to the land that is incapable of being removed.

■▬■

Marriage of Lucas

Cal. Sup. Ct., 27 Cal. 3d 808, 614 P.2d 285 (1980).

NATURE OF CASE: Appeal from an interlocutory judgment dissolving a marriage and dividing property.

FACT SUMMARY: At issue in the dissolution proceeding involving Gerald and Brenda Lucas was how to determine their separate and community property interests in the home they had purchased during their marriage with both separate property and community property funds.

🏛 RULE OF LAW
For the purpose of the division of property upon divorce or separate maintenance only, there is a statutory presumption that a single family residence acquired by a couple during marriage as joint tenants is community and it is overcome only by showing they had an agreement or understanding to the contrary.

FACTS: During their marriage, Gerald and Brenda Lucas purchased a home, Brenda using separate property funds for the down payment and some maintenance. Title was taken as "Gerald E. Lucas and Brenda G. Lucas, Husband and Wife as Joint Tenants." The evidence showed that they had very little discussion about their intentions in taking title as joint tenants. When they were undergoing dissolution, the court held that a certain portion was Brenda's separate property interest and another portion represented a community property interest.

ISSUE: Is there a statutory presumption in divorce or separate maintenance cases that a single family residence acquired during marriage as joint tenants is community property absent a showing of some agreement or understanding between spouses to the contrary?

HOLDING AND DECISION: (Manuel, J.) Yes. There is a statutory presumption, covering cases of dissolution and separate maintenance only, that a single family residence acquired during marriage as joint tenants is community property. Of course, that presumption can be overcome by evidence of an agreement or understanding between the parties to the contrary. However, merely tracing the funds used to purchase the residence to a separate property source is not sufficient to overcome this special statutory presumption (which arises only when there is an affirmative act specifying a form of ownership in the conveyance of title), although such tracing can overcome the general presumption that property acquired during marriage is community property. Reversed and remanded for a redetermination of the basis of those principles and rules.

▶ ANALYSIS

The special presumption highlighted in this case was the legislature's attempt to remedy the unhappy situation that developed because real estate brokers, title companies, and escrow companies habitually prepared their documents in joint tenancy form. As a result, the general presumption that property is held in a form consistent with that created by the form of legal title taken worked to keep most property from being properly considered community property upon dissolution or separation.

■▬■

Quicknotes

COMMUNITY PROPERTY In community property jurisdictions refers to all money or property acquired during the term of the marriage in which each spouse has an undivided one-half interest.

DISSOLUTION PROCEEDING AND DECREE A proceeding and resulting decree to terminate a marriage.

INTERLOCUTORY JUDGMENT An order entered by the court determining an issue that does not resolve the disposition of the case, but is essential to a proper adjudication of the action.

JOINT TENANCY An interest in property whereby a single interest is owned by two or more persons and created by a single instrument; joint tenants possess equal interests in the use of the entire property and the last survivor is entitled to absolute ownership.

PRESUMPTION A rule of law requiring the court to presume certain facts to be true based on the existence of other facts, thereby shifting the burden of proof to the party against whom the presumption is asserted to rebut.

SEPARATE PROPERTY Property owned by one spouse prior to marriage, or any income derived therefrom, and any property received by one spouse pursuant to a gift, devise, bequest or descent.

■▬■

Limitations on the Classification Process

Quick Reference Rules of Law

Todd v. Todd

Wife (P) v. Husband (D)

Cal. Ct. App., 272 Cal. App. 2d 786 (1969).

NATURE OF CASE: Appeal from an interlocutory decree of divorce.

FACT SUMMARY: Wife (P) appealed from an interlocutory decree of divorce after the trial court failed to base an award upon the value of husband's (D) education and allegedly failed to properly measure the value of husband's (D) law practice.

🏛 RULE OF LAW
(1) Education is an intangible property right, the value of which, because of its character, cannot have a monetary value placed upon it for division between spouses.
(2) The value of a practice at the time of dissolution of the community is community property.

FACTS: The parties married January 25, 1947, and separated December 26, 1964. Before marriage, husband (D) resumed college which had been interrupted by military service and after marriage entered law school and was admitted to the bar in 1951. His assets at the time were virtually nothing, but by 1965, the community's net assets exceeded $200,000 and his law practice brought in about $23,500 net per year. Wife (P) worked prior to marriage and continued to do so for several years after marriage. Her earnings were treated as community income and used for community purposes. At the time of dividing the community property, the court valued the law practice at $9,866.47 including $1,000 goodwill and awarded wife (P) no portion of it. Wife (P) appealed the interlocutory decree on grounds that husband's (D) education was a community asset and that it had an economic potential of substantial worth that should have been considered, and that husband's (D) law practice was community property, undervalued by the court, and divisible.

ISSUES:
(1) Is education a property right which can have a monetary value placed upon it for division between spouses?
(2) Is the value of a practice, at the time of dissolution of the community, community property?

HOLDING AND DECISION: (Bray, J.)
(1) No. Education is an intangible property right, the value of which, because of its character, cannot have a monetary value placed upon it for division between spouses. Community property does not encompass every property right acquired by either husband or wife during marriage. The right to practice a profession, while a property right, is not classed as community property. Here, the assets of

the community were the results of husband's (D) legal education, and in that sense, the wife (P) realized a portion of the educational value by being awarded more than $111,000 of those assets.

(2) Yes. The value of a practice at the time of dissolution of the community is community property. Where a lucrative law business has been built by the husband, as here, during marriage, "the business is community property and it has a substantial value." On dissolution of the community, the professional practice remains with the spouse who is licensed to practice it, but its existing economic potential may have substantial worth which must be considered in evaluating the community estate for divorce purposes. Here, the court's failure to take into account certain community property for division purposes requires the matter to be remanded for consideration of that property. While the assigned value of goodwill will not be disputed, the value given husband's (D) law practice seems unreasonably low and possibly falsified. Reversed in part and remanded.

▌ ANALYSIS

California has held that the right to practice medicine and similar professions is a property right but cannot be classified as community property. Similarly, the goodwill of a doctor's practice is community property. Generally, the California community property system applies to married persons domiciled in the state. This is rather simple when a couple is domiciled in California for all of their married life, but becomes more complicated when a couple, formerly domiciled elsewhere, settles for some permanent period of domicile in California. In the latter case, the California community property system takes effect as to all property acquired after acquisition of domicile. The character of property acquired before California domicile retains the character it acquired under the law of the place of domicile at the time it was obtained.

■■■

Quicknotes

COMMUNITY PROPERTY In community property jurisdictions refers to all money or property acquired during the term of the marriage in which each spouse has an undivided one-half interest.

GOODWILL An intangible asset reflecting a corporation's favor with the public and expectation of continued patronage.

Continued on next page.

INTANGIBLE RIGHT An interest in property that is not embodied in a physical object.

INTERLOCUTORY Intervening; temporary; refers to an issue that is determined during the course of a proceeding and which does not constitute a final judgment on the merits.

Marriage of Watt

Wife (P) v. Husband (D)

Cal. Ct. App., 214 Cal. App. 3d 340 (1989).

NATURE OF CASE: Appeal from judgment denying spousal support or reimbursement in marital dissolution action.

FACT SUMMARY: After Elaine (P) and David (D) Watt separated, the trial court denied Elaine's (P) request for spousal support and reimbursement to the community of contributions made to David's (D) education, even though Elaine (P) had shouldered a major portion of the community's living expenses during the time that David (D) was a full-time student.

🏛 RULE OF LAW
When awarding spousal support, a court must consider the totality of one spouse's contribution to the other spouse's attainment of a degree, including contributions for ordinary living expenses.

FACTS: For the entire 9½ years of their marriage, David Watt (D) was a full-time student, while Elaine Watt (P) worked full-time for Kaiser Foundation Hospital, using all of her income for family expenses. David (D) paid for his direct educational expenses with loan funds, with the remainder of his student loans going toward the couple's living expenses. David (D) received his medical degree five months after their separation. Elaine (P) testified that she had planned to attend school after David (D) finished his education and that she wanted to enroll in a sixteen-month program to become a chef. David (D) became an anesthesiologist, with an annual income in excess of $94,000. The trial court denied Elaine's (P) request for spousal support, retraining, or education, determining that there were no community contributions which should be reimbursed. David (D) was ordered to assume full responsibility for repayment of all student loans. Elaine (P) appealed.

ISSUE: Must a trial court consider the totality of one spouse's contribution to the other's attainment of a degree when awarding spousal support?

HOLDING AND DECISION: [Judge not stated in casebook excerpt.] Yes. When awarding spousal support, a trial court must consider the totality of one spouse's contribution to the other's attainment of a degree. Nothing in the statutory language regarding spousal support suggests that contributions should be limited to direct education expenses like tuition. Contrary to the finding of the trial court, Elaine's (P) contribution to the community's living expenses was more than a "de minimis" contribution since she shouldered the burden of approximately 64% of their living expenses for a six-year period. Thus, the trial court erred in denying her spousal support. However, the court did not err in denying Elaine's (P) reimbursement claim. Section 4800.3 of the Family Law

Act requires reimbursement only for expenses that are related to the education experience itself. David's (D) direct educational costs were covered by student loans. Elaine (P) has failed to show what living expenses, if any, were specially connected to David's (D) education. Furthermore, because the career change anticipated by Elaine (P) would not immediately or necessarily result in a material increase in income, she did not demonstrate a present need for retraining or education to attain more marketable skills. Finally, David's (D) medical degree is not property subject to division within the community property system. Affirmed in part and reversed in part and remanded.

▶ ANALYSIS

Elaine (P) pursued her reimbursement claim on the theory that § 4800.3 entitled the community to full reimbursement for all its contributions to living expenses during the time one spouse was pursuing an education. However, the court noted that a married couple would incur ordinary living expenses regardless of whether one spouse was attending school, staying home, or working. There is no constitutionally recognized property interest in the form of a right to reimbursement for community property earnings which a spouse voluntarily spends for the couple's living expenses during marriage.

■═■

Quicknotes

DE MINIMIS Insignificant; trivial; not of sufficient significance to require legal action.

SPOUSAL SUPPORT Payments made by one spouse to another in discharge of the spouse's duty pursuant to law, or in accordance with a written divorce or separation decree, in order to provide maintenance for the other spouse.

■═■

Marriage of Graham

Wife (D) v. Husband (P)

Cal. Ct. App., 109 Cal. App. 4th 1321 (2003).

NATURE OF CASE: Appeal of denial of request for reimbursement to the community for funds spent on education.

FACT SUMMARY: During divorce proceedings begun by a husband, the wife requested reimbursement to the community for funds spent on the husband's legal education. The court denied her request.

🏛 RULE OF LAW
A legal education does not substantially enhance earning capacity as a matter of law.

FACTS: Katherine (D) and Jeffrey (P) Graham were married in 1992. In 1994, Jeffrey (P) began law school, and while he was in school, the couple spent over $12,000 for tuition and related expenses. Jeffrey (P) filed for dissolution in 1999 while still in school. At the time his grade point average was approximately 2.2, he had no plan to take the bar exam, and he was employed as a police officer, making over $4400 per month. The trial court denied Katherine's (D) claim for reimbursement of the money spent on Jeffrey's (P) law school tuition and expenses. She appealed, and urged the appellate court to rule that legal, medical, dental, and accounting degrees will be presumed to result in a substantially enhanced earning capacity as a matter of law.

ISSUE: Does a legal education substantially enhance earning capacity as a matter of law?

HOLDING AND DECISION: (Moore, J.) No. A legal education does not substantially enhance earning capacity as a matter of law. The comment following Family Code section 2541, which provides that the community should be reimbursed for contributions to education or training that substantially enhances the earning capacity of the party, states that the requirement is a limitation intending to restrict litigation by requiring that the education or training must "demonstrably enhance" earning capacity. In this case, the evidence does not show that Jeffrey's (P) legal education had either substantially or demonstrably enhanced his earning capacity. He may or may not pass the bar, and may choose not to do anything with the law degree. Even if he does, not all lawyers are good at it, and not all make money. His future earnings derived by the degree are too speculative to support adoption of the rule proposed by Katherine (P).

▌ ANALYSIS

The court's ruling limits consideration of education as a measure of future earnings, where there is no evidence of enhanced earning. Had the husband begun law school during their marriage, and, when finished, enjoyed a steadily escalating income until the dissolution proceeding, the court might have reached a different result.

■■▬■

Quicknotes

EXPECTANCY INTEREST The expectation or contingency of obtaining possession of a right or interest in the future.

REIMBURSEMENT The tendering of payment to a party for expenditures made on his behalf.

■■▬■

Marriage of McTiernan & Dubrow

Husband (P) v. Wife (D)

Cal. Ct. App., 133 Cal. App. 4th 1090 (2005).

NATURE OF CASE: Appeal of trial court judgment in marriage dissolution.

FACT SUMMARY: The husband, a film director, appealed the court's decision that there was goodwill in his business valued at $1.5 million, and that it was community property.

⚖ RULE OF LAW
A person's expectation of future patronage in his profession does not constitute business goodwill that is community property.

FACTS: John McTiernan (P) directed blockbuster films, including "Die Hard," "The Hunt for Red October," and "The Thomas Crown Affair." During his eight-plus years of marriage to Donna Dubrow (D), he had earned approximately $15 million. The trial court found that there was goodwill in his profession, because of his "quantifiable expectation of future patronage." The court determined its value using the "excess earnings" method, by which his earnings were compared with that of a peer whose performance was "average." The trial court decided that McTiernan's (P) goodwill at the time of separation was $1.5 million. McTiernan (P) appealed, arguing that he does not have an asset that can properly be classified as goodwill.

ISSUE: Does a person's expectation of future patronage in his profession constitute business goodwill that is community property?

HOLDING AND DECISION: (Flier, J.) No. A person's expectation of future patronage in his profession does not constitute business goodwill that is community property. According to California's Business and Professional Code, the "good will" of a business is the expectation of continued public patronage, it constitutes property, and it is transferable. a "business" refers to a professional, commercial, or industrial enterprise with assets, not a natural person. California case and statutory law support this decision, which hold that goodwill is not separable from the physical assets of the business that generated the goodwill, but is separate and distinct from the person or persons who operate, own, or manage the business. The everyday meaning of the noun "a business" clearly indicates a commercial or industrial enterprise with assets, not a natural person. Had the law intended to include in the definition a natural person, the law could have expressly done so. In addition, property only qualifies as property if it is transferable, and if it is not, it cannot be divisible. The fact that McTiernan's (P) standing as a director is not transferable, refutes the trial court's conclusion that his practice is like the practice of an attorney or physician. The practice of an attorney or physician is transferable. The trial court erred in finding that there was goodwill in this case, and the judgment must be modified to eliminate the $1.5 million in assets that are subject to division.

CONCURRENCE: (Boland, J.) The Legislature defined goodwill as property only in connection with a business, and specified that the goodwill of a business is transferable. Since there is no transferable business, there is no property to divide, and there is no goodwill. If a broader definition of goodwill were intended, it would be for the Legislature to remedy.

CONCURRENCE AND DISSENT: (Cooper, J.) The majority's conclusion that the husband has no divisible goodwill is wrong. The limiting of goodwill to a "business," as opposed to an individual, is semantic and not a valid basis for overturning the trial court's judgment. Finding that McTiernan's (P) goodwill was not transferable also is not a valid ground for reversing. The use of the phrase "is transferable" in the statutory provision that "the good will of a business is property and is transferable" is meant to convey that goodwill may be transferred, not to qualify or define the term "goodwill." The trial court properly determined the existence and extent of the husband's goodwill.

▶ ANALYSIS

The value of goodwill is not so easy to grasp, because it is often not tangible. Businesses usually sell for more than their assets are worth, and the difference between the book value and the sale price is usually attributable to goodwill—customer loyalty, employee knowledge, and so on. Courts and accountants devise methods for valuing goodwill, but there's really no telling how much a willing buyer might pay for a business, because there's no telling how much it is worth to her.

■=■

Quicknotes

ASSET An item, of real or personal property, that is owned and has tangible value.

BOOK VALUE The value of an asset as reflected by a corporation's balance sheet.

EXPECTANCY INTEREST The expectation or contingency of obtaining possession of a right or interest in the future.

GOODWILL An intangible asset reflecting a corporation's favor with the public and expectation of continued patronage.

■=■

Marriage of Spengler

Wife (P) v. Beneficiary (D)

Cal. Ct. App., 5 Cal. App. 4th 288 (1992).

NATURE OF CASE: Appeal from ruling as to the community property character of an employment-related group term life insurance policy.

FACT SUMMARY: When Daniel Spengler's second wife, Rose (D), collected the full amount of an employment-related group term life insurance policy, his first wife, Barbara (P), contended it was community property subject to division upon the dissolution of her marriage to Daniel.

🏛 RULE OF LAW
The renewal right aspect of an employment-related group term life insurance policy is not "property" subject to division in a marital dissolution, where the employee has no enforceable right to renewal.

FACTS: During the marriage of Daniel and Barbara (P) Spengler, Daniel worked for an employer who insured his employees through a group term life insurance plan. Four years after Daniel was diagnosed with prostate cancer, he and Barbara (P) separated, and the marriage was dissolved. Daniel later married Rose (D), naming her as his beneficiary under the policy. He died three months later, and Rose (D) received approximately $100,000 from the policy. Barbara (P) sought half the proceeds as a community asset. The trial court, concluding that the insurance policy was community property and an omitted asset under Civil Code § 4353, entered judgment in Barbara's (P) favor for one-half of the policy proceeds. This appeal followed.

ISSUE: Is the renewal right aspect of an employment-related group term life insurance policy "property" subject to division in a marital dissolution, where the employee has no enforceable right to renewal?

HOLDING AND DECISION: (Sims, J.) No. The renewal right aspect of an employment-related group term life insurance policy is not "property" subject to division in a marital dissolution, where the employee has no enforceable right to renewal. In this case, since Daniel's prostate cancer rendered him uninsurable, Barbara (P) argued that renewed coverage under his existing policy without proof of insurability was a valuable community asset. However, the right to continued insurance protection under an employment-related insurance policy depends on the insured's continuing to work at that employment and on the employer's continuing to provide the group insurance plan. A benefit contingent on continued employment may or may not be property subject to the community property laws, depending on whether it is a mere expectancy or a contract right. Daniel's renewal right depended on his continued employment and also on the continued offering of the plan by his employer,

who could have terminated the policy at any time with thirty days' notice. Thus, although there was a contingent contract right to policy proceeds in the event of his death during the term, Daniel had no right to compel his employer to renew the coverage at the end of the term. In other words, the prospect of renewal of the policy by the employer was a beneficence to which Daniel had no enforceable right. Therefore, the trial court erred in finding the insurance policy to be a community property asset. Reversed.

▶ ANALYSIS

California courts of appeal are split on the issue of whether a term life insurance policy is community property. In this case, the Third District Court of Appeals adopted the ruling of the First District in *Estate of Logan* 191 Cal. App. 3d 319, 325 (1987). Although the court here agreed with the holding of *Logan*, it disagreed with dictum in *Logan* stating that if the insured becomes uninsurable during the marriage, the policy's renewal rights to continued coverage that cannot otherwise be purchased are a community asset to be divided upon dissolution.

■≡■

Quicknotes

COMMUNITY PROPERTY In community property jurisdictions refers to all money or property acquired during the term of the marriage in which each spouse has an undivided one-half interest.

■≡■

Marriage Cases

Would-be spouses (P) v. State (D)

Cal. Ct. App., 143 Cal. App. 4th 873 (2006).

NATURE OF CASE: Appeal of trial court judgment.

FACT SUMMARY: [Facts omitted from casebook excerpt.]

🏛 RULE OF LAW
California laws limiting marriage to unions between a man and a woman do not violate the state's constitution if they bear a rational relationship to a conceivable legitimate state purpose.

FACTS: [Facts omitted from casebook excerpt.]

ISSUE: Do California laws limiting marriage to unions between a man and a woman violate the state's constitution if they bear a rational relationship to a conceivable legitimate state purpose?

HOLDING AND DECISION: (McGuiness, J.) No. California laws limiting marriage to unions between a man and a woman do not violate the state's constitution if they bear a rational relationship to a conceivable legitimate state purpose. In equal protection and due process analyses, if a law does not abridge a fundamental right or employ a suspect classification, it is reviewed under the rational relationship test. Under the rational relationship test, a law is presumed to be constitutional if it bears some rational relationship to a conceivable legitimate purpose.

First, no fundamental right to marriage between same-sex partners has been recognized in the state of California. Marriage is a fundamental right under case law, but the right at issue here is the right to same-sex marriage, not simply marriage, and the right to marry is not abridged by this law. Because case law addressing marriage refers explicitly or implicitly to the union of a man and a woman, and there is no historical tradition of same-sex marriage in this country, acknowledging a fundamental right to marry between people of the same sex would require a redefinition of the term "marriage." The interracial marriage cases do not provide support for finding gays and lesbians have a fundamental right to marry their same-sex partners either, because those laws were based solely on the race of potential spouses, and race is a suspect classification, thus warranting the application by the court of strict scrutiny to the law. While same-sex marriage may some day enjoy the same constitutional protection afforded opposite-sex marriage, the court cannot compel the change asked for. The marriage laws do not infringe on other asserted constitutional rights either, including the right of privacy and intimate association and the right of free expression. Even if there is a protected right of privacy in having intimate relations with a same-sex partner, that does not mean the

right to marry has to be expanded to encompass such a constitutionally protected right. Moreover, the law does not intrude on their rights to privacy and intimacy, since it does not take away a right that existed before. And while there are expressive aspects to marriage, it is obviously much more than a communicative act, and if the law makes unavailable for same-sex couples this one form of expression while all others are intact, a constitutional violation does not exist.

Second, while classifications based on gender are considered "suspect" under the California Constitution, and laws that discriminate based on sex are therefore subject to strict scrutiny, the marriage laws at issue do not discriminate based on gender either. The law singles out as a class neither men nor women for unequal treatment. Strict scrutiny is not warranted where a law merely mentions gender, but does not treat either group differently. And while statutes prohibiting interracial marriage were struck down despite the fact that those laws treated all races similarly—the laws in question prohibited all races, not just some, from marrying outside their race—the analogy is inapt, because at issue in those laws were racial classifications, all of which had to be subjected to strict scrutiny. In addition, though facially neutral, anti-miscegenation laws' true purpose was to maintain "White Supremacy," according to the Supreme Court. California's opposite-sex definition of marriage was not intended to discriminate against males or females.

Third, sexual orientation is not a suspect classification for purposes of equal protection analysis, and the fact that the law has a disparate impact on gays and lesbians does not trigger strict scrutiny. A statutory classification can be considered "suspect" only where the defining characteristic (1) is based on an immutable trait, (2) bears no relation to a person's ability to perform or contribute to society, and (3) is associated with a stigma of inferiority and second-class citizenship. The latter two requirements are easily satisfied in the case of gays and lesbians, but the first is controversial. There is no precedent for subjecting laws to strict scrutiny which classify based on sexual orientation, and strict scrutiny is therefore not triggered by a classification based on sexual orientation.

Since the law does not abridge a fundamental right or involve a suspect classification, it must be reviewed under the rational basis test, and under that test, it is constitutional. The state's interest in preserving the traditional definition of marriage is legitimate, because the opposite-sex definition of marriage has existed throughout history and continues to represent the common understanding of marriage in most other countries and states. And the opposite-sex requirement

Continued on next page.

is rationally related to the state's interest. But California also provides equal rights and benefits to same-sex partners through a domestic partnership system, and the dual system is therefore not discriminatory. This is not an echo of the "separate but equal" era in our history of race relations, because there is no constitutionally suspect classification in this case. The state may legitimately support the two institutions—marriage and domestic partnership—while also acknowledging their differences.

And finally, the state's interest in carrying out the will of its citizens is legitimate. Voters passed Proposition 22, which enacted a law providing that only marriages between a man and a woman is valid or recognized in California. But California also enacted "sweeping" domestic partnership laws to provide substantially the same rights as marriage to same-sex couples, carefully balancing the needs and desires of Californians. Whether their reasoning is agreeable is beside the point, because, in any event, the court defers to the Legislature's judgment where a law is challenged under the rational basis test. Reversed.

DISSENT: (Kline, J.) The inalienable right to marry the person of one's choice is a fundamental constitutional right, and therefore may not be restricted by the state without a showing of compelling need. According to the Supreme Court, the right to marry cannot be taken from anyone—even the most violent criminal—because their characteristics do not render them unqualified for such a basic right. To uphold a law that denies the right of gay men and lesbians to enter society's most fundamental and sacred institution is incompatible with liberty and equality, inhumane, and wrong.

▶ ANALYSIS

In 2008, this decision was reversed by the California Supreme Court. See *In re Marriage Cases,* 43 Cal. 4th 757 (2008). The Court ruled in a 4–3 decision that laws directed at gays and lesbians are subject to strict scrutiny and that marriage is a fundamental right under the California Constitution, and that the state's ban on same-sex marriage through legislative action in 1977 and through Proposition 22 was unconstitutional. The Court's ruling also established that any law discriminating on the basis of sexual orientation is constitutionally suspect, making California the first state in the United States to set such a strict standard. The Court's ruling was nullified in large part by the amendment of the California Constitution through Proposition 8, which passed on Nov. 4, 2008. Proposition 8 required that the Constitution define marriage as a union between members of opposite sex. The amendment does not disturb that part of the Court's holding that gay men and lesbians constitute a suspect class for purposes of equal protection under the constitution.

Quicknotes

DUE PROCESS RIGHTS The constitutional mandate requiring the courts to protect and enforce individuals' rights and liberties consistent with prevailing principles of fairness and justice, and prohibiting the federal and state governments from such activities that deprive its citizens of a life, liberty or property interest.

EQUAL PROTECTION CLAUSE A constitutional provision that each person be guaranteed the same protection of the laws enjoyed by other persons in like circumstances.

FUNDAMENTAL RIGHT A liberty that is, either expressly or impliedly provided for in the United States Constitution, the deprivation or burdening of which is subject to a heightened standard of review.

LEGITIMATE STATE INTEREST Under a rational basis standard of review, a court will not strike down a statute as unconstitutional if it bears a reasonable relationship to the furtherance of a legitimate governmental objective.

MISCEGENATION Marriage between persons of different races.

RATIONAL BASIS REVIEW A test employed by the court to determine the validity of a statute in equal protection actions, whereby the court determines whether the challenged statute is rationally related to the achievement of a legitimate state interest.

STRICT SCRUTINY The method by which courts determine the constitutionality of a law when a law affects a fundamental right. Under the test, the Legislature must have had a compelling interest to enact the law and measures prescribed by the law must be the least restrictive means possible to accomplish its goal.

SUSPECT CLASSIFICATION A class of persons that have historically been subject to discriminatory treatment; statutes drawing a distinction between persons based on a suspect classification, i.e., race, nationality or alienage, are subject to a strict scrutiny standard of review.

Coats v. Coats

Wife (P) v. Husband (D)

Cal. Sup. Ct., 160 Cal. 671, 118 P. 441, 36 L.R.A.N.S. 844 (1911).

NATURE OF CASE: Appeal from division of property upon annulment of marriage.

FACT SUMMARY: Husband (D), after successfully seeking an annulment of his 18-year marriage, appealed the division of "community" property on grounds that as the marriage was void from its beginning and, therefore, no property rights depending on marriage existed.

🏛 RULE OF LAW

Upon annulment, property, even though it is no longer community, should be divided as community property would have been upon dissolution of the marriage by divorce or death.

FACTS: The parties were married in 1887. In 1906, husband (D) obtained an annulment of the marriage on the ground of the physical incapacity of the wife (P). Wife (P) then brought this action for a division of the property acquired during the marriage. During the marriage, husband (D) owned a farm with wife (P) rendering the usual services of a farmer's wife. In 1897, husband (D) entered the horse trading business and lost all his wealth by 1900, except for his $2,500 interest in his business. From 1901 to 1906, the parties lived in hotels and apartments, and husband (D), through his skill, increased his assets to $70,000. Wife's (P) services were of no pecuniary value in husband's (D) accumulation of this wealth during this period. The trial court awarded wife (P) $10,000. Husband (D) appealed on the grounds that as an annulment renders the marriage void ab initio (from the start) and makes children illegitimate, the property rights of either party must also be at an end so far as they depend on the marriage.

ISSUE: Upon annulment, should property, even though it is no longer community, be divided as community property would have been upon dissolution of the marriage by divorce or death?

HOLDING AND DECISION: (Sloss, J.) Yes. Upon annulment, property, even though it is no longer community, should be divided as community property would have been upon dissolution of the marriage by divorce or death. A woman who has in good faith entered into a marriage which may be voided at the insistence of the other party, is entitled, upon or after annulment, to any participation in the property which has been accumulated by the efforts of both parties during the existence of the supposed marriage, and while she in good faith believed that such marriage was valid. To say otherwise "would be contrary to the most elementary conceptions of fairness and justice." Husband (D) had the right to void the marriage, but in the absence of seeking an annulment, the marriage was good against everybody. Husband's (D) argument fails because the question does not involve property owned by him before marriage or acquired by him after termination of marriage, but involves acquisitions by husband (D) and wife (P) during marriage. If both contributed to the acquisitions, each has an interest which did not exist at the time of the marriage. In the absence of fraud or other grounds, there is no reason to say that one party over the other should have title to all the property by reason of an annulment. As the apportionment of property upon annulment is not provided by any statute, equitable principles must be followed. It is immaterial when the bulk of the property was acquired. Wife (P) does not sue here on a contract for services. She was a wife and her share must so be measured. There is no more equitable basis of apportionment than an equal division. As wife (P) was awarded much less than one-half, husband (D) had no reason to complain. Affirmed.

▶ ANALYSIS

A putative marriage is one entered into by the spouses in good faith without any knowledge that there is an impediment to it. At common law, a putative spouse was not protected by the marital property system. In California, an equitable system supplements the community property system and is known as "quasi-marital property." Civil Code § 4452 states the status of the putative spouse and outlines the division of quasi-marital property. The code section basically codifies the holding of this case by saying that quasi-marital property shall be divided in the same manner as community property. It is important to remember that the putative marriage must have been entered into in good faith.

Quicknotes

AB INITIO From its inception or beginning.

ANNULMENT To nullify a marriage; to establish that the marital status never existed.

COMMUNITY PROPERTY In community property jurisdictions refers to all money or property acquired during the term of the marriage in which each spouse has an undivided one-half interest.

EQUITY Fairness; justice; the determination of a matter consistent with principles of fairness and not in strict compliance with rules of law.

PUTATIVE SPOUSE A spouse who has a good faith belief in the existence of a valid marriage, when the marriage is in fact unlawful.

Estate of Leslie

Husband (P) v. Wife (D)

Cal. Sup. Ct., 37 Cal. 3d 186, 689 P.2d 133 (1984).

NATURE OF CASE: Appeal from distribution of estate of a putative spouse.

FACT SUMMARY: In Garvin's (P) action to determine his entitlement to distribution of the estate of his putative spouse, Leslie (D), Garvin (P), who believed that the couple has been validly married, contended that he was entitled to succeed to a share of Leslie's (D) separate property.

> **RULE OF LAW**
> A surviving putative spouse is entitled to succeed to a share of his or her decedent's separate property.

FACTS: Garvin (P) and Leslie (D) were married in Mexico. The marriage was invalid because it was never recorded as required by Mexican law. However, Garvin (P) believed that he and Leslie (D) were validly married. The couple lived together for nine years until Leslie's (D) death. Leslie (D) died intestate and was survived by Garvin (P) and four children from previous marriages. One of his sons, Smith, filed a petition for letters of administration and sought a determination as to who was entitled to distribution of the estate. Garvin (P) filed a petition in opposition to son's petition. The trial court decided to deny Garvin's (P) petition and determined that he was not entitled to any of Leslie's (D) separate property. Garvin (P) appealed.

ISSUE: Is a surviving putative spouse entitled to succeed to a share of his or her decedent's separate living property?

HOLDING AND DECISION: (Bird, C.J.) Yes. A surviving putative spouse is entitled to succeed to a share of his or her decedent's separate property. This result is inherently fair. By definition, a putative marriage is a union in which at least one partner believes in good faith that a valid marriage exists. As in this case, the couple conducts themselves as husband and wife throughout the period of their union. The right of separate property accorded to legal spouses should be afforded putative spouses. To accord a surviving putative spouse the status of "surviving spouse" simply recognizes that a good faith belief in the marriage should put the putative spouse in the some position as a survivor of a legal marriage. The couple involved here lived together for a substantial period of time, conducting themselves as husband and wife throughout their union. Therefore, this court holds that a surviving putative spouse is entitled to succeed to a share of the decedent's separate property. Reversed and remanded.

► ANALYSIS

In defining the rights of a putative spouse, California courts have stressed the essentially equitable character of the doctrine. The courts have also cautioned that the doctrine should not be applied where injustice would result, particularly where its application would deprive third persons of equitable community property (quasi-marital property). The situation is analogous to the division of legal community property.

━━■

Quicknotes

DUTY OF GOOD FAITH OF FAIR DEALINGS An implied duty in a contract that the parties will deal honestly in the satisfaction of their obligations and without intent to defraud.

INTESTATE To die without leaving a valid testamentary instrument.

PUTATIVE SPOUSE A spouse who has a good faith belief in the existence of a valid marriage, when the marriage is in fact unlawful.

SEPARATE PROPERTY Property owned by one spouse prior to marriage, or any income derived therefrom, and any property received by one spouse pursuant to a gift, devise, bequest or descent.

━━■

Estate of Hafner

First wife (P) v. Estate (D)

Cal. Ct. App., 184 Cal. App. 3d 1371 (1986).

NATURE OF CASE: Appeal from award of community property.

FACT SUMMARY: In Joan Hafner's (P) appeal against the estate of Hafner (D), Joan (P) contended that the trial court's award of the proceeds of the estate to Hafner's (D) putative spouse, Helen, was error and contrary to law in that the authorizing statute provided that the rights of the legal spouse should be established and protected.

🏛 RULE OF LAW
When a just distribution of an estate among the parties is not provided by any statute, equity should be used to resolve the issue of distribution.

FACTS: Joan Hafner (P) and Charles Hafner (D) were married and had three children. Shortly before the birth of their third child, Charles (D) abandoned Joan and did not supply her with any support. Charles (D) moved to California, met Helen, and married her without dissolving his marriage to Joan (P). Charles (D) told Helen that he and Joan (P) were divorced, and she, in good faith, relied on his representations. Helen had no actual knowledge or reasonable grounds to believe otherwise. Charles (D) was involved in a serious auto accident and received $600,000 in settlement. Charles (D) later died and his estate consisted of the remainder of the proceeds of his personal injury settlement. Helen, at Charles' (D) death, filed a petition for determination of entitlement to estate, claiming to be Charles' (D) surviving wife. Joan (P) also filed a petition, asserting her claim to the estate as Charles' (D) surviving wife. The court concluded that Helen had a legal right to succeed to Charles' (D) entire estate as Charles' (D) good faith putative spouse. Joan (P) appealed, contending that the award to Helen was error and contrary to law in that the law provided that the rights of the legal spouse should be established and protected.

ISSUE: When a just distribution of an estate among the parties is not provided by any statute, should equity be used to resolve the issue of distribution?

HOLDING AND DECISION: (Danielson, J.) Yes. When a just distribution of an estate among the parties is not provided by any statute, equity should be used to resolve the issue of distribution. The first duty of equity is to be equitable. In this case, equity demands and this court holds that one-half the estate should be distributed to Helen, the putative spouse, and one-half to Joan, the legal spouse. Every court which has considered the issue of succession to a decedent's intestate estate, as between a surviving legal spouse and a surviving putative spouse, has awarded one-half of the quasi-marital property to the putative spouse and one-half to the legal spouse. The statutes are not designed to provide for the unique circumstances present in such cases, and thus, equity must be relied upon here for the just distribution of the estate. Reversed and remanded.

DISSENT: (Lui, J.) The proper legal distribution of Charles' (D) estate should result in Helen, the surviving putative spouse, taking one-half of the decedent's entire estate as her quasi-marital property. As to the remainder of Charles' (D) estate, the putative and legal spouses should be treated equally: one-third of the estate divided equally between Helen and Joan (P); the remaining two-thirds should be distributed in equal shares to Charles' (D) four children by both relationships.

▶ ANALYSIS

There can be no community property in the absence of a valid marriage. The putative cases decided prior to the enactment of the Family Law Act struggled with the term to be applied to property which cannot be "community property" because there was no valid marriage but which otherwise has all the incidents of community property. In California Civil Code § 4452, the Legislature resolved the problem by directing that such property be called "quasi-marital property."

■■■■

Quicknotes

DUTY OF GOOD FAITH OF FAIR DEALINGS An implied duty in a contract that the parties will deal honestly in the satisfaction of their obligations and without intent to defraud.

INTESTATE To die without leaving a valid testamentary instrument.

PUTATIVE SPOUSE A spouse who has a good faith belief in the existence of a valid marriage, when the marriage is in fact unlawful.

SURVIVING SPOUSE The spouse who remains living after the death of the other spouse.

■■■■

Velez v. Smith

Domestic partner (P) v. Domestic partner (D)

Cal. Ct. App., 142 Cal. App. 4th 1154 (2006).

NATURE OF CASE: Appeal of dismissal of petition to dissolve a domestic partnership and divide property.

FACT SUMMARY: [Two women registered as domestic partners in the city and county of San Francisco, and received a domestic partnership certificate. They never registered as domestic partners with the state of California. The trial court dismissed a petition for dissolution on grounds that it was without legal basis. The petitioning partner appealed.]

🏛 RULE OF LAW
A domestic partner who failed to register her relationship in accordance with the family law of the state may not bring a petition for dissolution and division of property under the putative spouse doctrine.

FACTS: [Lena Velez (P) and Krista Smith (D) registered as domestic partners in the city and county of San Francisco, and received a domestic partnership certificate. They never registered as domestic partners with the state of California. For 10 years following their registration with the city and county, they lived together, bought real and personal property together, maintained joint bank accounts with commingled funds, and shared a health insurance plan. Lena (P) filed a petition for dissolution of domestic partnership, and an amended petition requesting dissolution, division of accumulated partnership property, terminating of jurisdiction to award support to Krista (D), and attorneys' fees. Krista moved to strike the petition as beyond the family court's jurisdiction. The trial court dismissed a petition for dissolution on grounds that it was without legal basis. The petitioning partner appealed.]

ISSUE: May a domestic partner who failed to register her relationship in accordance with the family law of the state bring a petition for dissolution and division of property under the putative spouse doctrine?

HOLDING AND DECISION: [Judge not identified in casebook excerpt.] No. A domestic partner who failed to register her relationship in accordance with the family law of the state may not bring a petition for dissolution and division of property under the putative spouse doctrine. The putative spouse doctrine allows an innocent party to relief where her marriage is invalid due to some legal infirmity. Domestic partners are not afforded the same rights and privileges as married partners. It must be assumed that the Legislature was aware of the putative spouse doctrine, and that it would have added to the Domestic Partner Act the rights granted to putative spouses had it been so inclined. The trial court did not err in granting the motion to strike Lena's (P) petition.

▶ ANALYSIS

The law regarding same-sex marriage and domestic partnership is changing quickly across the nation, and domestic partnership laws may be obsolete sooner rather than later. Nevertheless, for the moment, domestic partner laws are valid, and simply do not confer the same rights and responsibilities as marriage, including rights against, and responsibilities toward, each other.

Quicknotes

PUTATIVE SPOUSE A spouse who has a good faith belief in the existence of a valid marriage, when the marriage is in fact unlawful.

Vallera v. Vallera

Wife to a meretricious relationship (P) v. Husband to a meretricious relationship (D)

Cal. Sup. Ct., 21 Cal. 2d 681, 134 P.2d 761 (1943).

NATURE OF CASE: Appeal from an action for separate maintenance and for a division of community property.

FACT SUMMARY: "Wife" (P) alleged that she was a common law wife under the laws of Michigan even though she knew that husband (D) was already married, and while the trial court found that the parties were not married, it did find that they were tenants in common as to certain property.

> ### 🏛 RULE OF LAW
> A woman who lives with a man as his wife but with no genuine belief that she is legally married to him acquires by reason of cohabitation alone no rights of a co-tenant in his earnings and accumulations during the period of their relationship.

FACTS: "Wife" (P) brought this action for separate maintenance and for a division of community property amounting to $60,000. She alleged that a common-law marriage was contracted in Michigan, but the trial court found that no such marriage was entered into on December 16, 1938, or at any other time. It further found that there was never an attempt to agree to live as husband and wife, and that beginning in May 1936, and continuing for the next three years, the parties meretriciously cohabited. Furthermore, Vallera (D) was married to one Ethel Chippo from January 1933 to December 1938 and "wife" (P) knew of this legal disability to her alleged common-law marriage. The parties did not learn, however, of the dissolution of that marriage until November 1939. On July 6, 1940, Vallera (D) entered into a valid marriage with one Lido Cappello. While the trial court concluded that the parties were never married, that no separate maintenance was due, and that there was no community property, it held that all property acquired by the parties between December 16, 1938, and July 6, 1940, except such property acquired by gift, devise, bequest, or descent, was held by them as tenants in common, each owning an undivided one-half. Vallera (D) appealed on the ground that "wife" (P) could acquire no rights not having entered into the relationship in good faith.

ISSUE: Does a woman who lives with a man as his wife but with no genuine belief that she is legally married to him acquire by reason of cohabitation alone any rights of a co-tenant in his earnings and accumulations during the period of their relationship?

HOLDING AND DECISION: (Traynor, J.) No. A woman who lives with a man as his wife but with no genuine belief that she is legally married to him acquires by reason of cohabitation alone no rights of a co-tenant in his earnings and accumulations during the period of their relationship. Clearly, when a woman lives with a man as his

wife in the belief that a valid marriage exists, she has a right to share in the property acquired by them until termination of their relationship. However, the essential basis for a putative marriage is a belief in its validity as an actual marriage. Without such good faith belief, the equitable considerations arising from the reasonable expectation of the continuation of benefits attending the status of marriage are not present. This will not prevent a woman from recovering property to which she is entitled, such as where she and the man agree to pool their earnings and share equally in their joint accumulations. Even in the absence of such an express agreement, the woman would be entitled to share in jointly accumulated property in the proportion to which she contributed to it. Here, there was no evidence of any such agreement. The "meager evidence" regarding the accumulation of alleged community property can only support an inference it consisted totally of Vallera's (D) earnings. Accordingly, that portion of the decision appealed from is reversed.

DISSENT (IN PART): (Curtis, J.) The majority appears to believe that the value of "wife's" (P) services was no more than the cost of the maintenance of her and her two children while seemingly ignoring her value as a housekeeper, homemaker, and cook.

▶ ANALYSIS

The court has still not settled the problem brought out in the dissent to the extent to which contributions by way of services should be tied into the meretricious relationship in establishing property rights. As for agreements between persons during meretricious relationships to share in business acquisitions, they may be implied as well as expressed. The case above expresses a traditional approach to the question of meretricious relationships. The parties are left in the position in which they have placed themselves. Neither can claim a right to property held in the other's name.

▄▄▄

Quicknotes

COMMUNITY PROPERTY In community property jurisdictions refers to all money or property acquired during the term of the marriage in which each spouse has an undivided one-half interest.

CO-TENANT A tenant possessing property with one or more persons jointly or whose interest is derived from a common grantor.

Continued on next page.

GOOD FAITH RELIANCE Honest reliance on the representations of another.

MERETRICIOUS RELATIONSHIP A stable, marital-like relationship where both parties cohabit with knowledge that
a lawful marriage between them does not exist.

TENANCY IN COMMON An interest in property held by two
or more people, each with equal right to its use and
possession; interests may be partitioned, sold, conveyed,
or devised.

Marvin v. Marvin

Spouse to a meretricious relationship (P) v. Husband to a meretricious relationship (D)

Cal. Sup. Ct., 18 Cal. 3d 660, 557 P.2d 106 (1976).

NATURE OF CASE: Action seeking declaratory relief and imposition of a constructive trust.

FACT SUMMARY: Michelle Marvin (P) maintained that she and Lee Marvin (D) had entered into an express and/or implied agreement to share equally in all property acquired while they lived together.

🏛 RULE OF LAW
The courts should enforce express and implied contracts between non-marital partners except to the extent that they are explicitly founded on the consideration of meretricious sexual services and should also employ the doctrine of quantum meruit, or equitable remedies such as constructive or resulting trusts, in distributing property acquired during a non-marital relationship, when warranted by the focus of the case.

FACTS: Alleging that they had an oral agreement to share equally in all property acquired while they lived together without benefit of marriage, Michelle Marvin (P) sought a declaration of her contract and property rights once Lee Marvin (D) compelled her to leave the house they had shared and subsequently stopped supporting her. She also sought to impose a constructive trust on half of the property thus acquired. Furthermore, she insisted that part of the aforementioned oral agreement was that she would give up her singing career and devote full time to Lee Marvin (D) as homemaker, companion, housekeeper, cook, etc. and he would support her for the rest of her life. The trial court granted judgment to Lee Marvin (D) on the pleadings, leaving him with all the property accumulated by the couple during their live-in relationship.

ISSUE: Should the courts enforce express and implied contracts between parties living together without benefit of marriage?

HOLDING AND DECISION: (Tobriner, J.) Yes. In light of the changes that have occurred in this society, it seems appropriate that the courts should enforce express and implied contracts between non-marital partners except to the extent that they are explicitly founded on the consideration of meretricious sexual services. So long as the agreement does not rest upon illicit meretricious consideration, the parties may order their economic affairs as they choose, and no policy precludes the courts from enforcing such agreements. Furthermore, the courts should employ the doctrine of quantum meruit, or equitable remedies such as constructive or resulting trusts in distributing property acquired during a non-marital relationship (when warranted by the facts of the case). Reversed and remanded for further proceedings.

CONCURRENCE AND DISSENT: (Clark, J.) The majority is correct in permitting recovery on the basis of either an express or implied in fact agreement between the parties and it is at this point that the majority should end its analysis. All anticipated rights, duties and remedies within every meretricious relationship should not be attempted to be determined, but rather they should be decided as each arises in a concrete case. The majority fails to advise us of the circumstances permitting recovery, limitations on recovery, or whether their numerous remedies are cumulative or exclusive. The majority's opinion also raises, but does not answer, many other questions.

▌ ANALYSIS

On remand, the court found that no express or implied agreement between the parties existed. However, the judge seized upon the equitable remedies portion of the Supreme Court's decision and awarded Michelle Marvin (P) $104,000 for "rehabilitation purposes so that she may have the economic means to reeducate herself." The award was reversed on appeal.

Quicknotes

CONSTRUCTIVE TRUST A trust that arises by operation of law whereby the court imposes a trust upon property lawfully held by one party for the benefit of another, as a result of some wrongdoing by the party in possession so as to avoid unjust enrichment.

EQUITABLE REMEDY A remedy that is based upon principles of fairness as opposed to rules of law; a remedy involving specific performance rather than money damages.

IMPLIED CONTRACT An agreement between parties that may be inferred from their general course of conduct.

MERETRICIOUS RELATIONSHIP A stable, marital-like relationship where both parties cohabit with knowledge that a lawful marriage between them does not exist.

ORAL CONTRACT A contract that is not reduced to written form.

QUANTUM MERUIT Equitable doctrine allowing recovery for labor and materials provided by one party, even though no contract was entered into, in order to avoid unjust enrichment by the benefited party.

RESULTING TRUST An equitable trust that is established from the inferred intent of the parties to create a trust.

Rozan v. Rozan

Wife (P) v. Husband (D)

Cal. Sup. Ct., 49 Cal. 2d 322, 317 P.2d 11 (1957).

NATURE OF CASE: Appeal from an action for divorce and a division of community property.

FACT SUMMARY: Husband (D), who with his wife (P), moved to California in 1948, contended that certain North Dakota real property was his separate property, not community.

🏛 RULE OF LAW
Property acquired while domiciled in California as the result of a spouse's work, efforts, ability, and skills is community property.

FACTS: Wife (P) brought this action against husband (D) for divorce, support, custody of their minor child, and division of their community property. Wife (P) contended that the parties established their domicile in California in May 1948, when husband (D) sent her to California from Colorado to set up a home. Husband (D) claimed that there was no evidence that he was ever in California before July 1948, and that he did not intend to establish California domicile by sending wife (P) to California. Further, it appeared that the parties acquired some money and property after acquiring California domicile due to husband's efforts, work, ability, and skill as an oil broker and operator, but that they lost it all between late 1948 and early 1949. After 1949, husband (D) acquired certain North Dakota properties which were purchased with "movables" for he had made a lot of money on Canadian oil ventures as an oil operator. The parties at this time still owned everything they had brought with them from California. The trial court awarded a 65% interest in the title to the North Dakota properties to wife (P) and husband (D) appealed.

ISSUE: Is property acquired while domiciled in California as the result of a spouse's work, efforts, ability, and skills community property?

HOLDING AND DECISION: (Traynor, J.) Yes. Property acquired while domiciled in California as the result of a spouse's work, efforts, ability, and skills is community property. The first finding essential to a division of property is that the parties established domicile in California, in this case in May 1948, and not later than July 1948. Marital interests in movables acquired during marriage are governed by the law of their domicile at the time of acquisition. These interests do not change even when the movables are taken into another state or are used to purchase land in another state. The evidence supported a finding of domicile in July 1948, and it is unnecessary to find any earlier domicile because all property was acquired after that date. As for the North Dakota properties, it was undisputed that they were acquired after 1949 when the parties had no funds. "It thus appears that the purchase money for the North Dakota properties was acquired by the efforts and skill of (husband [D]) as an oil operator subsequent to the establishment of the California domicile and was therefore community property." Furthermore, a presumption arises that all property acquired by the husband after marriage is community property in the absence of evidence of gift, bequest, devise, or descent. As no such evidence was presented, there was sufficient evidence to uphold the trial court's ruling. Affirmed.

▶ ANALYSIS

In a companion case of the same name, the courts of North Dakota gave full faith and credit to the California judgment that the North Dakota land was community property. However, North Dakota did not recognize that portion of the judgment entitling wife (P) to 65% of the interest in the property, *Rozan v. Rozan*, 129 N.W. 2d 694 (N.D., 1964). It must be kept in mind that the law of the domicile of the parties at the time of acquisition of the property governs the nature of the property in question. Parties who have had several domiciles can create difficult questions upon divorce. When the parties are domiciled in California and receive no separate income, all property accumulated during such time is presumed to be community.

Quicknotes

COMMUNITY PROPERTY In community property jurisdictions refers to all money or property acquired during the term of the marriage in which each spouse has an undivided one-half interest.

DOMICILE A person's permanent home or principal establishment to which he has an intention of returning when he is absent therefrom.

SEPARATE PROPERTY Property owned by one spouse prior to marriage, or any income derived therefrom, and any property received by one spouse pursuant to a gift, devise, bequest or descent.

Grappo v. Coventry Financial Corporation

Husband (P) v. Wife (D)

Cal. Ct. App., 235 Cal. App. 3d 496 (1991).

NATURE OF CASE: Appeal from judgment rejecting community property claim.

FACT SUMMARY: After Michael Grappo (P) and his wife Tillie (D) separated, she moved to her separate property on the Nevada side of Lake Tahoe, for which Michael (P) had lent her the funds to construct a house, and Michael (P) brought this action, claiming an interest in the real property.

🏛 RULE OF LAW
The laws of the domicile of the parties at the time property was acquired govern in determining the characterization of the property as separate or community.

FACTS: During their marriage, Michael Grappo (P) and Tillie Grappo (D) resided in California, both acquiring property in their own names and agreeing to keep their separate property separate and not to commingle it with or transmute it to community property. They also agreed that any increase in value to each party's separate property attributable to their personal time and effort would also be separate property. Through a bank loan in her name, Tillie (D) acquired three unimproved lots on the Nevada side of Lake Tahoe as her separate property in 1977. Michael (P) supplied the money for the costs of construction of the house on the property through loans from his own funds. Tillie (D) moved into the house after they separated in 1979. Michael (P) filed for dissolution of the marriage in 1983 but did not prosecute it. In this action, Michael (P) did not seek to recover indebtedness on the basis of a loan transaction but claimed an interest in the Nevada property. The trial court found that Michael (P) was not entitled to an equitable lien on the Lake Tahoe property and that he had no community property interest in that property. Micheal (P) appealed, claiming the court erred in applying California, rather than Nevada, law.

ISSUE: Do the laws of the domicile of the parties at the time property was acquired govern in determining the characterization of the property as separate or community?

HOLDING AND DECISION: (Merrill, J.) Yes. The laws of the domicile of the parties at the time property was acquired govern in determining the characterization of the property as separate or community. This rule applies even when the acquired property is located in another state. In this case, the parties resided in California during the time Tillie (D) purchased the property in Nevada and Michael (P) supplied the money for the costs of construction of the house. It is apparent that California has the most significant relationship to the parties and issues in this case. Therefore, the characterization of the parties'

respective marital interests in the Nevada property must be determined under the community property law of California. Michael (P) states that his claim is not a contractual one but is based on the fact that he was married to Tillie (D) and that he acquired a community interest as a result of his advancement of funds and his contribution of time, labor, and skill to the property. Thus, the trial court's choice of California law was correct. Affirmed.

▶ ANALYSIS

The excerpt omits any discussion of the California community property law applicable to this situation. Under California law, the parties in a marriage have the right to agree to keep their property segregated to preserve its separate character. However, under California law applicable at the time the Grappos were married, the parties in a marriage could, by oral or written contract, change property from community to separate. Current law requires such agreements to be in writing. Because husbands previously had sole management and control of community property, prior California law treated a husband's voluntary improvement of his wife's separate property as a gift, with no right of reimbursement unless there was an agreement to compensate. Although the nonretroactive family law amendments of 1973, giving both spouses equal right of management and control, removed the underlying theory of the prior rule, *In re Marriage of Camire*, 105 Cal. App. 3rd 859 (1980), involving the husband's use of community funds to improve the wife's separate property, held that the traditional rule denying reimbursement to the community in this situation was still good law. The court in *Grappo* appears to have applied the presumption that Michael (P) had made a gift to Tillie's (D) separate property since Michael (P) had sole management and control over his own separate property as a result of their agreement.

■=■

Quicknotes

COMMINGLED ASSETS The combining of money or property into a joint account or asset.

COMMUNITY PROPERTY In community property jurisdictions refers to all money or property acquired during the term of the marriage in which each spouse has an undivided one-half interest.

DOMICILE A person's permanent home or principal establishment to which he has an intention of returning when he is absent therefrom.

Continued on next page.

EQUITABLE LIEN An equitable right to have specified property applied to payment of a debt.

SEPARATE PROPERTY Property owned by one spouse prior to marriage, or any income derived therefrom, and any property received by one spouse pursuant to a gift, devise, bequest or descent.

TRANSMUTATION The conversion of the separate property of one spouse into separate property of the other spouse or into community property, or the conversion of community property into the separate property of one spouse, by either an agreement or transfer made in a writing signed by the spouse whose interest is adversely affected and without the payment of consideration.

Addison v. Addison

Wife (P) v. Husband (D)

Cal. Sup. Ct., 62 Cal. 2d 558, 399 P.2d 897 (1965).

NATURE OF CASE: Appeal from an action for divorce.

FACT SUMMARY: Wife (P), in her action for divorce, sought to show that husband (D) had orally transmuted his separate property, and that the separate property should be divided as quasi-community property.

🏛 RULE OF LAW
The concept of quasi-community property, which is applicable only if a divorce or separate maintenance action is filed after the parties have become domiciled in California, does not abridge privileges and immunities of national citizenship because valid independent reasons bearing a close relation to the resultant discrimination exist in its support.

FACTS: The parties were married in Illinois in 1939. Husband (D) was engaged in the used car business and conflicting evidence showed his net worth at the time of marriage ranging from nothing to $20,000. In 1940, the parties moved to California, bringing $149,000 in cash and personal property. In 1961, wife (P) sought a divorce and an equitable division of the marital property. She advanced two theories in support of her claimed property interest. First, wife (P) alleged that husband (D) had verbally recognized her interest (oral transmutation), and, second, she argued that the marital property was quasi-community property, contending that property presently in husband's (D) name was acquired by use of property brought from Illinois, and that property would have been community had it originally been acquired while the parties were domiciled in California. The trial court found no oral transmutation and held the quasi-community property statute unconstitutional on grounds that it abridged the privileges and immunities of national citizenship. Wife (P) appealed.

ISSUE: Does the concept of quasi-community property, which is applicable only if a divorce or separate maintenance action is filed after the parties have become domiciled in California, abridge the privileges and immunities of national citizenship?

HOLDING AND DISSENT: (Peters, J.) No. The concept of quasi-community property, which is applicable only if a divorce or separate maintenance action is filed after the parties have become domiciled in California, does not abridge the privileges and immunities of national citizenship because valid independent reasons bearing a close relation to the resultant discrimination exist in its support. The quasi-community property statute makes no attempt to alter property rights merely upon crossing the boundary into California. It is only applicable if, after the acquisition of California domicile, certain acts or events occur, which give rise to an action for divorce or separate maintenance, acts or events not necessarily connected with a change of domicile at all. Neither does the statute violate due process. Vested rights may be impaired with due process of law whenever reasonably necessary to protect the health, safety, morals, and general well being of the people. Where an innocent party would otherwise be left unprotected, the state has a substantial interest in equitably dividing marital property without violating due process. As for the disparity in treatment, the inquiry into whether valid independent reasons for it exist must be conducted in view of the principle that states have considerable leeway in analyzing local evils and prescribing appropriate cures. Here, wife (P), a former non-domiciliary of California, is a member of a class of persons who have lost the protection of Illinois law had they sought a divorce there. California must provide that protection. Additionally, the fact that the statute was not passed until after the action was filed is of no consequence because the law at the time of judgment is controlling. Nor is the statute being applied retroactively because it neither creates nor alters rights except upon divorce or separate maintenance. Reversed and remanded.

DISSENT: (McComb, J.) Dissents for reasons found in *Addison v. Addison*, 40 Cal. Rptr. 330.

▶ ANALYSIS

The quasi-community property concept arises also in the following situations: (1) when a wife's obligation to her husband is argued; (2) when a homestead is being established; (3) when a probate homestead is demanded; (4) when a homestead is distributed in probate; and (5) in questions of gift and inheritance taxation. The civil and probate codes provide for wealth classification in its original and changed forms, but do not mention how rents, profits, or income from such wealth should be classified. It has been held that such wealth has the same classification as the wealth that produced it.

▬▬

Quicknotes

DUE PROCESS The constitutional mandate requiring the courts to protect and enforce individuals' rights and liberties consistent with prevailing principles of fairness and justice and prohibiting the federal and state governments from such activities that deprive its citizens of life, liberty, or property interest.

Continued on next page.

MARITAL PROPERTY Property accumulated by a married couple during the term of their marriage.

PRIVILEGES AND IMMUNITIES CLAUSE Refers to the guarantee set forth in the Fourteenth Amendment to the United States Constitution recognizing that any individual born in any of the United States is entitled to both state and national citizenship and guaranteeing such citizens the privileges and immunities thereof.

SEPARATE PROPERTY Property owned by one spouse prior to marriage, or any income derived therefrom, and any property received by one spouse pursuant to a gift, devise, bequest or descent.

TRANSMUTATION The conversion of the separate property of one spouse into separate property of the other spouse or into community property, or the conversion of community property into the separate property of one spouse, by either an agreement or transfer made in a writing signed by the spouse whose interest is adversely affected and without the payment of consideration.

Marriage of Roesch

Cal. Ct. App., 83 Cal. App. 3d 96 (1978).

NATURE OF CASE: Appeal from portions of an interlocutory judgment of dissolution.

FACT SUMMARY: William Roesch separated from his wife and moved to California, where the court hearing his petition for dissolution characterized the assets he and his wife had accumulated while living in Pennsylvania as quasi-community property and divided them accordingly.

🏛 RULE OF LAW
A statute purporting to change the classification of property acquired during marriage on the basis of a subsequent change in domicile can be constitutionally applied only in cases meeting two prerequisite conditions: (1) both parties have changed their domicile to the state enacting the statute, and (2) subsequent to the change of domicile the spouses sought a legal alteration of their marital status in a court of that state.

FACTS: For their 27 years of married life, William and Helen Roesch lived in Pennsylvania and acquired numerous assets there. Eventually, William Roesch separated from his wife and moved to California, where he filed for dissolution six months later. The trial court characterized the Pennsylvania assets as quasi-community property, pursuant to a statute authorizing such, and divided them accordingly. Helen Roesch appealed certain portions of that judgment.

ISSUE: Can a statute change the classification of property acquired during marriage merely on the basis of a subsequent change in domicile?

HOLDING AND DECISION: (Christian, J.) No. California has passed a statute that attempts to change the classification of property acquired by those living elsewhere upon a change in domicile to California by treating it as "quasi-community" property if it would have been community property had the acquiring spouse been domiciled in California at the time of its acquisition. Vested property rights can be diminished by such retrospective application of changes in marital property only if such application is demanded by a sufficiently important state interest. The Privileges and Immunities and Due Process Clauses preclude reclassification of property based upon a mere change of domicile except in cases where two prerequisite conditions are met: (1) both parties have changed their domicile to California, and (2) subsequent to the change of domicile the spouses sought in a California court legal alteration of their marital status. California's quasi-community property statute cannot, therefore, be constitutionally applied in this case.

▶ ANALYSIS

In the absence of a statute, personal property acquired by a spouse during marriage and while domiciled in a common law state does not lose its character as the separate property of the acquiring spouse upon a change of domicile to a community property state. Furthermore, all property which has as its traceable source such common law separate property is likewise deemed separate property.

Quicknotes

COMMUNITY PROPERTY In community property jurisdictions refers to all money or property acquired during the term of the marriage in which each spouse has an undivided one-half interest.

DUE PROCESS RIGHTS The constitutional mandate requiring the courts to protect and enforce individuals' rights and liberties consistent with prevailing principles of fairness and justice, and prohibiting the federal and state governments from such activities that deprive its citizens of a life, liberty or property interest.

PRIVILEGES AND IMMUNITIES CLAUSE Refers to the guarantee set forth in the Fourteenth Amendment to the United States Constitution recognizing that any individual born in any of the United States is entitled to both state and national citizenship and guaranteeing such citizens the privileges and immunities thereof.

SEPARATE PROPERTY Property owned by one spouse prior to marriage, or any income derived therefrom, and any property received by one spouse pursuant to a gift, devise, bequest or descent.

Marriage of Bouquet

Husband (P) v. Wife (D)

Cal. Sup. Ct., 16 Cal. 3d 583, 546 P.2d 1371 (1976).

NATURE OF CASE: Action by husband declaring that his earnings while living apart be deemed his separate property.

FACT SUMMARY: Bouquet (D) argued that since Civil Code § 5118 became effective prior to the entry of the interlocutory decree, his earnings while living apart should be deemed his separate property.

🏛 **RULE OF LAW**
The state may impair vested property rights by finding community property legislation is retroactive in the interest of equal property division and to eliminate inequities.

FACTS: Bouquet (D) and his wife (P) were married in 1941 and separated in 1969. In 1971, Bouquet's wife (P) petitioned for dissolution. An interlocutory decree was entered in 1972. After the filing of the petition, but before the granting of the interlocutory decree, § 5118 of the Civil Code was amended. The state had allowed the wife (P) to retain her earnings and accumulations while living separate and apart as her separate property. The husband's (D) earnings and accumulations during this same period were deemed community property. The new law provided that earnings and accumulations of both spouses were deemed separate property. The wife (P) argued that the law was prospective based on statutory construction; that it was an unconstitutional impairment of vested property rights without due process of law. The court found that the statute was prospective and affirmed the property division.

ISSUE: May the state impair vested property rights by finding community property legislation, such as Civil Code § 5118, retroactive?

HOLDING AND DECISION: (Tobriner, J.) Yes. First, with respect to the statute itself, it is neutral on its face, i.e., neither prospective nor retroactive. Next, there is no announced congressional intent. However, several letters from individual congressmen, including the initiator of the legislation, indicate that the Legislature may have intended it to be retroactive. The legislation was passed to eliminate the probable prior unconstitutional aspects of former § 5118. Finally, § 5118 as originally enacted operated to defeat the announced Legislative intent to effectuate an equal division of community property. Where the Legislative intent is evidenced and a retroactive application is necessary to remedy past evils, the statute may be deemed retroactive. While Mrs. Bouquet's (P) interests had vested, they must give way to a valid state interest in the equal division of community property. There is no impermissible impairment of property rights in such cases, especially where there have been past inequities. Reversed.

▶ *ANALYSIS*

Where the state has an overwhelming interest in an area it may legislate retroactively. Here there was no real detrimental reliance on the previous legislation. Mrs. Bouquet (P) would have earned the money regardless of the state of the law. The reallocation of property rights is often held to be retroactive (see *Addison v. Addison*, 62 Cal. 2d 558 (1965)). Statutes are often held to be retroactive where past injustice needs to be remedied, e.g., the whole line of school desegregation cases.

■■■

Quicknotes

COMMUNITY PROPERTY In community property jurisdictions refers to all money or property acquired during the term of the marriage in which each spouse has an undivided one-half interest.

CONSTRUCTION The examination and interpretation of statutes.

INTERLOCUTORY ORDER An order entered by the court determining an issue that does not resolve the disposition of the case, but is essential to a proper adjudication of the action.

SEPARATE PROPERTY Property owned by one spouse prior to marriage, or any income derived therefrom, and any property received by one spouse pursuant to a gift, devise, bequest or descent.

■■■

Marriage of Heikes

Cal. Sup. Ct., 10 Cal. 4th 1211, 899 P.2d 1349 (1995).

NATURE OF CASE: Marital dissolution proceeding.

FACT SUMMARY: Husband sought a petition for review of the proper classification of two parcels of land which he reconveyed to himself and his wife as joint tenants during the marriage.

🏛 RULE OF LAW
Retroactive application of the requirement that separate property contributions to community property in dissolution proceedings commenced after January 1, 1984 be reimbursed would unconstitutionally deprive the noncontributing spouse of vested property interests.

FACTS: Husband owned a home in Santa Barbara and a vacant lot near Boron as his separate property. While married to his wife, he conveyed both parcels to wife and himself as joint tenants. The trial court found there was no oral or written agreement preserving the interest of husband in the parcels. The judgment in the present dissolution action classified both parcels as community property. Six days after that judgment, this court filed *In re Marriage of Hilke*, which gave retroactive effect to the presumption that property acquired during marriage in joint tenancy is community property. Here the husband moved for a partial new trial. The trial court ordered a new trial and the court of appeal affirmed. Wife petitioned for review.

ISSUE: Would retroactive application of the requirement that separate property contributions to community property in dissolution proceedings commenced after January 1, 1984 be reimbursed unconstitutionally deprive the noncontributing spouse of vested property interests?

HOLDING AND DECISION: (Werdegar, J.) Yes. Retroactive application of the requirement that separate property contributions to community property in dissolution proceedings commenced after January 1, 1984 be reimbursed would unconstitutionally deprive the noncontributing spouse of vested property interests. Family Code § 2640 provides that when community property is divided upon dissolution of marriage, either spouse is to be reimbursed for contributions of separate property to the acquisition of any property being divided as community property, unless the contributing spouse has waived the right to reimbursement in writing. Prior to that time, any such contribution was an outright gift in the absence of an agreement as to reimbursement. In *Fabian*, 715 P.2d 253 (1986), the court held that in dissolution proceedings commenced before January 1, 1984 (the effective date of the section) to apply § 2640 retroactively would deprive the other spouse of a vested property right in violation of the California Constitution. The Legislature soon thereafter amended the section to expressly provide that it applied to actions commenced after January 1, 1984. The issue here is whether the Constitution permits the statutorily authorized reimbursement of a husband for separate property contributions he made in 1976 to property divided as community property in 1992. We conclude that such reimbursement would deprive the wife of a vested property interest without due process of law. Husband claims reimbursement for the conveyance of the two parcels he owned separately to his wife and himself in joint tenancy, thereby making both presumptively community property for purposes of dissolution. In *Fabian*, we held that retroactive application of the section to cases pending on January 1, 1984 impaired vested property rights without due process of law. This court denied reimbursement in that case, noting that for more than 20 years prior to the enactment of section 2640, it was well established that absent an agreement to the contrary, separate property contributions to a community asset were deemed gifts to the community. Since the Fabians had no such agreement, retroactive application of the reimbursement requirement would have impaired the wife's vested property interest. The court pointed out however, that impairment of a vested property interest does not necessarily invalidate a statute's retroactive application if such impairment does not violate due process. With respect to the relevant state interest prong, the court concluded that the need to enhance fairness by complementing the community property presumption with a right of reimbursement for separate property contributions does not represent a sufficiently significant state interest to mandate retroactivity. With respect to the extent of the reliance on the former law, the legitimacy of such reliance was clear. Husband's transfer of his separate property to the joint ownership of his wife and himself gave the wife a vested property interest that cannot constitutionally be impaired through the retroactive application of the reimbursement provisions of § 2460. Reversed.

▶ ANALYSIS

All courts to consider the issue of retroactive application of the reimbursement requirement have held that it would violate due process. The court of appeal here refused to follow such decisions on the basis of what it characterized as dictum in the *Hilke* case limiting the holding in *Fabian*.

■=■

Quicknotes

COMMUNITY PROPERTY In community property jurisdictions refers to all money or property acquired during the term of the marriage in which each spouse has an undivided one-half interest.

Continued on next page.

DUE PROCESS RIGHTS The constitutional mandate requiring the courts to protect and enforce individuals' rights and liberties consistent with prevailing principles of fairness and justice, and prohibiting the federal and state governments from such activities that deprive its citizens of a life, liberty or property interest.

JOINT TENANCY An interest in property whereby a single interest is owned by two or more persons and created by a single instrument; joint tenants possess equal interests in the use of the entire property and the last survivor is entitled to absolute ownership.

SEPARATE PROPERTY Property owned by one spouse prior to marriage, or any income derived therefrom, and any property received by one spouse pursuant to a gift, devise, bequest or descent.

Wissner v. Wissner

Wife (P) v. Deceased husband's parents (D)

338 U.S. 655 (1950).

NATURE OF CASE: Appeal from finding that proceeds of insurance policy was community property.

FACT SUMMARY: In Marilyn Wissner's (P) action against the Wissners (D), her deceased husband's parents, Marilyn (P) contended that the proceeds of a National Service Life insurance policy were community property and she was entitled to one-half thereof.

RULE OF LAW
The proceeds of a National Service Life Insurance policy belong to the named beneficiary and are not subject to state community property laws.

FACTS: Leonard Wissner died while serving in the U.S. Army. When he enlisted in the Army, he had taken out a National Service Life Insurance policy which remained in effect at the date of his death. Leonard and his wife, Marilyn, (P) were estranged at the time he entered the Army, or shortly thereafter. Without the knowledge or consent of Marilyn (P), Leonard named his parents, the Wissners (D), as beneficiaries of the policy. After Leonard's death, the U.S. Veteran's Administration began paying the Wissners (D) the proceeds of the policy. Marilyn (P) then brought action, contending that the proceeds were community property and that she was entitled to one-half thereof. The trial court and the appellate court ruled in Marilyn's (P) behalf, deciding that the proceeds were and are the community property of the widow and the decedent, and that Marilyn (P) was entitled to one-half of the proceeds. The Wissners (D) appealed.

ISSUE: Do the proceeds of a National Service Life Insurance policy belong to the named beneficiary and are they subject to state community property laws?

HOLDING AND DECISION: (Clark, J.) Yes. The proceeds of a National Service Life Insurance policy belong to the named beneficiary and are not subject to state community property laws. Congress has spoken with force and clarity in the National Service Life Insurance Act of 1940 in directing that the proceeds of a National Service Life Insurance policy belong to the designated beneficiary. Pursuant to the congressional command, the government contracted to pay the insurance to the insured's choice. He chose his parents. The federal statute establishes the fund in issue, and forestalls the existence of any "vested" right under state law in the proceeds of federal insurance. Reversed and remanded.

DISSENT: (Minton, J.) The husband's earnings are community property under § 161a of the California Civil Code. The wife has a vested interest in one-half of such earnings. The source of the premium paid on the policy was Leonard's army pay and so the proceeds of the policy should be community property.

ANALYSIS

Employee retirement benefits have long been considered property classifiable as community property under the California community property system. Even non-vested pension benefits may be so considered. Where retirement benefits have been created by federal legislation and a conflict arises between federal and state law, federal law preempts state law.

Quicknotes

COMMUNITY PROPERTY In community property jurisdictions refers to all money or property acquired during the term of the marriage in which each spouse has an undivided one-half interest.

Boggs v. Boggs

First wife's sons (P) v. Second wife and widow (D)

520 U.S. 833 (1997).

NATURE OF CASE: Review of summary judgment upholding validity of testamentary transfer in favor of plaintiffs.

FACT SUMMARY: The widow (D) of Isaac Boggs sought a declaratory judgment that the Employee Retirement Income Security Act (ERISA), a federal regulatory scheme, preempted the application of state community property and succession laws.

🏛 **RULE OF LAW**
The purpose of ERISA is to provide a minimum stream of income to a plan participant's surviving spouse in cases where state law defining property interest is contrary.

FACTS: Dorothy Boggs predeceased her husband Isaac; by her will, her share in Isaac's retirement benefits went to Isaac. Isaac held a lifetime interest in two-thirds of Dorothy's estate, with the ownership interest going to her sons (P). When Isaac died, Sandra (D), Isaac's second wife, contested the validity of the transfer to the sons (P).

ISSUE: Does ERISA control where state law does not guarantee a plan participant's surviving spouse the minimum stream of income provided for by ERISA?

HOLDING AND DECISION: (Kennedy, J.) Yes. The purpose of ERISA is to provide a minimum stream of income to a plan participant's surviving in cases where state law defining property interests is contrary. ERISA requires that a surviving spouse be paid 50% of the annuity payable during the joint lives of the participant and spouse. If state law were allowed to control in this case, Sandra's (D) share could be reduced well beneath that level. Even more troubling, the funds could be diverted to support an unrelated stranger. This would defeat the purpose of ERISA; where a conflict between federal and state law clearly exists, the state law cannot stand. Reversed.

DISSENT: (Breyer, J.) If Dorothy had divorced Isaac, she would have been entitled to her community share of the retirement benefits, leaving a later-appearing Sandra (D) with a diminished share. I cannot believe that Congress intended to effectively strip Dorothy of her community property rights through ERISA simply because, instead of divorcing Isaac, she remained his wife until she died. Moreover, the law in question concerns family, property, and probate; all traditionally areas of state concern.

▶ *ANALYSIS*

The preemption analysis in *Boggs* was applied in situations involving military disability benefits elected in lieu of retirement, and Social Security benefits. The courts have generally

held the distribution of any benefits potentially within the jurisdiction of federal law to be governed by federal law, despite the fact that family law and property law are traditional areas of state concern.

■■■

Quicknotes

COMMUNITY PROPERTY In community property jurisdictions refers to all money or property acquired during the term of the marriage in which each spouse has an undivided one-half interest.

DECLARATORY JUDGMENT A judgment of the court establishing the rights of the parties.

ERISA 29 U.S.C. § 1001 Enacted in 1974, a comprehensive statute designed to benefit the interests of employees and their beneficiaries in employee benefit plans.

TESTAMENTARY REMAINDER An interest created by a testamentary instrument that remains after the termination of the immediately preceding estate.

■■■

Selected Problems in Classification

Quick Reference Rules of Law

See v. See

Husband (P) v. Wife (D)

Cal. Sup. Ct., 64 Cal. 2d 778, 415 P.2d 776 (1966).

NATURE OF CASE: Appeal of interlocutory divorce decree.

FACT SUMMARY: In the 21 years of his marriage, See (P) extensively commingled community and separate property assets and claimed on divorce that the fact that aggregate community expenses exceeded aggregate community income during marriage justified a finding that no community property remained.

> 🏛 **RULE OF LAW**
> In order to overcome the presumption that all property acquired during marriage is community property, a spouse must prove that each and every item he claims as separate property was acquired for separate property and (absent concrete proof of such) in order to be able to implicitly trace any such item to separate property, such spouse must prove that community expenses exceeded community income at the time of acquisition of "that particular item."

FACTS: Laurance (P) and Elizabeth (D) See were married for 21 years, from 1941 to 1962. During that period, two See family corporations flourished, See's Candies, Inc. and See's Candy Shops, Inc., both of which paid Laurance See (P) salaries aggregating over $1 million during the 21 years of his marriage. These salaries were paid into the two accounts primarily at issue here. "Account 13," a corporate account for Laurance's (P) personal use into which his See's Candies salary was paid and out of which many community expenses were paid, and the "Security Account," a bank account primarily for Laurance's (P) separate property, into which, however, his Candy Shops salaries were sometimes paid and out of which many community expenses were paid. In addition, to the above-described commingling, money from both accounts was from time to time transferred from one to the other, without ever earmarking whether Laurance's (P) separate or community property was being used. At the proceedings for the dissolution of the See marriage in 1962, Laurance (P), over Elizabeth's (D) objection, was permitted to aggregate both community income and expenses and subtract the latter from the former to prove that no net community property had been generated by the marriage. This appeal followed.

ISSUE: May a spouse be permitted to prove that his marriage generated no net community property (to be divided on dissolution) by merely subtracting aggregate community expenses during marriage from aggregate community income, regardless of how any particular item of marital property was acquired?

HOLDING AND DECISION: (Traynor, C.J.) No. In order to overcome the presumption that all property acquired during marriage is community property, a spouse must prove that each and every item he claims as separate property was acquired for separate property, and (absent concrete proof of such) in order to be able to implicitly trace any such item to separate property, such spouse must prove that community expenses exceeded community income at the time of acquisition of "that particular item." The formula which the court permitted Laurance (P) here to use was based on an incorrect reading of past cases. It is true that such a formula was used by one appeals court in *Estate of Ades*, 184 P.2d 1 (1947), but that case involved a special problem, the determination of whether assets "discovered" after marriage could be traced to property acquired before it. The aggregation there employed is wholly inapplicable to the case at bar. Here, the problem is the tracing of extensively and indiscriminately commingled assets. The law affords Laurance (P) no special help in straightening this problem out, neither by permitting aggregation nor even any right of reimbursement for any separate property he may have commingled with community property here. The cause is therefore remanded to determine whether Laurance (P) can do this. Reversed.

▶ *ANALYSIS*

This case established the general rule that income and expenses may not be aggregated for the purpose of making any "net community property" computations for characterization of property on death or dissolution. Practically, this requires an item-by-item analysis of all marital property for which a separate property classification is sought. Note also that *See v. See* stands for the proposition that where community and separate funds are commingled the entire fund will be characterized as community property, unless the separate property owner can specifically identify which particular funds are separated-property. Note, however, the rationale for this grew out of the old rule that the husband in any marriage had management and control over all community property. It was felt that this power should be subjected to a duty to keep records of separate and community property, to protect wives from abuse. The sanction used to enforce this latter rule was the presumption of community property.

◼▬◼

Continued on next page.

Quicknotes

COMMINGLED ASSETS The combining of money or property into a joint account or asset.

COMMUNITY PROPERTY In community property jurisdictions refers to all money or property acquired during the term of the marriage in which each spouse has an undivided one-half interest.

INTERLOCUTORY ORDER An order entered by the court determining an issue that does not resolve the disposition of the case, but is essential to a proper adjudication of the action.

SEPARATE PROPERTY Property owned by one spouse prior to marriage, or any income derived therefrom, and any property received by one spouse pursuant to a gift, devise, bequest or descent.

■≡■

Marriage of Mix

Husband (P) v. Wife (D)

Cal. Sup. Ct., 14 Cal. 3d 604, 536 P.2d 479 (1975).

NATURE OF CASE: Action to classify property purchased with commingled funds as community property.

FACT SUMMARY: Mrs. Mix (D) commingled the community earnings from her law practice with her separate property funds in several accounts.

🏛 RULE OF LAW
A spouse may trace the source of funds withdrawn from a commingled account where separate property deposits exceed separate property withdrawals.

FACTS: Mrs. Mix (D) was an attorney. Mrs. Mix (D) also owned a large amount of separate property. Mrs. Mix (D) commingled her community earnings with separate property funds in several bank accounts. Mrs. Mix (D) purchased certain items from these commingled accounts. In a subsequent dissolution action, Mr. Mix (P) declared these items to be community property. Mrs. Mix (D) attempted to trace the source of the funds used to purchase the property. She showed that her separate property deposits to these accounts exceeded her withdrawals. However, Mrs. Mix (D) could not associate which deposits and withdrawals went with which account. The court believed her testimony and declared the items to be her separate property.

ISSUE: May items purchased with commingled funds be traced by establishing an excess of separate deposits over separate withdrawals?

HOLDING AND DECISION: (Sullivan, J.) Yes. Since both spouses now have equal rights to the management and control of the community, the presumption is that all property acquired during marriage is community. This presumption may be overcome by either of two methods of tracing. It may be established by showing the exact source of the funds used to acquire the property or by showing that all of the community funds were exhausted. Mrs. Mix (D) could not establish that the community had been exhausted. The proof submitted as to the excess of separate fund deposits over withdrawals is persuasive, but her failure in establishing from which account the funds were taken or deposited will not support a finding that the property acquired was separate property. However, based on Mrs. Mix's (D) testimony in support of her records, the trial court could and did hold that she had sufficiently traced the funds. We cannot say that the decision was not supported by adequate proof. Affirmed.

▶ ANALYSIS

Mix involves three presumptions. First, property acquired during marriage is community property. Secondly, earnings and accumulations from separate property remain separate property. Finally, funds used for living expenses are first deemed to have been paid for by community funds. In any commingled funds case, first look to see whether community expenses exceed community income. If so, then any remaining funds are deemed separate property. The converse of greater deposits than withdrawals of separate funds also is a method of proving separate property.

Quicknotes

COMMINGLED ASSETS The combining of money or property into a joint account or asset.

COMMUNITY PROPERTY In community property jurisdictions refers to all money or property acquired during the term of the marriage in which each spouse has an undivided one-half interest.

SEPARATE PROPERTY Property owned by one spouse prior to marriage, or any income derived therefrom, and any property received by one spouse pursuant to a gift, devise, bequest or descent.

TRACING The process whereby the court determines the source of funds to be divided in a marital dissolution proceeding by tracing the funds back to their original source.

Marriage of Frick

Wife (P) v. Husband (D)

Cal. Ct. App., 181 Cal. App. 3d 997 (1986).

NATURE OF CASE: Appeal from division of community property.

FACT SUMMARY: In Mrs. Frick's (P) dissolution action against Jerome Frick (D), Mrs. Frick (P) contended that funds used by Jerome (D) to reduce the principal balance of an encumbrance on real property purchased by Jerome (D) prior to his marriage were community property as they were paid from a commingled account.

🏛 RULE OF LAW
Where funds are paid from a commingled account, the presumption is that the funds are community funds.

FACTS: Prior to marriage, Jerome Frick (D) owned real property which he used to operate a hotel and restaurant. During his marriage to Mrs. Frick (P), Jerome used certain funds to reduce the principal balance of any encumbrance on the property. Upon dissolution, Mrs. Frick (P) contended that the funds so used were community property. The trial court agreed with Mrs. Frick (P), stating that because Jerome (D) commingled rents which were received from a separate property source with community property funds, all the funds commingled would be considered community property. Jerome (D) appealed.

ISSUE: Where funds are paid from a commingled account, is the presumption that the funds are community funds?

HOLDING AND DECISION: (Johnson, J.) Yes. Where funds are paid from a commingled account, the presumption is that the funds are community funds. In order to overcome this presumption, a party must trace the funds expended to a separate property source. The burden of establishing a spouse's separate interest in presumptive community property is not simply records. The husband may protect his separate property by not commingling community and separate assets and income. Once he commingles, he assumes the burden of keeping records adequate to establish the balance of the community income and expenditures at the time an asset is acquired with commingled property. Here, Jerome (D) neither kept clear records showing that payments made were made from separate property funds nor presented sufficient evidence to demonstrate it was his intent to use only separate property to make loan payments. As such, he did not meet his burden of tracing monthly loan payments to his separate property income. Affirmed.

▶ ANALYSIS

Under the basic tracing principle, separate assets produce separate property and community assets produce community property. Where the two types of property combine in the production of something new, California courts have decided that the new production should be apportioned according to relative separate and community contribution. The appointment rule was first developed in cases involving the use of a spouse's time, energy, and skill in connection with a separately owned business.

Quicknotes

COMMINGLED ASSETS The combining of money or property into a joint account or asset.

COMMUNITY PROPERTY In community property jurisdictions refers to all money or property acquired during the term of the marriage in which each spouse has an undivided one-half interest.

ENCUMBRANCE An interest in property that operates as a claim or lien against its title potentially, making it unmarketable.

SEPARATE PROPERTY Property owned by one spouse prior to marriage, or any income derived therefrom, and any property received by one spouse pursuant to a gift, devise, bequest or descent.

TRACING The process whereby the court determines the source of funds to be divided in a marital dissolution proceeding by tracing the funds back to their original source.

Pereira v. Pereira

Wife (P) v. Husband (D)

Cal. Sup. Ct., 156 Cal. 1, 103 P. 488, 23 L.R.A.N.S. 880 (1909).

NATURE OF CASE: Appeal of interlocutory divorce decree.

FACT SUMMARY: Mr. Pereira's (D) principle occupation during the nine years of his marriage was the management of his separate property saloon.

🏛 RULE OF LAW
Where one spouse during marriage renders substantial community services to his separate property, the amount of the income, profits, etc. generated thereby which he will be entitled to retain as his separate property is equal to the amount of his original capital outlay for such separate property times a reasonable rate of return (7%—in absence of evidence establishing some other figure).

FACTS: At the time of his marriage to Mrs. Pereira (P), in 1900, Mr. Pereira (D) owned as separate property a saloon and cigar business worth about $15,500 and producing an annual net income of about $5,000. Throughout the marriage, Mr. Pereira's (D) principal occupation was the management of said business. In 1902, he purchased the property on which his business was located for $40,000, paid for out of income from the business itself. In 1909, Mrs. Pereira (P) filed this action for a divorce. The hearing court listed all the income from Mr. Pereira's (D) business and all property purchased with that income among the community property assets available for division. Mr. Pereira (D) appealed on the ground that, though it is true that such income is community property to the extent it represents the fruits of his community services to his separate property, he is entitled to some return on his original capital investment (separate property) in the business.

ISSUE: Where a spouse renders community property services during marriage to his separate property, is he entitled to recognition of a reasonable rate of return on his initial separate property investment, upon divorce?

HOLDING AND DECISION: (Shaw, J.) Yes. Where one spouse during marriage renders substantial community services to his separate property, the amount of the income, profits, etc. generated thereby which he is entitled to retain as his separate property is equal to the amount of his original capital outlay for such separate property times a reasonable rate of return (7%—in absence of evidence establishing some other figure). One of the most elementary presumptions of community property law is that income generated by work during marriage is community income—the result of a legal determination that such work is the result of community efforts. This rule, however, does not require that a spouse abdicate all separate interest in his separate property. Certainly, such a spouse retains a right to all income generated, not by community work effort, but rather by his separate capital. Such is the case here. Reversed, and though the court had originally intended to remand this case for rehearing on the extent of reasonable return to which Mr. Pereira (D) is entitled, his subsequent agreement to the legal interest rate of 7% removes the necessity for a new hearing.

▶ ANALYSIS

This case points up the *Pereira* rule for determining the extent to which income from community services on separate property is separate property. This rule is applied in cases in which the court determines that the community services to the business were the "greater factor" in generating the income in question. Note, however, that where a court determines that the greater factor in generating such income is not the community services of one of the spouses (e.g., where another person could have rendered the same services for a salary) then the court will compute the community property interest in such income as the reasonable value of the rendering spouse's services. This is the so-called *Van Camp* rule, from the case of the same name, (199 P. 885 (1921)).

Quicknotes

COMMUNITY PROPERTY In community property jurisdictions refers to all money or property acquired during the term of the marriage in which each spouse has an undivided one-half interest.

INTERLOCUTORY ORDER An order entered by the court determining an issue that does not resolve the disposition of the case, but is essential to a proper adjudication of the action.

SEPARATE PROPERTY Property owned by one spouse prior to marriage, or any income derived therefrom, and any property received by one spouse pursuant to a gift, devise, bequest or descent.

Marriage of Koester

Cal. Ct. App., 73 Cal. App. 4th 1032 (1999).

NATURE OF CASE: Appeal of property disbursement in a dissolution action.

FACT SUMMARY: Frederick argued that a business he owned prior to his marriage, but incorporated after his marriage, should be dispersed as separate and not community property in the dissolution proceedings.

🏛 RULE OF LAW

The *Pereira* analysis, which awards the value of separate property at the time of marriage plus a reasonable return to represent the appreciation of separate capital with the balance going to the community, applies when business property is at issue in a dissolution proceeding because the reimbursement statute was never designed to apply to separate property businesses, and is inherently not applicable to businesses when the requirements for transmutation have not been met, and because the mere incorporation of a business is not a change in its charter.

FACTS: Prior to getting married, Frederick owned Koester Electric as a sole proprietorship. A few years after his marriage to Jeanne, the business was incorporated, but no stock was ever issued. The couple eventually divorced, and the trial judge held that the incorporation of the business made the business community property because the community "acquired" the incorporated business during the marriage. The business was valued at $622,000. Frederick was allowed a credit of $337,500 for the value of the business at the time of marriage, and was charged $284,000 in community assets when the business was awarded to him. Frederick appealed.

ISSUE: Should the *Pereira* analysis, which would have awarded the value of the separate property at the time of marriage plus a reasonable return to represent the appreciation of separate capital with the balance going to the community, or the reimbursement statute, which reimburses the spouse for separate money contributed to what is now a community asset, be applied?

HOLDING AND DECISION: (Sills, J.) The *Pereira* analysis should have been applied because the reimbursement statute was never designed to apply to separate property businesses and is inherently not applicable to a business when the requirements for transmutation have not been met, and because the mere incorporation of a business is not a change in its charter. The *Pereira* case, 103 P. 488 (1909), involved a separate saloon and cigar business. In contrast, the reimbursement statute arose out of a case of a residence and, therefore, published decisions involving the statute arise out of conveyances

of residences. In addition, the incorporation of a sole proprietorship business is usually done for reasons having nothing to do with the marital relationship. Certainly if a married couple uses the occasion of the incorporation of a separate business to expressly transmute that business into community property, more than just the incorporation without the issuance of stock certificates would be involved. Furthermore, separate property does not change its character because of a change in form or identity. In the present case, there is nothing to indicate that the incorporation of the separate property business represented anything other than a mere change in the legal form under which the business was conducted, as the customers and accounts receivable were the same after the incorporation as before. Reversed and remanded.

▶ ANALYSIS

As the court in this case notes, in *Kenney v. Kenney*, 97 Cal. App.2d 60 (1950), shares in a business interest acquired before marriage, but not issued to a spouse until after marriage, did not even transmute them into community property. It is therefore unlikely for the court to have considered in the present case that a transmutation would have occurred if no stock at all had been issued.

■═■

Quicknotes

APPRECIATION The increase in the fair market value of property over either an earlier value or the taxpayer's basis.

COMMUNITY PROPERTY In community property jurisdictions refers to all money or property acquired during the term of the marriage in which each spouse has an undivided one-half interest.

SEPARATE PROPERTY Property owned by one spouse prior to marriage, or any income derived therefrom, and any property received by one spouse pursuant to a gift, devise, bequest or descent.

TRANSMUTATION The conversion of the separate property of one spouse into separate property of the other spouse or into community property, or the conversion of community property into the separate property of one spouse, by either an agreement or transfer made in a writing signed by the spouse whose interest is adversely affected and without the payment of consideration.

■═■

Tassi v. Tassi

Wife (P) v. Deceased husband's relatives and others (D)

Cal. Dist. Ct. App., 160 Cal. App. 2d 680, 325 P.2d 872 (1958).

NATURE OF CASE: Action to set aside transfers of marital property.

FACT SUMMARY: Mr. Tassi, now deceased, made certain transfer of property, without Mrs. Tassi's (P) consent, to other relatives, such as Tassi (D).

🏛 RULE OF LAW
Two approaches are available to a court for the allocation of earnings from a separate property business between separate and community property: (1) to compute interest on the capital investment in such business and allocate that amount to separate property, or (2) to compute the reasonable value of the spouse's services to his separate property and allocate that amount to community property, and the court is free to choose whichever formula "will achieve substantial justice between the parties."

FACTS: Prior to his death, Mr. Tassi transferred various properties to certain relatives, among them Tassi (D). Upon his death, Mrs. Tassi (P) filed this action to have these transfers set aside on the ground that they involved community property and she had not participated in them. At trial, it was adduced that all the property had been purchased with profits, etc., from Mr. Tassi's separate property wholesale meat business, which he operated and managed as his sole occupation. The trial court ordered the transactions set aside to the extent of Mrs. Tassi's (P) community property interest therein. They computed this interest as the reasonable value of her husband's services to his business (by taking testimony regarding comparable salaries in the industry) and then divided the Tassi (D) property 73% as separate property (all of which was properly transferred) and 27% community property (which could be set aside and returned, in part). This appeal followed.

ISSUE: Is it within the discretion of the court to determine by what approach, or formula, community and separate property interests in profits, etc., derived from one spouse's separate property are to be allocated?

HOLDING AND DECISION: (Dooling, J.) Yes. Two approaches are available to a court for the allocation of earnings from a separate property business between separate and community property: (1) to compute interest on the capital investment in such business and allocate that amount to separate property, or (2) to compute the reasonable value of the spouse's services to his separate property and allocate that amount to community property; and the court is free to choose whichever formula "will achieve substantial justice between the parties." The court's choice, here, of formula 2 above was wholly within its discretion. The evidence and testimony which it took regarding the value of Mr. Tassi's services to his business was wholly competent. It appears, here, that the court based its decision to use the formula it chose on its conclusion that the increase in the value of and profits from Mr. Tassi's business were attributable more to market conditions than Mr. Tassi's efforts. Such is a proper exercise of discretion. Affirmed.

▶ ANALYSIS

The two rules pointed up by this case and their manner of application by the court represents a classic case of the *Pereira/Van Camp* dichotomy in community property law. Note, however, that with either approach, before a final distribution can be made, a deduction for family living expenses (presumed to be community property) must be made from the aggregate amount of community property acquired during marriage. Only the balance remaining after such deduction is community property. Note, also, that the court's statement above that the *Pereira/Van Camp* choice is wholly within the court's discretion to make is a bit broad. Rather, the court should properly exercise its discretion to determine whether or not the community services to the separate property involved has been the key to the income generated.

■■■

Quicknotes

COMMUNITY PROPERTY In community property jurisdictions refers to all money or property acquired during the term of the marriage in which each spouse has an undivided one-half interest.

SEPARATE PROPERTY Property owned by one spouse prior to marriage, or any income derived therefrom, and any property received by one spouse pursuant to a gift, devise, bequest or descent.

■■■

Marriage of Imperato

Cal. Ct. App., 45 Cal. App. 3d 432 (1975).

NATURE OF CASE: Appeal from portion of a judgment in a marital dissolution action.

FACT SUMMARY: Louis Imperato admitted that the business he ran was community property but insisted it should be valued as of the date he and his wife separated and that any increase in value thereafter should constitute his separate property.

🏛 RULE OF LAW
In a marital dissolution action, asset values and liabilities should be determined as near to the date of trial as reasonably practicable, with the increase in value of a community property business being apportioned between the community property interest that arises from the inherent increase in value and the separate property interest that arises from the increase in value due to the devotion of time and effort to the business by one of the spouses.

FACTS: Having admitted the business he ran was community property, Louis Imperato nonetheless insisted that the valuation date should have been set on the date he and his wife separated (December 30, 1971) rather than June 30, 1973, the date closest to the date of trial for which proof of value existed. He further argued that he essentially ran the business, that it should be treated as a sole partnership, and that his efforts after separating of the parties were responsible for any increase in value after the separation. Thus, he claimed, such increase would be his separate property, as it would constitute his earnings or accumulations while living separate and apart from his wife.

ISSUE: Does the fact that a spouse devoted his time and effort to running a community property business after a couple separated entitle him to treat the entire increase in value of the business from the date of separation as his separate property?

HOLDING AND DECISION: (Hastings, J.) No. The rule is that in a marital dissolution, asset values and liabilities should be determined as near to the date of the trial as reasonably practicable. Any increase in the value of a community property business run by one of the spouses subsequent to their separation should be apportioned between community and separate property interests. That is, whatever portion of the increase is due to the inherent growth of the business is community property. However, that portion attributable to the personal efforts and services rendered by the spouse operating the business is clearly separate property. Reversed and remanded.

▶ ANALYSIS

The court refused to choose between the two approaches that have developed for allocating earnings between separate and community income. The *Pereira* approach is to first allocate a fair return on the investment and then treat the rest as increase due to personal services. The *Van Camp* approach is to first determine the reasonable value of the personal services (less draws or salary taken) and then treat the rest as return on investment.

Quicknotes

COMMUNITY PROPERTY In community property jurisdictions refers to all money or property acquired during the term of the marriage in which each spouse has an undivided one-half interest.

SEPARATE PROPERTY Property owned by one spouse prior to marriage, or any income derived therefrom, and any property received by one spouse pursuant to a gift, devise, bequest or descent.

Vieux v. Vieux

Wife (P) v. Husband (D)

Cal. Dist. Ct. App., 80 Cal. App. 222, 251 P. 640 (1926).

NATURE OF CASE: Action to determine ownership of real property.

FACT SUMMARY: Prior to his marriage, Mr. Vieux (D) executed an installment contract to purchase real property and, after his marriage, he used some community property funds to pay installments on this contract.

🏛 RULE OF LAW
When one spouse before marriage executes an installment contract to purchase property and then uses community funds after marriage to pay some of the installments, the community property is entitled to an interest in such property in the proportion that community funds were used for installments.

FACTS: Prior to marriage, Mr. Vieux (D) executed an installment contract for land and paid $280 as a down payment. After marriage to Mrs. Vieux (P), Mr. Vieux (D) used $553.68 of community funds to make installment payments on the purchase price of the land. Subsequently, Mrs. Vieux (P) filed for divorce from Mr. Vieux (D) and claimed that the land was partially community property (i.e., she was entitled to an interest in it). The trial court, however, awarded the land to Mr. Vieux (D) since title was in his name alone and since the contract for purchase was executed before his marriage. Thereafter, Mrs. Vieux (P) appealed.

ISSUE: When one spouse executes an installment contract to purchase property before marriage, is such spouse entitled to full ownership of that property even if community funds are used after marriage to pay some of the installments?

HOLDING AND DECISION: (Houser, J.) No. When one spouse before marriage executes an installment contract to purchase property and then uses community funds after marriage to pay some of the installments, the community property is entitled to an interest in such property in the proportion that community funds were used for installments. Furthermore, this is true even if title to the property is in the name of the contracting spouse only. As such, the non-contracting spouse is entitled to an interest in the property (i.e., one-half of the community property interest). Here, therefore, the community property is entitled to an interest in the land in the proportion that community funds were used for installments, and Mrs. Vieux (P) is entitled to one-half of such community property interest. Reversed and remanded.

▶ ANALYSIS

This case again illustrates the "apportionment theory" followed in California. Note, however, that if Mr. Vieux (P) here had taken out a full loan before marriage and received title to the land before marriage, such land would have remained his separate property even if he subsequently used community funds to repay the purchase loan. However, the community would have been entitled to "reimbursement" for any community funds used. Note, finally, that a few community property states follow the "inception of right" theory. Under such theory, the status of property depends upon the marital status of the acquiring party at the inception of his right to the property, e.g., when the contract of purchase is made.

Quicknotes

APPORTIONMENT The division of property costs in proportion to the parties' respective interests therein.

COMMUNITY PROPERTY In community property jurisdictions refers to all money or property acquired during the term of the marriage in which each spouse has an undivided one-half interest.

INSTALLMENT CONTRACT A contract pursuant to which the parties are to render performance or payment in periodic intervals.

SEPARATE PROPERTY Property owned by one spouse prior to marriage, or any income derived therefrom, and any property received by one spouse pursuant to a gift, devise, bequest or descent.

Gudelj v. Gudelj

Wife (P) v. Husband (D)

Cal. Sup. Ct., 41 Cal. 2d 202, 259 P.2d 656 (1953).

NATURE OF CASE: Action to declare property as a community asset in a suit for divorce.

FACT SUMMARY: Mr. Gudelj (D) purchased a one-quarter interest in a dry-cleaner with $1,500 in cash and a note for $10,000.

🏛 RULE OF LAW
Unless evidence can be adduced that a loan was granted or property was sold on the sole basis of a spouse's separate property or credit, the property is presumed to be a community asset.

FACTS: Gudelj (D) owned a dry-cleaner prior to marriage. After marriage, Gudelj (D) sold the store, apparently netting $1,500 in cash. Gudelj (D) bought into a new dry-cleaner for $1,500 in cash plus a $10,000 note. He obtained a one-quarter interest in the new business. Mrs. Gudelj (P) sued for divorce and the court awarded the business to Mr. Gudelj (D) as his separate property. Even though no evidence was adduced at trial as to the basis for the granting of the $10,000 note, the court found that the $1,500 was Gudelj's (D) separate property and therefore the note must have been granted solely on the basis of his separate property.

ISSUE: Must a spouse establish that property was sold to him solely on the basis of his separate property and credit?

HOLDING AND DECISION: (Edmonds, J.) Yes. A presumption exists that property acquired during marriage is community property. To overcome the presumption, it is necessary to adduce evidence that the sale or loan was granted solely on the basis of the spouse's separate property and credit. Gudelj (D) argues that his previous business failure clearly establishes that the sale was not made on the basis of his skill or management ability. He further contends that the seller must have been aware that Gudelj (D) had an interest in the proceeds from the sale of property owned by Gudelj (D) and his mother. The answer to this is that there was no proof that the seller knew of such proceeds. No testimony was given at trial concerning the seller's motivation. Having failed to adduce such evidence, Gudelj (D) has not overcome the presumption that the property was a community asset. Reversed and remanded.

▶ ANALYSIS

The holding in this case is the chief stumbling block to those who are attempting to prove that the proceeds are their separate property. How many creditors totally ignore the existence of community assets in making credit decisions? When a controversy arises at a later date between the spouses, how many creditors would exculpate the community from any liability for repayment of the obligation? Finally, how many creditors would remember exactly what considerations passed through their minds, possibly years earlier, as to which property was being relied on by them?

◼︎▬◼︎

Quicknotes

ASSET An item of real or personal property that is owned and has tangible value.

COMMUNITY PROPERTY In community property jurisdictions refers to all money or property acquired during the term of the marriage in which each spouse has an undivided one-half interest.

INSTALLMENT CONTRACT A contract pursuant to which the parties are to render performance or payment in periodic intervals.

SEPARATE PROPERTY Property owned by one spouse prior to marriage, or any income derived therefrom, and any property received by one spouse pursuant to a gift, devise, bequest or descent.

◼︎▬◼︎

Bank of California v. Connolly

Mortgage holder (P) v. Real estate partnership (D)

Cal. Ct. App., 36 Cal. App. 3d 350 (1974).

NATURE OF CASE: Action to declare a profit sharing agreement null and void as to the wife's community property interest.

FACT SUMMARY: Latimer transferred his community property interest in real property to Connolly (D) in exchange for a profit sharing agreement.

RULE OF LAW
A spouse may dispose of community assets for valuable consideration without the consent of the other spouse.

FACTS: Latimer, Connolly (D), and Seward (D) formed a real estate partnership. Latimer and the others borrowed money on their personal credit to purchase one section of land. Latimer borrowed funds on another parcel using the parcel and some separate property as collateral. Both loans were primarily granted based on the personal credit of Latimer and the others. Mrs. Latimer (P) signed an agreement that property held solely in Mr. Latimer's name would be deemed his separate property with respect to purchasers and encumbrancers. Mr. Latimer later transferred his interest to Connolly (D) and Seward (D) in exchange for a profit sharing agreement. Mrs. Latimer (P) brought suit with the mortgage holder, Bank of California (P), to have the transfer set aside as an attempt to dispose of her community interest without her permission. The court found that Mrs. Latimer (P) had a community interest in the property, but held that her husband had the right to dispose of the property for a valuable consideration.

ISSUE: May one spouse arbitrarily dispose of community assets for valuable consideration without the permission of the other spouse?

HOLDING AND DECISION: (Tamura, J.) Yes. Money borrowed during marriage is deemed to be community property. This presumption applies where the lender looks to the personal credit of the borrower. Therefore, the funds borrowed must be deemed to be community property. The agreement signed by Mrs. Latimer (P) did not alter the nature of the property between Mr. and Mrs. Latimer, merely as to encumbrancers and purchasers. Connolly (D) and Seward (D) were neither. Therefore the agreement is immaterial. While the property may be deemed community, a spouse has the right to unilaterally dispose of the community for a valuable consideration. The other spouse cannot set aside the transaction even if the arrangement is unwise so long as consideration was actually received. Affirmed.

ANALYSIS

A spouse cannot make a gift of community property. The nonconsenting spouse has the right to set the entire transaction aside prior to the death of the other spouse. After death one-half the transaction may be set aside. However, as *Connolly* holds, if there is any consideration present, of more than a token nature, the nonconsenting spouse cannot object. To hold otherwise would frustrate most contractual transactions. A man operating a community property business would need his wife's signature on most sales agreements.

Quicknotes

COMMUNITY PROPERTY In community property jurisdictions refers to all money or property acquired during the term of the marriage in which each spouse has an undivided one-half interest.

Marriage of Grinius

Wife (P) v. Husband (D)

Cal. Ct. App., 166 Cal. App. 3d 1179 (1985).

NATURE OF CASE: Appeal from property distribution in dissolution action.

FACT SUMMARY: In Joyce Grinius' (P) action against her husband, Victor (D), for dissolution of their marriage, Joyce (P) contended that the real property on which their restaurant was situated, the restaurant, and all rents, issues, and profits thereof were community property.

🏛 RULE OF LAW
Loan proceeds acquired during marriage are presumptively community property, and this presumption may be overcome by showing the lender intended to rely solely upon a spouse's separate property and did, in fact, do so.

FACTS: Shortly after Victor (D) and Joyce Grinius (P) were married, they purchased a restaurant with money secured through several loans, including an $80,000 Small Business Administration (SBA) loan. The SBA loan was secured by both community and separate property; both Victor (D) and Joyce (P) negotiated the original purchase offer. Without Joyce's (P) knowledge, Victor (D) placed title to the property in his name alone. Victor (D) and Joyce (P) separated, and before trial, Victor (D) stipulated the restaurant business was community property, and the business was sold. At trial, Joyce (P) contended that the restaurant real property, the restaurant itself, and all rents, issues, and profits thereof were community property. The trial court disagreed, finding all the contested assets, except the restaurant real property, to be community property. The restaurant real property, worth $340,000, was determined to be Victor's (D) separate property. Joyce (P) appealed.

ISSUE: Are loan proceeds acquired during marriage presumptively community property, and may this presumption be overcome by showing the lender intended to rely solely upon a spouse's separate property and did, in fact, do so?

HOLDING AND DECISION: (Work, J.) Yes. Loan proceeds acquired during marriage are presumptively community property, and this presumption may be overcome by showing the lender intended to rely solely upon a spouse's separate property and did in fact do so. Without satisfactory evidence of the lender's intent, the general presumption prevails. Here, Victor (D) presented no direct evidence of lender intent and instead offered circumstantial evidence to prove lender reliance on his separate property. In fact, approval for the SBA loan required Joyce's (P) signature on the note and the instruments of hypothecation,

suggesting the lender did look toward community assets for security. In sum, Victor (D) failed to present sufficient evidence to rebut the presumption property acquired during marriage is community property. Therefore, the restaurant property and all rents, issues, and profits thereof are properly characterized as community property. Reversed and remanded.

▶ ANALYSIS

Property acquired during marriage through a credit or loan transaction comes within the general presumption of community property. The general presumption can be rebutted by using the tracing principle, establishing that separate property produced the acquisition. The general presumption may also be overcome by showing that a contract controls the classification.

◼▬◼

Quicknotes

COMMUNITY PROPERTY In community property jurisdictions refers to all money or property acquired during the term of the marriage in which each spouse has an undivided one-half interest.

REAL PROPERTY Land, an interest in land, or anything attached to the land that is incapable of being removed.

TITLE The right of possession over property.

◼▬◼

Marriage of Lucas

Cal. Sup. Ct., 27 Cal. 3d 808, 614 P.2d 285 (1980).

NATURE OF CASE: Appeal from an interlocutory judgment dissolving a marriage and dividing property.

FACT SUMMARY: At issue in the dissolution proceeding involving Gerald and Brenda Lucas was how to determine their separate and community property interests in the home they had purchased during their marriage with both separate property and community property funds.

🏛 **RULE OF LAW**
For the purpose of the division of property upon divorce or separate maintenance only, there is a statutory presumption that a single family residence acquired by a couple during marriage as joint tenants is community and it is overcome only by showing they had an agreement or understanding to the contrary.

FACTS: During their marriage, Gerald and Brenda Lucas purchased a home, Brenda using separate property funds for the down payment and some maintenance. Title was taken as "Gerald E. Lucas and Brenda G. Lucas, Husband and Wife as Joint Tenants." The evidence showed that they had very little discussion about their intentions in taking title as joint tenants. When they were undergoing dissolution, the court held that a certain portion was Brenda's separate property interest and another portion represented a community property interest.

ISSUE: Is there a statutory presumption in divorce or separate maintenance cases that a single family residence acquired during marriage as joint tenants is community property absent a showing of some agreement or understanding between spouses to the contrary?

HOLDING AND DECISION: (Manuel, J.) Yes. There is a statutory presumption, covering cases of dissolution and separate maintenance only, that a single family residence acquired during marriage as joint tenants is community property. Of course, that presumption can be overcome by evidence of an agreement or understanding between the parties to the contrary. However, merely tracing the funds used to purchase the residence to a separate property source is not sufficient to overcome this special statutory presumption (which arises only when there is an affirmative act specifying a form of ownership in the conveyance of title), although such tracing can overcome the general presumption that property acquired during marriage is community property. Reversed and remanded for a redetermination of the basis of those principles and rules.

▶ *ANALYSIS*

The special presumption highlighted in this case was the legislature's attempt to remedy the unhappy situation that developed because real estate brokers, title companies, and escrow companies habitually prepared their documents in joint tenancy form. As a result, the general presumption that property is held in a form consistent with that created by the form of legal title taken worked to keep most property from being properly considered community property upon dissolution or separation.

■≡■

Quicknotes

COMMUNITY PROPERTY In community property jurisdictions refers to all money or property acquired during the term of the marriage in which each spouse has an undivided one-half interest.

INTERLOCUTORY ORDER An order entered by the court determining an issue that does not resolve the disposition of the case, but is essential to a proper adjudication of the action.

JOINT TENANCY An interest in property whereby a single interest is owned by two or more persons and created by a single instrument; joint tenants possess equal interests in the use of the entire property and the last survivor is entitled to absolute ownership.

SEPARATE PROPERTY Property owned by one spouse prior to marriage, or any income derived therefrom, and any property received by one spouse pursuant to a gift, devise, bequest or descent.

TRACING The process whereby the court determines the source of funds to be divided in a marital dissolution proceeding by tracing the funds back to their original source.

■≡■

Marriage of Moore

Cal. Sup. Ct., 28 Cal. 3d 366, 618 P.2d 208 (1980).

NATURE OF CASE: Appeal from an interlocutory judgment of dissolution of marriage.

FACT SUMMARY: Mr. Moore did not like the method the trial court used to determine the community interest in a house his wife had purchased before marriage but on which the community made payments.

🏛 RULE OF LAW
Amounts paid by the community for interest, taxes, and insurance are not figured in when calculating the community's interest in property that was purchased by one of the spouses prior to marriage but as to which the community made payments.

FACTS: Eight months before she married Mr. Moore, Mrs. Moore put $16,640.57 down on a house and secured a loan for the balance of the $56,640.57 purchase price. In entering an interlocutory judgment dissolving their marriage, the trial court figured the community interest in said house by multiplying the equity value of the house by the ratio of the community's reduction of principal (via payments made on the house during marriage) to the total amount of principal reduction by both community and separate property. Mr. Moore, on appeal, continued to argue that the community property interest should have been based on the full amount of payments made, including interest, taxes, and insurance, rather than only on the amount by which community payments reduced the principal.

ISSUE: In calculating the community interest in property purchased by a spouse prior to marriage but on which the community made payments, are payments for interest, taxes, and insurance figured in?

HOLDING AND DECISION: (Manuel, J.) No. There is no basis for departing from the present rule that excludes amounts paid for interest, taxes, and insurance in calculating separate community interests in property by a spouse prior to marriage. Here, the down payment is attributable to Mrs. Moore alone, as is the loan since it was based on separate assets. Accordingly, the community interest would be found by (1) dividing the amount by which the community property payments reduced the principal balance of the loan by the purchase price, then (2) multiplying that community percentage interest by the equity value of the house to find the capital appreciation due to community funds, and (3) adding to that the amount of equity paid by community funds. While this was not the formula used by the trial court the error was in Mr. Moore's favor. Since Mrs. Moore did not appeal and Mr. Moore was not prejudiced by the error, reversal is unwarranted. Affirmed.

▶ ANALYSIS

A simpler approach is advocated by Professor Bruch, who suggests that rents, profits, and natural appreciation be considered the "fruits" of separate property and that all the "fruits" of separate property be considered assets to the extent they are acquired during the marriage. Bruch, "The Definition and Division of Marital Property in California: Towards Parity and Simplicity," 33 Hastings L.J. 769, 789-798 (1982).

Quicknotes

APPRECIATION The increase in the fair market value of property over either an earlier value or the taxpayer's basis.

COMMUNITY PROPERTY In community property jurisdictions refers to all money or property acquired during the term of the marriage in which each spouse has an undivided one-half interest.

INTERLOCUTORY JUDGMENT An order entered by the court determining an issue that does not resolve the disposition of the case, but is essential to a proper adjudication of the action.

SEPARATE PROPERTY Property owned by one spouse prior to marriage, or any income derived therefrom, and any property received by one spouse pursuant to a gift, devise, bequest or descent.

Marriage of Frick

Wife (P) v. Husband (D)

Cal. Ct. App., 181 Cal. App. 3d 997 (1986).

NATURE OF CASE: Action to distribute community property upon dissolution of a marriage.

FACT SUMMARY: In Hiroko Frick's (P) dissolution action against her husband, Jerome (D), Jerome (D) contended that the parties' respective interest in a hotel and restaurant run by Jerome (D) should be determined by the fair market value of the property at the time of marriage rather than by calculating the separate and community property percentage interest based on the purchase price of the property at the time of marriage.

RULE OF LAW
The community and separate property's respective interest should be based on the ratio of capital contribution to purchase price of property acquired before and during marriage.

FACTS: Jerome Frick (D) owned certain real property prior to his marriage of Hiroko Frick (P) which he used to operate a hotel and restaurant. During the marriage, he used community property funds to reduce the principal balance of the encumbrance on the real property. In determining the parties' respective interests in the real property, the trial court calculated the separate and community property percentage interest based on the purchase price of the property rather than on the fair market value of the property at the time of the marriage. Jerome (D) appealed the trial court's decision, contending that the parties' interests should have been determined by the fair market value of the property at the time of marriage rather than by calculating the separate and community property percentage interest based on the purchase price of the property at the time of marriage.

ISSUE: Should the community and separate property's respective interest be based on the ratio of capital contribution to purchase price of property acquired before or during marriage?

HOLDING AND DECISION: (Johnson, J.) Yes. The community and separate property's respective interest should be based on the ratio of capital contribution to purchase price of property acquired before or during marriage. Fairness dictates that this should be so. It is the ratio which best reflects the parties' respective interests in the property at the time the appreciation at issue is accruing. The community should share in the appreciation that accrues during the marriage in the same proportion that its capital contribution bears to the total capital contribution required to own the property outright. This is the method of computation that has been historically followed in this study, and this court believes it is the appropriate

one. To do as Jerome (D) asks would give him double credit for premarital appreciation in the value of this property. There is no justification for this approach. It fails the test of fundamental fairness. Affirmed.

ANALYSIS

The approach used in the above case involved classification of the down payment, the loan proceeds, and the principal payments made on a loan. Whether the purchase or loan transaction occurred before or after marriage is of major importance in classifying the loan proceeds. In many cases, classification of the loan proceeds will be the critical factor in deciding which estate will receive the major share of appreciation.

Quicknotes

APPRECIATION The increase in the fair market value of property over either an earlier value or the taxpayer's basis.

CAPITAL In tax, is often used synonymously with basis; in accounting, refers to an account that represents the equity (ownership) interests of the owners, i.e., the amounts they would obtain if the business were liquidated.

COMMUNITY PROPERTY In community property jurisdictions refers to all money or property acquired during the term of the marriage in which each spouse has an undivided one-half interest.

FAIR MARKET VALUE The price of particular property or goods that a buyer would offer and a seller would accept in the open market following full disclosure.

SEPARATE PROPERTY Property owned by one spouse prior to marriage, or any income derived therefrom, and any property received by one spouse pursuant to a gift, devise, bequest or descent.

Marriage of Walrath

Cal. Sup. Ct., 17 Cal. 4th 907, 952 P.2d 1124 (1998).

NATURE OF CASE: Marital dissolution proceeding.

FACT SUMMARY: Gilbert reconveyed a separate property house to himself and his wife Gladys as joint tenants.

🏛 RULE OF LAW
A party's entitlement to a separate property contribution reimbursement is not limited to the original community property to which the contribution was made, and when that original property is refinanced and the proceeds used in part to purchase or pay down the indebtedness on the original and other assets, the contributing spouse can trace the contribution to, and be reimbursed from, those assets.

FACTS: Gilbert and Gladys Walrath were married in 1992 and separated less than three years later. Prior to the marriage Gilbert owned a house in Lucerne which he deeded to himself and Gladys as joint tenants. In 1993 they refinanced the home borrowing $180,000 against their equity interest. They used the money to pay off the existing loan, the mortgage on some property in Nevada, and to acquire additional property in Utah. They placed the remainder in a joint savings account. The trial court ruled that the parties were each entitled to reimbursement on a proportionate basis (88% and 12% respectively) for their contributions to the Lucerne property. Reimbursement was limited to the equity value of the property at the time of division. Based on the reduced market value this amount came to only $1,000. In its statement of decision, the court found that there was no reimbursable claim pursuant to Family Code § 2640 for the loan proceeds traced into the Nevada and Utah properties. The court of appeal affirmed and this court granted Gilbert's petition for review.

ISSUE: Is a party's entitlement to a separate property contribution reimbursement limited to the original community property to which the contribution was made, and when that original property is refinanced and the proceeds used in part to purchase or pay down the indebtedness on the original and other assets, can the contributing spouse trace the contribution to, and be reimbursed from, those assets?

HOLDING AND DECISION: (Brown, J.) Yes. A party's entitlement to a separate property contribution reimbursement is not limited to the original community property to which the contribution was made, and when that original property is refinanced and the proceeds used in part to purchase or pay down the indebtedness on the original and other assets, the contributing spouse can trace the contribution to, and be reimbursed from, those assets. Section 2640(b) states that "in the division of the

community estate . . . unless a party has made a written waiver of the right to reimbursement or has signed a writing that has the effect of a waiver, the party shall be reimbursed for the party's contributions to the acquisition of property to the extent the party traces the contributions to a separate source. The contributions include "down payments, payments for improvements, and payments that reduce the principal of a loan used to finance the purchase or improvement of the property." The separate property contribution is reimbursable prior to the division of the community property. If there is insufficient equity at the time of dissolution to fully reimburse the contribution, the entire asset is awarded to the contributing spouse. The issue here is whether a party's entitlement to a separate property contribution reimbursement is limited to the original community property to which the contribution was made or whether, when that original property is refinanced and the proceeds used in part to purchase or pay down the indebtedness on the original and other assets, the contributing spouse can trace the contribution to, and be reimbursed from, those assets. This depends on the meaning of the word "property" as used in § 2640. We conclude that phrase includes not only the particular community property to which the separate property is originally contributed, but also any other community property that is subsequently acquired from the proceeds of the initial property and to which the separate property contribution can be traced. The trial court must ascertain what percentage of the loan proceeds traceable to each asset are based on each party's separate property contributions. Reversed and remanded.

CONCURRENCE AND DISSENT: (Kennard, J.) I agree that § 2640(b) permits a spouse, upon dissolution of marriage, to obtain reimbursement for separate property contributions not only from the property to which the contribution was originally made but also from property acquired later with funds traceable to the original contribution. I do not agree with the tracing method that the court adopts. It is unnecessarily complicated and insufficiently protective of the separate property reimbursement right.

CONCURRENCE AND DISSENT: (Baxter, J.) I concur in the majority's conclusion that a spouse's statutory right to reimbursement is not limited to reimbursement from the specific asset to which the contribution was originally made. The statute seems to contemplate that the right of reimbursement extends to the value of the entire community estate as it exists at the time of division, up to the full amount of separate property contributions. The method of tracing used by the majority unfairly insulates portions of the community estate and of assets

Continued on next page.

specifically traceable to the original contribution from the burden of reimbursement.

▶ *ANALYSIS*

Family Code § 2640 was enacted in order to overrule the common law rule that separate property contributions to community property were deemed as gifts to the community absent an agreement otherwise.

■≡■

Quicknotes

COMMUNITY PROPERTY In community property jurisdictions refers to all money or property acquired during the term of the marriage in which each spouse has an undivided one-half interest.

JOINT TENANCY An interest in property whereby a single interest is owned by two or more persons and created by a single instrument; joint tenants possess equal interests in the use of the entire property and the last survivor is entitled to absolute ownership.

RECONVEYANCE The restoration of title to real property to an individual, who previously owned it.

REIMBURSEMENT The tendering of payment to a party for expenditures made on his behalf.

SEPARATE PROPERTY Property owned by one spouse prior to marriage, or any income derived therefrom, and any property received by one spouse pursuant to a gift, devise, bequest or descent.

TRACING The process whereby the court determines the source of funds to be divided in a marital dissolution proceeding by tracing the funds back to their original source.

■≡■

Marriage of Wolfe

Wife (P) v. Husband (D)

Cal. Ct. App., 91 Cal. App. 4th 962 (2001).

NATURE OF CASE: Appeal of the property issues in a judgment of dissolution.

FACT SUMMARY: In a dissolution proceeding, the wife (P) moved to have reimbursed one-half of the funds she contributed, out of community assets, to the improvements made on her husband's (D) separate property.

🏛 RULE OF LAW
When a spouse contributes community funds to improvements on their spouse's separate land, the contributing spouse is entitled to reimbursement.

FACTS: When Phillip (D) and Joyce (P) separated, they held as community property a single family residence in Newcastle, and a vineyard near Fresno. Philip (D) also owned real property adjacent to the vineyard as his separate property. Just prior to the couple divorcing, the community paid $8,935 in improvements on the adjoining land that Philip (D) held as his separate property. The trial court ordered Philip (D) to reimburse Joyce (P) for the community funds used to pay for improvements on Phillip's (D) separate property. Philip (D) appealed.

ISSUE: Did the court err in ordering Phillip (D) to reimburse Joyce (P) for her share of community funds used to install a drip irrigation system on Philip's (D) separate real property?

HOLDING AND DECISION: (Callahan, J.) No. The court did not err in reimbursing Joyce (P) for her share of community funds spent on a drip irrigation system for Phillip's (D) separate parcel during the marriage. Although the use of community funds to improve the separate property of one spouse does not alter the character of the separate property, unless there is an agreement stating otherwise, the community funds must still be reimbursed to the contributing spouse. Prior to this case, there was in California a presumption that if a spouse expends community funds to improve his spouse's separate property, it is a gift. There is, however, no logical basis for denying a spouse reimbursement for a community-funded improvement to the other spouse's separate property. Such a presumption is outside of the mainstream of community property principles applied in other American jurisdictions and, therefore, it will be discarded by this court. Moreover, since there is no such gift presumption for community funds which are used to contribute to the purchase or reduce an encumbrance on a separate asset, there should not be such a presumption for improvements. Spouses simply would not want their spouse to walk away from a marriage with property enriched by community funds with

no obligation to reimburse. It is also contrary to public policy, which presumes acquisitions during a marriage to be community. In the present case, Joyce (P) seeks only to recover one-half of the initial expenditure and she is entitled to that. Affirmed.

▌ *ANALYSIS*

As the opinion notes, in the 1800s, California was at one time in the mainstream of community property law and, at that time, when a husband used community funds to improve his own separate property, there was a general rule of reimbursement and no gift presumption. Over time, an inference based on the evidence in one particular case was distorted into a presumption of law in later California decisions. Those later decisions in the 1930s erroneously went on to use the gift presumption. From that point on it was the court of appeal which continuously adopted the gift presumption. Since it was not the Supreme Court who also adopted it, the court in the present case was free to disregard it.

■=■

Quicknotes

COMMUNITY PROPERTY In community property jurisdictions refers to all money or property acquired during the term of the marriage in which each spouse has an undivided one-half interest.

GIFTED PROPERTY Property, transferred to another person voluntarily, and without consideration.

REIMBURSEMENT The tendering of payment to a party for expenditures made on his behalf.

SEPARATE PROPERTY Property owned by one spouse prior to marriage, or any income derived therefrom, and any property received by one spouse pursuant to a gift, devise, bequest or descent.

■=■

Marriage of Smith

Wife (P) v. Husband (D)

Cal. Ct. App., 79 Cal. App. 3d 725 (1978).

NATURE OF CASE: Appeal from portions of inter-locutory judgment of dissolution.

FACT SUMMARY: In a dissolution action, Sieglinde Smith (P) contended that the trial court's decision that she was not entitled to reimbursement for her separate property ex-penditures on community items was incorrect and that she was entitled to reimbursement.

🏛 RULE OF LAW
A spouse who uses his or her separate property for community purposes is entitled to reimbursement from the community property of the other spouse only if there is an agreement between the parties to that effect.

FACTS: When Sieglinde Smith (P) and her husband Wayde Smith (D) separated, they owned a custom sign-making business. At the dissolution proceeding, the court gave Wayde (D) exclusive use, occupancy, and control of the family business and excluded Sieglinde (P) therefrom. Sieglinde (P) then appealed, contending that she had spent money she had received from an inheritance for communi-ty purchases such as a down payment on real property, the construction costs of a swimming pool added to the family residence, and equipment and machinery used in the fami-ly business. She argued that because she had made these expenditures from a separate property source, the court should have reimbursed her from the community property or given her a portion of the family business.

ISSUE: Is a spouse who uses his or her separate prop-erty for community purposes entitled to reimbursement from the community property or separate property of the other spouse only if there is an agreement between the parties to that effect?

HOLDING AND DECISION: (Kaufman, J.) Yes. A spouse who uses his or her separate property for com-munity purposes is entitled to reimbursement from the community property or separate property of the other spouse only if there is an agreement between the parties to that effect. Here, the trial court's finding is that Sie-glinde's (P) separate funds used in the purchase and improvement of the community properties were intended to be a gift to the community and that the properties were listed as subject to disposition by the court and there was no request to confirm any property as her separate proper-ty. At trial, however, Sieglinde's (P) position was that she was entitled to reimbursement. Her testimony that no gift was intended by her only created a conflict in the evidence for resolution by the trial court. There is no evidence

whatsoever of any agreement for Sieglinde's (P) reimburse-ment, and the court's finding that Sieglinde (P) intended these expenditures of her separate funds to be gifts to the community is entirely inconsistent with the existence of such an agreement. Affirmed.

▶ ANALYSIS

Cases involving the use of separate funds to improve community property are similar in some ways to cases involving the use of separate property to pay a community obligation or expense, in which the owner of the separate property is presumed to have made a gift to the communi-ty. This presumption is rebuttable. If the presumption of a gift is rebutted, then the separate property estate would not be entitled to any ownership interest in the improved property, but would have a right to reimbursement.

Quicknotes

COMMUNITY PROPERTY In community property jurisdic-tions refers to all money or property acquired during the term of the marriage in which each spouse has an undi-vided one-half interest.

GIFTED PROPERTY Property transferred to another person voluntarily and without consideration.

INTERLOCUTORY JUDGMENT An order entered by the court determining an issue that does not resolve the disposition of the case, but is essential to a proper adju-dication of the action.

REIMBURSEMENT The tendering of payment to a party for expenditures made on his behalf.

SEPARATE PROPERTY Property owned by one spouse prior to marriage, or any income derived therefrom, and any property received by one spouse pursuant to a gift, devise, bequest or descent.

Marriage of Devlin

Cal. Ct. App., 138 Cal. App. 3d 804 (1982).

NATURE OF CASE: Appeal from an order dividing community property.

FACT SUMMARY: All of the community property the Devlins had acquired had been purchased with funds Mr. Devlin received during marriage as damages from a car accident that rendered him a paraplegic.

🏛 RULE OF LAW
Personal injury damages received or to be received from a cause of action during marriage are community property, but statute provides that they shall be assigned to the party who suffered the injuries (upon dissolution or separation) unless the court determines that the interests of justice require another disposition, except that at least one-half of such damages must be assigned to the spouse who suffered the injuries.

FACTS: The realty and mobile home that made up the Devlin's community property had been acquired by using funds Mr. Devlin received during marriage as damages for personal injuries he sustained in a car accident that left him a paraplegic. Upon dissolution, the trial court awarded Mr. Devlin the bulk of the community property, and Mrs. Devlin appealed.

ISSUE: In general, are community property personal injury damages to be awarded to the spouse who suffered the injuries unless the court determines that the interests of justice require another disposition?

HOLDING AND DECISION: (Evans, J.) Yes. By statutory provision, personal injury damages received or to be received from a cause of action arising during marriage, are community property. However, statutes also provide that upon dissolution or separation these community property personal injury damages are to be assigned to the injured spouse, unless the court considering the facts of the case (including the economic condition and needs of each party and the time that has elapsed since the recovery of damages or the accrual of the cause of action) determines that the interests of justice require another disposition. In such case, the community property personal injury damages may be assigned to respective parties in such proportion as the court determines to be fair, except that at least one-half of such damages must be assigned to the spouse who suffered the injuries. The court below followed these statutory guidelines. Affirmed.

▶ ANALYSIS

The case illustrates one of the main statutory exceptions to the basic rule which says that there shall be an equal division of community and quasi-community property upon dissolution. Another statutory exception exists as to community property estates whose net value is less than $5,000. When the estate is that small and, despite reasonable diligence, one of the spouses cannot be located, all of the community property can be awarded to the appearing spouse.

■=■

Quicknotes

COMMUNITY PROPERTY In community property jurisdictions refers to all money or property acquired during the term of the marriage in which each spouse has an undivided one-half interest.

DAMAGES Monetary compensation that may be awarded by the court to a party who has sustained injury or loss to his person, property or rights due to another party's unlawful act, omission or negligence.

■=■

Marriage of Brown

Wife (P) v. Husband (D)

Cal. Sup. Ct., 15 Cal. 3d 838, 544 P.2d 561 (1976).

NATURE OF CASE: Action to declare a non-vested pension as community property.

FACT SUMMARY: Brown (D), a telephone company employee, had worked for 24 years and needed two more years for retirement.

🏛 RULE OF LAW
A spouse should be granted a contingent interest in a non-vested pension which, if vested, would be deemed community property.

FACTS: Mr. and Mrs. Brown were married for 23 years. Mr. Brown (D) was employed by General Telephone during this period. Mr. Brown (D) was two years away from early retirement. Mr. Brown's (D) pension at that time would be $310.94 per month. If Mr. Brown (D) continued to work until age 63, he would receive $485 per month. In a dissolution action, Mrs. Brown (P) asked the court to overrule *French v. French*, 17 Cal. 2d 775 (1941). This case held that non-vested pensions were a mere expectancy and were not subject to community property division. The court affirmed the decision in *French* and awarded Mrs. Brown (P) nothing with respect to the pension.

ISSUE: May a spouse be awarded an interest in a non-vested pension as part of a community property division?

HOLDING AND DECISION: (Tobriner, J.) Yes. Employer funded pension plans are not mere expectancies. They are contractual in nature and are funded as an incident of employment. So long as the employee continues to work, the employer is contractually obligated to make pension contributions. They are in the nature of additional compensation. While the pension may not have been vested at the time of the interlocutory judgment, it would be grossly unfair to allow Mr. Brown (D) to retain all of the benefits upon its vesting. Twenty-three out of his 24 years with General Telephone were during his marriage. We expressly overrule *French*. If the pension finally vests, Mrs. Brown (P) is to receive her community property share. This spreads the risk of Mr. Brown's (D) death or change in employment equally between the parties. Mr. Brown (D) is free to continue or change his position. However, if he continues to work for General, upon the receipt of pension payments, Mrs. Brown's (P) community share must be paid to her. Our decision is retroactive to all similar cases in which no final judgment has been rendered. This is required to effectuate the legislature's announced policy of equal division of community property between the spouses. Reversed and remanded.

▶ ANALYSIS

Perhaps the true rationale behind this decision lies in the legislature's announced policy of "no-fault" and the equal division of community assets. Equity would deem this approach just in order to effectuate these policies. The rationale in *Brown* would probably apply to causes of action arising during marriage, which affect community business. While contingent on the outcome of the lawsuit, the cause of action had damaged a community asset during marriage. It is arguable that *French* was not overruled by this decision because the court has implied that since there is an existing contract this fact is equivalent to vesting.

■═■

Quicknotes

CONTINGENCY INTEREST An interest that is based on the uncertain happening of another event.

EQUITABLE ESTATE An interest in property that is only recognized in equity.

INTERLOCUTORY JUDGMENT An order entered by the court determining an issue that does not resolve the disposition of the case, but is essential to a proper adjudication of the action.

VESTED INTEREST A present right to property, although the right to the possession of such property may not be enjoyed until a future date.

■═■

Marriage of Bergman

Wife (P) v. Husband (D)

Cal. Ct. App., 168 Cal. App. 3d 742 (1985).

NATURE OF CASE: Appeal from distribution of community property.

FACT SUMMARY: In Joan Bergman's (P) dissolution action against her husband, Elmer Bergman, (D), Elmer (D) claimed that the trial court abused its discretion by failing to divide the community interest in his defined benefits pension plan on an in-kind basis.

🏛 RULE OF LAW
Upon dissolution of a marriage, the trial court has broad discretion in the division of the community property interest in a spouse's pension rights and can exercise its discretion in that division as it sees fit.

FACTS: Joan Bergman (P) and her husband, Elmer Bergman (D), were separated in April, 1980. Elmer (D) had been employed in the federal civil service from 1961 to 1976. Prior to marriage, he had performed almost two years of military service which counted as service towards his federal longevity retirement. In 1976, as a result of developing severe hypertension, Elmer (D) became permanently and totally disabled. He has been receiving a disability pension since that time. During the marriage, Joan (P) worked at several jobs, one of which was a school teacher. As a teacher, she made contributions to the California State Teachers Retirement System. At trial, the court used the cash-out method to define the community interest in Elmer's (D) defined benefit pension plan. It determined the present value of the interest of the community in Elmer's (D) pension plan, awarded it to him, and gave an offsetting award of other community property to Joan (P). Elmer (D) appealed, claiming that the court abused its discretion by failing to divide the community interest in the pension on an in-kind basis.

ISSUE: Upon dissolution of a marriage, does the trial court have broad discretion in the division of the community property interest in a spouse's pension rights and can it exercise its discretion in that division as it sees fit?

HOLDING AND DECISION: (King, J.) Yes. Upon dissolution of a marriage, the trial court has broad discretion in the division of the community property interest in a spouse's pension rights and can exercise its discretion in that division as it sees fit. Here, both parties presented evidence from experts on the present value of Elmer's (D) pension benefits and his probability of receipt of them. The court exercised its discretion in favor of awarding the community interest in those benefits solely to Elmer (D), awarding offsetting assets to Joan (P) to accomplish an equal division. It is clear the court did in fact exercise its discretion, since it utilized the cash-out method to dispose of Elmer's (D) pension, while it divided the community interest in Joan's (P) pension benefits in kind. Appellate courts should not second guess the exercise of the broad discretion of trial courts in the absence of a clear showing of an abuse of that discretion. No such abuse of discretion has been demonstrated in this case. The award to Elmer (D) of the community property interest in his pension plan must therefore stand. Affirmed.

CONCURRENCE: (Haning, J.) The result should stand based on the view that the trial courts should have broad discretion in dissolution cases.

▶ ANALYSIS

Two methods are usually used by the courts in dividing the community property interest in a spouse's pension rights: the cash-out method and the division in-kind method. The cash-out method entails the award of the entire community interest at its present value to the employee spouse with offsetting assets awarded to the other spouse to accomplish an equal division. In the division in-kind method, the community interest is divided between the parties, and the plan, when benefits become payable, usually makes separate payments to each according to their proportionate interests.

■═■

Quicknotes

COMMUNITY PROPERTY In community property jurisdictions refers to all money or property acquired during the term of the marriage in which each spouse has an undivided one-half interest.

IN-KIND Belonging to the same type or class.

PRESENT CASH VALUE METHOD A means of evaluating property by determining its actual or market value.

■═■

Marriage of Gillmore

Wife (P) v. Husband (D)

Cal. Sup. Ct., 29 Cal. 3d 418, 629 P.2d 1 (1981).

NATURE OF CASE: Appeal from denial of order of payment of retirement benefits in a dissolution action.

FACT SUMMARY: In Vera Gillmore's (P) action for dissolution against her husband, Earl Gillmore (D), Vera (P) appealed from the decision of the trial court refusing to order immediate payment to her of a share in Earl's (D) retirement benefits.

🏛 RULE OF LAW
Under California law, retirement benefits earned by a spouse during a marriage are community property, subject to equal division upon the dissolution of the marriage.

FACTS: Earl Gillmore (D) and his wife, Vera (P), separated in 1978, after a marriage of 14 years. The trial court issued an interlocutory decree dissolving their marriage and then entered a final judgment of dissolution. The community property was divided evenly, with the exception of Earl's (D) interest in a retirement plan managed by his employer. The court specifically reserved jurisdiction over the retirement plan. Earl (D) continued to work after he became eligible to retire in 1979. He represented that he was a "healthy, active man" and that he intended to work for some time to come. Vera (P) then requested an order directing Earl (D) to pay her share of the pension benefits immediately, retroactive to the date Earl (D) became eligible to collect them. The court held that it had discretion to delay distribution of the benefits until Earl (D) actually retired. Vera (P) appealed, contending that she was entitled to immediate payment of her share of Earl's (D) pension benefits.

ISSUE: Under California law, are retirement benefits earned by a spouse during marriage community property, subject to equal division upon the dissolution of the marriage?

HOLDING AND DECISION: (Bird, C.J.) Yes. Under California law, retirement benefits earned by a spouse during a marriage are community property, subject to equal division upon the dissolution of the marriage. This is true whether the benefits are vested or non-vested, matured or immature. Trial courts have considerable discretion to determine the value of the community property and to formulate a practical way in which to divide property equally. However, that discretion has been strictly circumscribed by the statutory requirement that all community property be divided equally between the parties. A trial court has been held to abuse its discretion when it improperly classifies property as the separate property of one of the spouses or fails to arrive at an equal division of the community property. Thus, under the law, Earl (D) cannot time his retirement to deprive Vera (P) of an equal share of the community's interest in his pension. Compensation is possible here because the value of Vera's interest (P) is known to the court. Also, the pension benefits have already vested and matured. There are no uncertainties affecting vesting or maturation that could lead the trial court to conclude that distribution of the pension must be delayed. Therefore, the trial court abused its discretion when it refused to order the immediate distribution of Earl's (D) vested and matured retirement benefit. Reversed and remanded.

▶ ANALYSIS

Civil Code § 4800.8 requires that the court, in dividing community property interests in any retirement plan, make whatever orders are necessary to assure that each party receives a full community property share of any retirement plan. In an uncodified section, the legislature expressed its intent to abolish the terminable interest rule in order that retirement benefits shall be divided in accordance with § 4800. The retroactivity in application of § 4800.8 has been held to be constitutional.

■=■

Quicknotes

COMMUNITY PROPERTY In community property jurisdictions refers to all money or property acquired during the term of the marriage in which each spouse has an undivided one-half interest.

EQUITABLE DISTRIBUTION The means by which a court distributes all assets acquired during a marriage by the spouses equitably upon dissolution.

INTERLOCUTORY Intervening; temporary; refers to an issue that is determined during the course of a proceeding and which does not constitute a final judgment on the merits.

VESTED RIGHT Rights in pension or other retirement benefits that are attained when the employee satisfies the minimum requirements necessary in order to be entitled to the receipt of such benefits in the future.

■=■

Marriage of Lehman

Cal. Sup. Ct., 18 Cal. 4th 169 (1998).

NATURE OF CASE: Marital dissolution proceeding.

FACT SUMMARY: Marietta sought to assert a community property interest in Jack's retirement benefits as enhanced.

🏛 RULE OF LAW
A nonemployee spouse who owns a community property interest in an employee spouse's retirement benefits under a defined benefit retirement plan owns a community property interest in the retirement benefits as enhanced.

FACTS: Jack and Marietta married in 1960 and in 1962 Jack began to participate in PG & E's defined retirement plan and began accruing retirement benefits thereunder. The couple separated in 1977 and divorced in 1979. In 1993 PG & E offered an enhanced retirement program to avoid discharging certain employees. After Jack retired, Marietta made various motions in the Superior Court seeking a determination that she owned a community property interest in the enhanced retirement benefits. The Superior Court concluded that Marietta owned a community property interest in the benefits as enhanced and the court of appeal affirmed.

ISSUE: Does a nonemployee spouse who owns a community property interest in an employee spouse's retirement benefits under a defined benefit retirement plan own a community property interest in the retirement benefits as enhanced?

HOLDING AND DECISION: (Mosk, J.) Yes. A nonemployee spouse who owns a community property interest in an employee spouse's retirement benefits under a defined benefit retirement plan owns a community property interest in the retirement benefits as enhanced. As a general rule, all property acquired by a spouse during marriage is community property. Such property may include the right to retirement benefits accrued by the employee spouse as deferred compensation for services rendered. The right to retirement benefits represents a property interest; to the extent that right accrues from employment during marriage and before separation, it comprises a community asset. That the nonemployee spouse might enjoy an increase or suffer a decrease in retirement benefits because of post-separation events or conditions is justified by the nature of the right to retirement benefits as a right to draw from a stream of income that begins to flow, and is defined, upon retirement. The nonemployee spouse bears the risk of loss or gain equally with the employee spouse. Thus, if the right to retirement benefits accrues during the marriage before separation, it is a community asset. If follows that a non-employee spouse who owns a community property interest in an employee spouse's retirement benefits also owns a

community property interest in those benefits as enhanced. This does not mean that the enhancement is a community asset in its entirety; the issue of characterization is one of apportionment. The Superior Court must apportion an employee spouse's retirement benefits between the community property interest of the employee spouse and the nonemployee spouse and any separate property interest of the employee spouse alone. Reflecting the husband's length of service of 17.39 years during the marriage before separation and his length of service of 32.67 years total, the community's interest in the retirement benefits as enhanced was fixed at 53.23% and his separate property interest at 46.77%. Affirmed.

DISSENT: (Baxter, J.) A marital community has a contractual entitlement to all benefits earned by a spouse during the marriage under the terms and conditions of the employment in effect. A dissolved community has no stake in any "enhancement" of benefits that was first offered after separation and was not in effect during the marriage. This should especially be the rule when the enhanced benefits are a new subsidy for the purpose of inducing a voluntary termination of employment. The community here is entitled to a pro rata share in the monthly benefit the husband would receive for early retirement under the previous pension plan, but has no interest in the additional monthly amount attributable to the enhancement.

▶ ANALYSIS

The majority here defines the retirement benefit as a community asset once the right accrues prior to separation. The various events and conditions that occur thereafter have no effect on the character of the asset, but may have an effect on the amount of benefits the employee spouse may receive. The court takes the view that any enhancement in the benefit is a "modification of an asset not the creation of a new one."

■■■

Quicknotes

APPORTIONMENT The division of property costs in proportion to the parties' respective interests therein.

COMMUNITY PROPERTY In community property jurisdictions refers to all money or property acquired during the term of the marriage in which each spouse has an undivided one-half interest.

DEFERRED COMPENSATION Earnings that are to be taxed at the time they are received by, or distributed to, the employee, and not when they are in fact earned.

■■■

Marriage of Hug

Wife (P) v. Husband (D)

Cal. Ct. App., 154 Cal. App. 3d 780 (1984).

NATURE OF CASE: Appeal from division of community property.

FACT SUMMARY: In Maria Hug's (P) dissolution action against her husband, Paul (D), Paul (D) contended that the court used an erroneous formula to value stock options Paul (D) was granted by his employer and that each annual option was separate and distinct and was compensation for services during that year and thus accrued after the date of separation from Maria (P) and were separate.

▥ RULE OF LAW
No single characterization can be given to employee stock options, and whether they can be characterized as compensation for future services, for past services, or for both depends upon the circumstances involved in the grant of the employee stock option.

FACTS: Maria (P) and Paul Hug (D) separated in 1976, after being married 20 years. In 1972, Paul (D) had left a position with IBM to begin employment at Amdahl. While employed at Amdahl, he was granted options to purchase 3,100 shares of Amdahl's stock. These options were granted in 1972, 1974, and 1975. At the dissolution trial, since portions of the options were exercisable only after the parties' separation, the court sought to allocate the options to reflect the relationship between periods of Paul's (D) community contribution in comparison to his overall contribution to earning the option rights. In other words, the court tried to fairly allocate the stock options between compensation for services prior to and after the date of separation. The court found that the community portion of the unexercised shares was the product of a fraction whose numerator is the length of service (months) by Paul (D) with Amdahl from the beginning of service to date of separation and whose denominator is the length of service (months) from the date of commencement of service to the date when an option could be exercised, multiplied by the number of shares that could be purchased on the date of exercise. Paul (D) appealed the court's decision, contending that the formula was erroneous, that each annual option was separate and distinct and was compensation for services during that year, accruing after the date of the Hugs' separation and, thus, separate property.

ISSUE: Can any single characterization be given to employee stock options, and does whether they can be characterized as compensation for future services, for past services, or for both, depend on the circumstances involved in the grant of the employee stock option?

HOLDING AND DECISION: (King, J.) No. No single characterization can be given to employee stock options. Whether they can be characterized as compensation for future services, for past services, or for both, depends on the circumstances involved in the grant of the employee stock option. Here, the trial court found that the stock option agreement arose from the standard corporate purpose of attracting and retaining the services of selected employees. Since the options are keyed to periods of employment after the date of each grant, Paul (D) argues that the options were earned from the outset of Paul's (D) service with Amdahl. Nothing in the makeup of the option plan requires the options to be construed as compensation for future services. The trial court properly exercised its discretion in fashioning the time formula it used to equitably allocate the separate and community property interests in the options. Paul's (D) arguments to the contrary overlook the community interests in contractual rights earned during the marriage as a factor of employee compensation. Affirmed.

▶ ANALYSIS

An employer's reasons for granting stock options may be an important factor in their classification as community or separate property. It will also affect the apportionment method the court will use. If an employer's intent is to compensate the employee for future as opposed to past efforts, courts have indicated that this factor could properly be considered in devising an apportionment formula.

■=■

Quicknotes

APPORTIONMENT The division of property costs in proportion to the parties' respective interests therein.

COMMUNITY PROPERTY In community property jurisdictions refers to all money or property acquired during the term of the marriage in which each spouse has an undivided one-half interest.

SEPARATE PROPERTY Property owned by one spouse prior to marriage, or any income derived therefrom, and any property received by one spouse pursuant to a gift, devise, bequest or descent.

STOCK OPTIONS The right to purchase or sell a particular stock at a specified price within a certain time period.

■=■

Marriage of Elfmont

Cal. Sup. Ct., 9 Cal. 4th 1026, 891 P.2d 136 (1995).

NATURE OF CASE: Marital dissolution proceeding.

FACT SUMMARY: John Elfmont challenged the ruling of the trial court finding that $5,000 of a $9,000 per month disability benefit payment to be community property.

🏛 RULE OF LAW
If the insured spouse does not become disabled during the last policy term before the parties' separation, the community will have no interest in benefits produced by renewals of the policy for subsequent terms because the renewal premium will not have been paid during the marriage with community funds and with the intent of providing community retirement income.

FACTS: John and Edie Elfmont were married in 1975 and separated in 1987. During the marriage John practiced medicine as an obstetrician and gynecologist. In 1977 he incorporated his medical practice, established a corporate pension and profit sharing plan and took out disability insurance. In 1989 John became disabled from a lower back disorder. He sold his practice and applied for disability benefits of $9,000 per month. The trial court found the disability coverage as originally purchased ($4,000 per month) was his separate property as it was intended as a wage replacement. However, the additional $5,000 was community property because he increased the amount of the policy due to changed circumstances. John appealed that portion of the judgment finding $5,000 per month of disability benefits to be community property.

ISSUE: If the insured spouse does not become disabled during the last policy term before the parties' separation, will the community have an interest in benefits produced by renewals of the policy for subsequent terms?

HOLDING AND DECISION: (Werdegar, J.) No. If the insured spouse does not become disabled during the last policy term before the parties' separation, the community will have no interest in benefits produced by renewals of the policy for subsequent terms because the renewal premium will not have been paid during the marriage with community funds and with the intent of providing community retirement income. In *Saslow*, 710 P.2d 346 (1985), where disability insurance benefits were paid wholly out of community property and payment of the benefits commenced during the marriage, this court held benefits received after separation were community property insofar as they were intended to replace the disabled spouse's post dissolution earnings. Here the disability term insurance was paid out of community funds during the marriage; however, payment of the benefits did not commence until 32 months after separation, during which time the husband

paid renewal premiums from his separate property. There was evidence the premium payments made during the marriage were made with an intent to provide retirement income and that the husband's physical condition at the time of separation might have precluded him from enjoying comparable disability coverage without the automatic policy renewal rights that were purchased by the community. The court must look to the spouse's intent at the time the insurance was originally purchased and at all time that decisions were made to renew such insurance. No evidence here indicates an intent that the renewal was to provide community retirement income. Post separation disability benefits may be treated as community property to the extent they were purchased during marriage with community funds, even if intended to provide retirement income. If during the marriage the insured becomes disabled, the benefits received are community property because they replace community earnings. If the benefits continue after the spouses have separated, they are the separate property of the insured spouse whose earnings they replace, unless during the marriage premiums were paid out of community funds with the intent the benefits provide retirement income. If the insured spouse does not become disabled during the last policy term before the parties' separation, the community will have no interest in benefits produced by renewals of the policy for subsequent terms because the renewal premium will not have been paid during the marriage with community funds and with the intent of providing community retirement income. Since the husband became entitled to draw the benefits only after he had renewed all three term policies following the parties' separation with premiums paid out of his separate funds, all the benefits are his separate property. Affirmed.

CONCURRENCE: (Baxter, J.) Instead of distinguishing *Saslow*, we should overrule it. With respect to the private disability insurance context, there is no logic in the notion that disability benefits are intended as a replacement for community retirement income.

CONCURRENCE AND DISSENT: (George, J.) The husband is entitled to retain the disability benefits as his separate property because he chose to maintain such policies after separation by paying the premium renewals from his separate property and thereafter became disabled. However, the opinion fails to require the husband to reimburse the community for the value at the time of separation of the contractual right to renew the disability policies.

DISSENT: (Kennard, J.) Although disability insurance is rarely purchased for the purpose of providing community retirement income, when a couple has bought such a policy

Continued on next page.

with this intent the court should recognize the community's interest in the policy. Awarding all the interest in the benefits to the insured spouse disregards the substantial sums paid by the community to purchase the policy. To the extent a married couple intended the disability policy to provide for retirement income, the policy proceeds are community property, in an amount proportional to the percentage of the policy premiums paid for with community funds.

▶ ANALYSIS

The court distinguishes the case of term disability benefits from that of term life insurance benefits. In the case of term life insurance upon which premiums were paid from community funds such insurance has no value after the term has ended if the insured is not deceased. If the insured remains insurable, the right to renew the policy has no value since the insured could have obtained comparable term insurance elsewhere. If the insured is no longer insurable, however, and the insured pays renewal premiums with his or her separate property, the community has an interest in the life insurance proceeds commensurate with its contributions to the right of renewal.

Quicknotes

COMMUNITY PROPERTY In community property jurisdictions refers to all money or property acquired during the term of the marriage in which each spouse has an undivided one-half interest.

SEPARATE PROPERTY Property owned by one spouse prior to marriage, or any income derived therefrom, and any property received by one spouse pursuant to a gift, devise, bequest or descent.

Marriage of Gram

Cal. Ct. App., 25 Cal. App. 4th 859 (1994).

NATURE OF CASE: Marital dissolution proceeding.

FACT SUMMARY: Marilyn Gram sought an order to show cause as to why the enhanced portion of Allen's retirement benefits should not be treated as community property.

> 🏛 **RULE OF LAW**
> If an early retirement benefit is a form of deferred compensation for services rendered, then it is a community asset includable in the calculation of Marilyn's share of the monthly retirement benefit; if it is a present compensation for present loss of earnings, then it is the earning spouse's separate property.

FACTS: Marilyn and Allen Gram were married on May 28, 1960. Allen started work for the San Diego Union-Tribune Newspapers and began accumulating retirement credit. The couple separated in 1981. The parties entered into a marital termination agreement giving the superior court jurisdiction over the community interest in Allen's employment benefits. The San Diego Union and San Diego Tribune announced plans to merge and offered its employees early retirement incentives. Allen was credited with 27 years of service and deemed to be 64 years of age. He elected to retire under the plan and receive a monthly benefit. Marilyn sought an order to show cause as to why Allen's enhanced benefits for early retirement should not be treated as community property. The trial court determined the enhanced portion of the retirement benefits was Allen's separate property and Marilyn appealed.

ISSUE: If an early retirement benefit is a form of deferred compensation for services rendered, then is it a community asset includable in the calculation of Marilyn's share of the monthly retirement benefit?

HOLDING AND DECISION: (Benke, J.) Yes. If an early retirement benefit is a form of deferred compensation for services rendered, then it is a community asset includable in the calculation of Marilyn's share of the monthly retirement benefit; if it is a present compensation for present loss of earnings, then it is the earning spouse's separate property. Courts are divided as to whether the proceeds of severance plans constitute community property. We conclude the trial court erred in finding the enhanced early retirement benefit selected by Allen to be his separate property. While no preexisting contractual obligation gave rise to the benefit, this factor is not determinative. The enhanced early retirement option selected by Allen reflected the most likely plan of an employee of his age and years of service. The plan merely accelerated the process by immediately granting him additional age and service credit. The plan essentially gave the employee a reasonable version of the benefit he expected had the merger not occurred. Thus it was not a present payment for loss of earnings but the realization of Allen's retirement expectation and a form of deferred compensation for services rendered. As such it should have been included in the computation of Marilyn's interest in the community estate. The enhanced benefit is computed by adding five years to service, thus resulting in a higher percentage of the monthly retirement benefit attributable to Allen's years of service after the marriage. The computation of the community interest should take those additional years into account by adding them to Allen's total years of employment in the benefit share formula. Reversed and remanded.

▶ ANALYSIS

Note that the rule in the present case applies equally to other forms of fringe benefits earning by the working spouse. Several courts have held that accrued vacation pay likewise constitutes deferred compensation for services rendered and are includable in the community estate.

━━■

Quicknotes

COMMUNITY PROPERTY In community property jurisdictions refers to all money or property acquired during the term of the marriage in which each spouse has an undivided one-half interest.

DEFERRED COMPENSATION Earnings that are to be taxed at the time they are received by, or distributed to, the employee, and not when they are in fact earned.

SEPARATE PROPERTY Property owned by one spouse prior to marriage, or any income derived therefrom, and any property received by one spouse pursuant to a gift, devise, bequest or descent.

━━■

Spousal Management and Creditors' Rights

Quick Reference Rules of Law

Tyre v. Aetna Life Insurance Co.

Life insurance beneficiary (P) v. Life insurance company (D)

Cal. Sup. Ct., 54 Cal. 2d 399, 353 P.2d 725 (1960).

NATURE OF CASE: Action to determine ownership of insurance proceeds.

FACT SUMMARY: Although Mr. Tyre named Mrs. Tyre (P) as beneficiary of a life insurance policy purchased with community property funds, he specified that she could receive the policy benefits only in the form of an annuity.

🏛 RULE OF LAW
A husband cannot interfere with his wife's vested one-half interest in the community property, either by bequeathing more than half of the community property to third persons or by bequeathing more than half of the community property to his wife under conditions which restrict her management and control over such property.

FACTS: During his marriage to Mrs. Tyre (P), Mr. Tyre purchased a life insurance policy from Aetna Life Insurance Co. (D) with community property funds. Under this policy, Mr. Tyre named Mrs. Tyre (P) as the sole beneficiary and directed that she receive the policy benefits in the form of an annuity. After Mr. Tyre's death, however, Mrs. Tyre (P) requested payment of the face amount of the policy (i.e., $20,000) in cash. When Aetna (D) refused to alter Mr. Tyre's directions, Mrs. Tyre (P) brought an action against Aetna (D) to determine ownership of the insurance benefits. In this action, Mrs. Tyre (P) specifically asked for $10,000 in cash representing her community property interest in the policy and for a declaration that the remaining $10,000 be paid according to the policy in the form of an annuity. After the trial court ruled for Aetna (D), Mrs. Tyre (P) appealed.

ISSUE: Can a husband bequeath the community property to his wife under conditions which restrict her control over her one-half interest in such property?

HOLDING AND DECISION: (Traynor, J.) No. A husband cannot interfere with his wife's vested one-half interest in the community property either by bequeathing more than half of the community property to third persons or by bequeathing more than half of the community property to his wife under conditions which restrict her management and control over such property. In either of these situations the wife can "elect" to take what her husband has given her or to take her community property rights (i.e., her vested one-half interest). Here, therefore, Mrs. Tyre (P) may either take the $10,000 in cash as her community property interest or take the entire insurance proceeds (as her husband's gift) in annuity form. She cannot, however, take both. Reversed and remanded.

▶ ANALYSIS

"Although the payment of insurance proceeds is a matter of contract between the insured and the insurer, the insured's exercise of his unilateral right under the contract to select the beneficiary is testamentary in character. Similarly, the insured's exercise of his unilateral right under the terms of the policy to determine whether the proceeds shall be paid as a lump sum or in the form of an annuity is testamentary in character. . . . (T)he probate code gives the husband testamentary control over only one-half of the community property, and the word 'testamentary' as used . . . is not limited to formal testaments. Thus, although a wife can set aside a husband's unauthorized gift of community property in its entirety during his lifetime, she is limited to recovery of her one-half share after his death on the theory that his testamentary powers validate the gift of his half interest."

Quicknotes

ANNUITY The payment or right to receive payment of a fixed sum periodically, for a specified time period.

COMMUNITY PROPERTY In community property jurisdictions refers to all money or property acquired during the term of the marriage in which each spouse has an undivided one-half interest.

Marriage of Stitt

Cal. Ct. App., 147 Cal. App. 3d 579 (1983).

NATURE OF CASE: Appeal of debt responsibility determination in a dissolution proceeding.

FACT SUMMARY: Mr. Stitt argued that his wife individually, and not the community, should be responsible for the attorney fees she incurred in defending a civil and criminal action.

🏛 RULE OF LAW
The accused spouse, and not the community, is solely responsible for any unpaid attorney fees incurred by the accused spouse in her defense against criminal charges and a related civil action.

FACTS: Mrs. Stitt settled a fraud and misappropriation of funds action her ex-employer filed against her. She was also tried and convicted of embezzlement. Mr. Stitt made partial payments out of a joint account, amounting to $4,287.68, towards the attorney fees incurred by his wife. After the couple separated, Mrs. Stitt executed a second trust deed on community real property in favor of the law firms which represented her for the remaining $10,989.20 owed to them. The trial court found that Mrs. Stitt was solely responsible for the attorney fees and she appealed.

ISSUE: Should the community be responsible for unpaid attorney fees incurred by the wife in her defense against embezzlement charges?

HOLDING AND DECISION: (Woolpert, J.) No. The wife, and not the community, is solely responsible for any unpaid attorney fees incurred by her in her defense against embezzlement charges. Generally, if a married person employs an attorney, the contractual obligation to the attorney would be the responsibility of both spouses. However, the court could find the obligation to be the wife's alone because the Family Code states that a married person is generally not liable for damages caused by a tortfeasor spouse. In this case, since Mr. Stitt did not participate in his wife's embezzlement and no benefit to the community was shown, the employer first looked to Mrs. Stitt's separate property for recovery and then the employer and the attorneys looked to satisfy their claims from the community property. Mr. Stitt's community interest in the trust deed property was therefore at risk from the creditor's standpoint; however, in the settlement of marital rights the court could seek an equitable result because of the separate nature of the obligation. It was thus appropriate for the trial court to assign the full financial responsibility for Mrs. Stitt's embezzlement to her, preventing her assertion of community debt from diminishing Mr. Stitt's share of the community property. This is because the actor is solely responsible for willful and negligent acts unless shared, mitigated or excused because of other principles of law. Moreover, the mere fact of marriage does not change the usual rules of personal responsibility for the consequence of criminal or tortuous activity. Furthermore, Mr. Stitt had not waived his right to receive his share of the community property free from any loss attributable to Mrs. Stitt's separate conduct. Affirmed.

▶ ANALYSIS

The court noted in this case that it was unclear whether the embezzlement took place prior to or during the marriage, and that there was no evidence that the embezzlement jointly benefited both spouses.

■══■

Quicknotes

COMMUNITY PROPERTY In community property jurisdictions refers to all money or property acquired during the term of the marriage in which each spouse has an undivided one-half interest.

EMBEZZLEMENT The fraudulent appropriation of property lawfully in one's possession.

EQUITABLE REMEDY A remedy that is based upon principles of fairness as opposed to rules of law; a remedy involving specific performance rather than money damages.

TORTFEASOR Party that commits a tort or wrongful act.

■══■

Marriage of Duffy

Cal. Ct. App., 91 Cal. App. 4th 923 (2001).

NATURE OF CASE: Appeal of finding of breach of fiduciary duty in managing community assets pre-dissolution in dissolution proceeding.

FACT SUMMARY: Patricia alleged that Vincent had breached his fiduciary duty in managing their community assets.

🏛 **RULE OF LAW**
(1) **A managing spouse will have breached his fiduciary duty of full disclosure upon request to the non-managing spouse, if there is evidence that the non-managing spouse sought information about investment assets and the managing spouse failed or refused to provide such information.**
(2) **There is no duty of care in the fiduciary duty owed by a spouse in managing community assets.**

FACTS: Vincent managed his and his wife Patricia's financial affairs. Patricia knew of Vincent's investment in an auto body shop, but had not asked him how much he had invested because he usually answered her questions about finances with dismissive answers. She did know, however, that the auto body shop was not making money, that enough money had to be produced each month to pay the rent and knew that the investment was tied up for a five-year lease term. Patricia also participated in the couple's purchase of property in Leona Valley. In addition, she knew about their investment in a house in Arizona prior to it taking place, and knew the purchase and sales price and that litigation was taking place between the parties to the transaction regarding the sale. She also had some information about an Atlanta nightclub for which Vincent had made a loan, although she asked no detailed questions. The couple also discussed ahead of time their purchase of a timeshare, including its price. Upon his termination from MCA Records, Vincent received his interest in MCA's profit-sharing plan which he rolled over into an IRA, and Patricia accompanied him in doing so. Vincent also received shares of MCA stock. Vincent invested these assets without consulting Patricia. Although Patricia was aware that Vincent had opened a brokerage account and had seen some statements, MCA stock was not reflected on these statements. She, however, asked no questions about this. Over time, the MCA investments substantially decreased in value. The trial court found that Vincent breached his fiduciary duty of full disclosure as to the MCA investment and Vincent appealed.

ISSUE:
(1) Did Vincent breach his fiduciary duty of full disclosure?
(2) Does the fiduciary duty owed by a spouse in managing community assets include a duty of care?

HOLDING AND DECISION: (Spencer, J.)
(1) No. Vincent did not breach his fiduciary duty of full disclosure upon request because there is no evidence, substantial or insubstantial, that Patricia ever sought information about the investment of MCA assets, which information Vincent failed or refused to provide.
(2) No. the fiduciary duty owed by a spouse in managing community assets does not include a duty of care. (1) The Family Code gives to either spouse the ability to manage and control the community's personal property. In doing so, however, the spouses must act in a fiduciary capacity towards one another by making full disclosures of all material facts and information regarding the characterization of all assets in which the community has an interest. The fiduciary duty imposes a duty of good faith and fair dealing on the spouses in which each spouse must have access at all times to any books, and upon request, the rendering of true and full information of all things affecting any transaction which concerns the community property must be provided, as well as an accounting. In this case, there is no evidence that Vincent ever refused to provide information about the investment of the MCA assets or that Patricia had asked questions regarding the investment of these assets. Indeed, Patricia testified that she had asked no questions concerning the MCA assets. Moreover, there is no evidence that Vincent treated any of Patricia's questions in a dismissive manner after 1983. Patricia could get pertinent investment information when she sought it as is evidenced by the information she received regarding the Arizona property, the time share and the auto body investment. (2) As evidenced by legislative intent, the fiduciary duty owed by a spouse in managing community assets does not include a duty of care. Historically, although the husband owed a duty of loyalty in managing community property, he did not owe a duty of care. When both spouses received the right to jointly manage the community's personal property, the managing spouse had a duty to act in good faith in doing so. Later legislation ruled that a spouse does not owe to the other spouse the duty of care that one business partner owes to another. In this case, Vincent did not owe Patricia a duty of care in investing the community assets. Reversed and remanded.

▶ **ANALYSIS**

Vincent would have been found to have violated his fiduciary duty of disclosure if Patricia had asked for information, but Vincent had refused to give it.

■═■

Continued on next page.

Quicknotes

COMMUNITY PROPERTY In community property jurisdictions refers to all money or property acquired during the term of the marriage in which each spouse has an undivided one-half interest.

DISSOLUTION PROCEEDING AND DECREE A proceeding and resulting decree to terminate a marriage.

DUTY OF CARE A principle of negligence requiring an individual to act in such a manner as to avoid injury to a person to whom he or she owes a duty.

DUTY OF LOYALTY A director's duty to refrain from self-dealing or to take a position that is adverse to the corporation's best interests.

FIDUCIARY DUTY A legal obligation to act for the benefit of another, including subordinating one's personal interests to that of the other person.

Wilcox v. Wilcox

Husband (P) v. Wife (D)

Cal. Ct. App., 21 Cal. App. 3d 457 (1971).

NATURE OF CASE: Action to recover community funds.

FACT SUMMARY: After Mrs. Wilcox (D) secreted and took control over certain community funds, Mr. Wilcox (P) demanded that she return such funds to his control.

🏛 **RULE OF LAW**
The husband has a right to maintain an action against his wife to protect his property rights in community funds, including his "right to manage, control, and dispose of such with the incident right to possession thereof for this purpose."

FACTS: Some time after Mr. Wilcox (P) and Mrs. Wilcox (D) became husband and wife, Mrs. Wilcox (D) took exclusive possession of, and secreted, $30,000 of community funds. Thereupon, Mr. Wilcox (P) demanded that such funds be returned to his possession and control. When Mrs. Wilcox (D) refused to return such funds, Mr. Wilcox (P) brought an action to recover them. In response, Mrs. Wilcox (D) filed a demurrer to the complaint on the ground that there was no statutory authority for the action. After the trial court sustained the demurrer, Mr. Wilcox (P) appealed.

ISSUE: Can the husband maintain an action against his wife to protect his right to manage, control, and dispose of community funds?

HOLDING AND DECISION: (Coughlin, J.) Yes. The husband has a right to maintain an action against his wife to protect his property rights in community funds, including his "right to manage, control, and dispose of such with the incident right to possession thereof for this purpose." The Civil Code gives the husband "management and control" over community funds and, of course, such power would be meaningless without any right of enforcement. As such, even though there is no specific statutory authority for the husband to sue his wife for interference with the power of management and control, he has such a right. Here, Mrs. Wilcox (D) interfered with Mr. Wilcox's (P) power of control over community funds by secreting such funds. As such, Mr. Wilcox (P) is entitled to bring an action to recover the funds. Reversed.

▶ *ANALYSIS*

This case illustrates the rule prior to 1975. Under the rule established in 1975 (which is still valid today), each spouse has the right to manage and control the community property. Note, however, that the powers of management and control which either spouse may exercise are subject to limitations. For example, neither spouse may sell community

real property without the written consent of the other spouse. Furthermore, although a spouse may transfer community personal property for value without consent of the other spouse, he or she cannot make a gift of such property without consent. If either spouse exceeds such limitations, the other spouse may bring an action for damages or other relief.

■=■

Quicknotes

COMMUNITY PROPERTY In community property jurisdictions, refers to all money or property acquired during the term of the marriage in which each spouse has an undivided one-half interest.

DEMURRER The assertion that the opposing party's pleadings are insufficient and that the demurring party should not be made to answer.

PROPERTY RIGHTS A legal right in specified personal or real property.

■=■

Spreckels v. Spreckels

Cal. Sup. Ct., 172 Cal. 775, 158 P. 537 (1916).

NATURE OF CASE: Probate action for accounting.

FACT SUMMARY: Claus Spreckels made gratuitous transfers of community property without his wife's consent.

🏛 RULE OF LAW
The Civil Code § 172 right of a husband to gratuitously transfer community property at any time is always subject to the right of the wife to revoke such transfers within the statutory period; but this right of the wife to revoke such gifts does not prevent their immediate vesting in the donee.

FACTS: During their marriage, Claus and Anna Spreckels had five children, Claus (P), Rudolph (P), Emma (P), John (D), and Adolph (D). Between 1896 and 1905, Claus, gratuitously and without Anna's consent, transferred some $25 million in community property assets to John (D) and Adolph (D). Upon Claus' death in 1909, there was some $10 million left in the estate. At that time, Anna executed her own will, dividing the $10 million between Claus (P), Rudolph (P) and Emma (P)—expressly omitting John (D) and Adolph (D) because of the $25 million already "given and advanced" to them. Upon Anna's death, Claus (P), Rudolph (P), and Emma (P) all filed this probate action (as executors of both Anna's and Claus' estates) to have the $25 million in gratuitous transfers set aside under Civil Code § 172 because Anna never consented to them "in writing." A demurrer was sustained and this followed.

ISSUE: Does the mere fact that a wife has not consented in writing to certain gratuitous transfers of community property by her husband automatically mean that those transfers are void?

HOLDING AND DECISION: (Shaw, J.) No. The Civil Code § 172 right of a husband to gratuitously transfer community property at any time is always subject to the right of the wife to revoke such transfers within the statutory period, but this right of the wife to revoke such gifts does not prevent their immediate vesting in the donee. Section 172 does not require written consent of the wife before any transfer of community property by the husband—it merely gives her a right to revoke it within the period of the statute of limitations. If this right accrued at the time of the transfers therefore, Anna's failure to revoke within the period clearly validates them. Even if the right did not accrue until Claus' death, however, the will that Anna executed, recognizing John's (D) and Adolph's (D) right to the $25 million, is sufficient to constitute a ratification of the gifts which no later revocation would have effected. The demurrer is affirmed.

▶ ANALYSIS

This case points up the early 20th century position of the courts on the development of the rights of a wife in the management and control of community property. Note that § 172 at that time unequivocally stated that a husband "cannot make a gift of . . . community property . . . unless the wife, in writing, consent thereto." The traditional right of management and control as vested in the husband was so strong, however, that to keep it inviolate was considered of such great importance that the courts decided that the legislature could not have meant what it said in § 172. Note that, following this case, in 1917, the legislature amended § 172 to provide, in accordance with *Spreckels*, a one-year statute of limitations period for revocation of gratuitous transfers.

■≡■

Quicknotes

COMMUNITY PROPERTY In community property jurisdictions refers to all money or property acquired during the term of the marriage in which each spouse has an undivided one-half interest.

DEMURRER The assertion that the opposing party's pleadings are insufficient and that the demurring party should not be made to answer.

DONEE A person to whom a gift is made.

GRATUITOUS TRANSFER A transfer of property that is accomplished without any consideration being received therefor.

STATUTE OF LIMITATIONS A law prescribing the period in which a legal action may be commenced.

VESTED INTEREST A present right to property, although the right to the possession of such property may not be enjoyed until a future date.

■≡■

Estate of Wilson

Ex-wife and others (P) v. Deceased's widow (D)

Cal. Ct. App., 183 Cal. App. 3d 67 (1986).

NATURE OF CASE: Appeal from award of community property.

FACT SUMMARY: In an action by Bowens (P) and Tolliver (P) action against Wilson (D), Bowens (P) and Tolliver (P) contended that Wilson (D), the surviving spouse of the decedent, Milburn Warren Wilson, was not entitled to any part of disputed trust accounts because decedent had the right to make a testamentary disposition of one-half of the entire community property taken as a whole, rather than merely one-half of each community property asset.

🏛 RULE OF LAW
If a spouse after the death of the decedent proves a lack of consent to a gift, it will be avoided to the extent of the non-consenting spouse's one-half interest in community property transferred.

FACTS: Decedent, Milburn Warren Wilson, died intestate on June 12, 1983, leaving a surviving spouse, Ruth Wilson (D), and nine children. Bowens (P), son of decedent, and Tolliver (P), mother of two minor children of decedent, brought an action contending that Ruth (D) should not be awarded half the funds in three separate "Totten trusts" created by decedent in favor of three of his children. Bowens (P) and Tolliver (P) further contended that Ruth (D) was not entitled to any part of the disputed trust accounts because decedent had the right to make a testamentary disposition of one-half of the entire community property taken as a whole, rather than merely one-half of each community property asset. The court awarded Ruth (D) half the funds of the trusts, and Bowens (P) and Tolliver (P) appealed.

ISSUE: If a spouse, after the death of the decedent, proves a lack of consent to a gift, will it be avoided to the extent of the non-consenting spouse's one-half interest in community property transferred?

HOLDING AND DECISION: (King, J.) Yes. If a spouse after the death of the decedent proves a lack of consent to a gift, it will be avoided to the extent of the non-consenting spouse's one-half interest in community property transferred. The rationale of this rule is founded in the nature of community property. Death of a spouse only dissolves the interest in the community property. Each spouse has a vested undivided one-half interest in the community property. Death of a spouse only dissolves the community; it does not affect the character of the property acquired or rights vested before the spouse's death. In sum, since each Totten trust is an individual community property asset in which the decedent had only a one-half

undivided interest at the time he died, he could pass on to third parties only his one-half of that asset—in this case one-half of the funds in each account. Although the practical effect of this rule limits the ability to make testamentary dispositions of community property through Totten trusts, individuals possess virtually unlimited ability to dispose of their share of the community assets at death by will. Affirmed.

▶ ANALYSIS

A Totten trust basically allows a decedent to make a testamentary disposition of cash assets without going through the formalities of drawing up a will. If a depositor merely opens a bank account in his own name as trustee for another, intending to reserve the power to withdraw funds during his lifetime, a tentative trust is created. This trust is revocable during the trustee's lifetime or by his will and at his death is presumptively absolute trust.

■■■

Quicknotes

COMMUNITY PROPERTY In community property jurisdictions, refers to all money or property acquired during the term of the marriage in which each spouse has an undivided one-half interest.

INTESTATE To die without leaving a valid testamentary instrument.

TESTAMENTARY DISPOSITION A disposition of property that is effective upon the death of the grantor.

TOTTEN TRUST A revocable trust that is created by depositing funds in a bank account in trust for the benefit of another.

■■■

Droeger v. Friedman, Sloan & Ross

Husband (P) v. Wife's divorce attorneys (D)

Cal. Sup. Ct., 54 Cal. 3d 26, 812 P.2d 931 (1991).

NATURE OF CASE: Appeal from reversal of a dismissal of an action to quiet title to community real property.

FACT SUMMARY: When Joanna Droeger executed a promissory note and deed of trust on community real property in order to satisfy her attorney fees and costs for her pending dissolution of marriage proceeding, John Droeger (P) brought this action against Joanna's attorneys (D) to quiet title to the encumbered community realty.

🏛 RULE OF LAW
Both spouses, either personally or by duly authorized agent, must join in executing any instrument by which community real property or any interest therein is sold, conveyed, or encumbered.

FACTS: During the Droegers' pending marital dissolution, Joanna executed a promissory note in favor of her attorney, Friedman (D), for attorney fees and costs and also executed a deed of trust on two parcels of the community's real property to secure the note. John (P) did not join in the execution of the note or the deed of trust. John (P) commenced this action to quiet title to the encumbered community realty. Friedman (D) demurred to John's (P) second amended complaint, claiming that the deed of trust was enforceable against Joanna's one-half interest in the property. The trial court sustained the demurrer without leave to amend, entering a judgment of dismissal. The court of appeal reversed, holding that John (P) was entitled to void the encumbrance in its entirety. Friedman (D) appealed.

ISSUE: Must both spouses, either personally or by duly authorized agent, join in executing any instrument by which community real property or any interest therein is sold, conveyed, or encumbered?

HOLDING AND DECISION: (Panelli, J.) Yes. Both spouses, either personally or by duly authorized agent, must join in executing any instrument by which community real property or any interest therein is sold, conveyed, or encumbered. The word "any" means "all" or "every." The language "any interest" would include the consenting spouse's one-half undivided interest. Under the plain language of Civil Code § 5127, both spouses "must join in executing any instrument" encumbering such interest. During the existence of the community, the nonconsenting spouse should be fully protected against efforts by the other spouse to transfer community real property in contravention of § 5127. A transfer of the community real property without consent of both spouses adversely affects the nonconsenting spouse's interests and the dissolution court's ability to make an equitable division of the community property. Allowing the transfer to stand

against a challenge by the nonconsenting spouse could have the effect of partitioning the community property during the marriage, an event the legislature has expressly sought to avoid. Community property principles of equal management and shared responsibility mandate that the nonconsenting spouse is entitled to invalidate in its entirety the other spouse's transfer of community real property. The judgment of the court of appeal is affirmed.

DISSENT: (Kennard, J.) Subdivision (a) of Code of Civil Procedure § 412.21 restrains both parties to a marital dissolution from encumbering any property, real or personal, without the written consent of the other party but provides for an exception where community property is used to pay reasonable attorney fees in order to retain legal counsel in the action. Giving full effect to the legislative intent in § 412.21(a) does not at all impair the purpose of § 5127. Accordingly, the correct rule should be that the parties to a dissolution action may encumber community real property to the extent of their interests to secure reasonable attorney fees in the dissolution action.

▶ ANALYSIS

After the 1975 reforms of the community property laws, giving control and management of the community assets to either spouse, a split of authority developed in the appellate courts concerning the extent of relief available when the nonconsenting spouse brought an action during the marriage. One line of decisions held that transfers were voidable only as to the nonconsenting spouse's one-half interest, regardless of when the action was brought. Another line of decisions, including the lower court's decision in the instant case, expressly disapproved the other line of authority, holding that if relief was sought during marriage, the entire transfer should be set aside. In its analysis, the Supreme Court concluded that the latter reasoning, following the decision of *Andrade Development Co. v. Martin*, 138 Cal. App. 3d 330 (1982), was the correct one.

■=■

Quicknotes

COMMUNITY PROPERTY In community property jurisdictions refers to all money or property acquired during the term of the marriage in which each spouse has an undivided one-half interest.

DEED OF TRUST A legal document that acts as a mortgage, placing a security interest in the deeded property with a trustee to insure the payment of a debt.

Continued on next page.

DEMURRER The assertion that the opposing party's pleadings are insufficient and that the demurring party should not be made to answer.

DISSOLUTION PROCEEDING AND DECREE A proceeding and resulting decree to terminate a marriage.

ENCUMBRANCE An interest in property that operates as a claim or lien against its title potentially making it unmarketable.

PROMISSORY NOTE A written promise to tender a stated amount of money at a designated time and to a designated person.

QUIET TITLE Equitable action to resolve conflicting claims to an interest in real property.

Lezine v. Security Pacific Financial Services, Inc.

Wife of debtor (P) v. Creditor and secured interest holder (D)

Cal. Sup. Ct., 14 Cal. 4th 56, 925 P.2d 1002 (1996).

NATURE OF CASE: Suit for declaratory relief, quiet title, and cancellation of deeds of trust.

FACT SUMMARY: During the marriage, husband unilaterally transferred a security interest in community real property to Security Pacific (D) with the knowledge or consent of the wife (P) in violation of former Civil Code § 5127; wife (P) sought to have the transfer set aside.

🏛 RULE OF LAW
A creditor who previously forfeited a security interest in community real property under § 5127 is placed in the position of any other unsecured creditor entitled to seek a judgment against a debtor spouse and to enforce its money judgment against the community property estate.

FACTS: In 1974 Lezine and his wife (P) purchased the Halm Avenue property as their marital residence. In 1989 Lezine forged wife's (P) signature on a quitclaim deed which purported to divest her of any interest in the property. The deed was recorded and husband obtained a loan form Guardian secured by a deed of trust in favor of San Clemente Savings and Imperial Thrift, as well as other community debts. In 1990 husband obtained a $100,000 line of credit from Security Pacific (D) secured by a deed of trust encumbering the Halm Avenue property. Wife (P) then learned of the two deeds of trust encumbering the property and filed suit seeking declaratory relief, quiet title, and cancellation of the deeds of trust. She also filed suit for dissolution of marriage. The trial judge entered judgment in favor of wife (P) declaring the deeds of trust void and canceled. In the marital dissolution action, the court awarded wife (P) the Halm Avenue property as her sole and separate property, subject to the lien. The court also entered judgment on favor of defendants which were recorded. Wife (P) then moved for clarification of the judgment that the abstracts of judgment did not create judgment liens that attached to the property. The court granted the motion and Security Pacific (D) appealed.

ISSUE: Is a creditor who previously forfeited a security interest in community real property under § 5127 placed in the position of any other unsecured creditor entitled to seek a judgment against a debtor spouse and to enforce its money judgment against the community property estate?

HOLDING AND DECISION: (George, C.J.) Yes. A creditor who previously forfeited a security interest in community real property under § 5127 is placed in the position of any other unsecured creditor entitled to seek a judgment against a debtor spouse and to enforce its money

judgment against the community property estate. The issue here is whether community real property remains liable for satisfaction of a debt after the transfer of a security interest, which secured repayment of the debt, is set aside pursuant to former § 5127. The general rule is that the community is liable for a debt incurred by either spouse before or during the marriage, regardless of which spouse has management and control of the property and of whether one or both spouses are parties to the debt or to a judgment for the debt. Although one spouse may be liable to the community for misuse of its assets, the community remains liable to third party creditors for any debt incurred as a result of such misuse. Code of Civil Procedure § 695.020 addresses the liability of community property for money judgments. Under that section all of the community property here was liable for the debts incurred by husband during the marriage and subject to enforcement of the money judgment prior to the property division. Under the judgment lien law, a judgment creditor's recordation of an abstract of judgment creates a lien that attaches to all real property situated in the county in which the judgment is recorded and that is otherwise subject to enforcement of the money judgment against the debtor. Last, former § 5120.160 provided that following property division, the community property awarded to one spouse no longer is liable for the marital debts assigned to the other, except that the award of community real property subject to a lien remains liable for satisfaction of the lien. The spouse would then have a right of reimbursement against the other. Under these rules, if a valid judgment in favor of Security Pacific (D) attached to the Halm Avenue property before it was awarded to wife (P), then the property was subject to the lien, even though the debt was assigned to the husband. If Security Pacific (D) satisfied the judgment by enforcing the lien, wife (P) has a right to reimbursement. The issue is whether these rules apply to property affected by former § 5127 or the circumstance that the deed of trust was set aside pursuant to § 5127. A court in equity may require as a condition to granting equitable relief under § 5127 the restoration of any consideration transferred by an innocent encumbrancer in exchange for the security interest, who acts without knowledge of the community status of the property. The plain language of the statute evidences an intent that both spouses must join in executing any instrument which a community real property interest is transferred. The statutory language does not refer to the liability of community real property for marital debts, nor does it evidence intent to exempt such property form liability for marital debts, even those incurred unilaterally

Continued on next page.

by one spouse. After Security Pacific's (D) deed of trust was set aside pursuant to § 5127 and it was awarded a money judgment against the husband, it was placed in the position of any other judgment creditor entitled to enforce its judgment against the community. By recording the abstract of judgment, it created a judgment lien that attached to all real property subject to the enforcement of the money judgment. Affirmed without prejudice to plaintiff.

▶ ANALYSIS

The decision in this case met with much criticism since the creditor's rights succeeded over the rights of the wronged wife.

■══■

Quicknotes

ABSTRACT OF JUDGMENT Summary of the history of an action.

COMMUNITY PROPERTY In community property jurisdictions, refers to all money or property acquired during the term of the marriage in which each spouse has an undivided one-half interest.

COURT OF EQUITY A court that determines matters before it consistent with principles of fairness and not in strict compliance with rules of law.

DEED OF TRUST A legal document that acts as a mortgage, placing a security interest in the deeded property with a trustee to insure the payment of a debt.

JUDGMENT CREDITOR A creditor who has obtained an enforceable judgment against a debtor and who may collect on that debt once the debtor has been given notice of the action.

JUDGMENT LIEN Lien filed by a judgment creditor against the property of a judgment debtor.

QUIET TITLE Equitable action to resolve conflicting claims to an interest in real property.

QUITCLAIM DEED A deed whereby the grantor conveys whatever interest he or she may have in the property without any warranties or covenants as to title.

SECURED TRANSACTION A transaction where security agreement provides for a security interest.

UNILATERAL One-sided; involving only one person.

■══■

Grolemund v. Cafferata

Married couple (P) v. Injured accident victim (D)

Cal. Sup. Ct., 17 Cal. 2d 679, 111 P.2d 641 (1941).

NATURE OF CASE: Appeal from denial of injunction against the sale of community property.

FACT SUMMARY: The Grolemunds (P), husband and wife, sought to enjoin the sale of community property under executions of a judgment for damages obtained by Cafferata (D), who was injured in an auto accident caused by Mr. Grolemund (P).

🏛 RULE OF LAW
All community property, whenever acquired, is liable for the satisfaction of the husband's debts including a judgment against the husband for his tort.

FACTS: Cafferata (D), in an earlier action where he was plaintiff, obtained a judgment for damages against Caesar Grolemund (P) and his wife, Lena (P), sued to enjoin the sale of community property under the executions in order to pay off the judgment. The community property included property acquired prior to and after 1927, the year in which wives were given a "present, existing and equal" interest in community property. From a judgment against them, the Grolemunds (P) appealed.

ISSUE: Is all community property, whenever acquired, liable for the satisfaction of the husband's debts, including a judgment against the husband for his tort?

HOLDING AND DECISION: (Curtis, J.) Yes. All community property, whenever acquired, is liable for the satisfaction of the husband's debts including a judgment against the husband for his tort. Prior to 1927, the rule was that community property acquired in California was always liable for the husband's debts. The 1927 amendment does not appear to change the rule that vests in the husband the entire management and control of the community property. The amendment was silent as to liability of the husband's separate property, but from this silence it can be inferred that it was intended that the husband, as the community's agent, should retain the power to divest the parties of community property by his own act in the same manner that he might divest himself of separate property, as long as he did not make a gift of community property without consideration. To say that the husband could not subject community property to his tort liability would be to say that he could not manage and control the community property. Caesar Grolemund (P), assuming this action had not been instituted, could have voluntarily settled his tort liability by payment from community funds or from a community bank account under his control. There is no logical distinction between voluntary satisfaction of judgment and satisfaction by levy of execution. Since the 1927 amendment has not altered the wife's interest remaining

subject to the husband's management and control, the date of acquisition of the property is immaterial and the rule applies equally to property acquired before or after the amendment. By affirming the judgment below, the court remains not only within legal principles, but meets practical considerations and public policy as well. Otherwise, a person injured by a husband's separate act would be unable to recover for his injury in a case where the causes only have community property. Such an "obviously unfair and unjust result would have a disastrous effect on the very foundation of our community system and would be entirely out of harmony with the general rule that the community property is liable for the husband's debts." Affirmed.

▶ ANALYSIS

This case, along with the *Stewart* case, suggests that while the 1927 changes to the community property system would be given their full effect, they would not affect other community property doctrines even though by not allowing such an effect, the system would be prevented from becoming more logical. For example, left unchanged was the provision that the entire community, upon the husband's death, is subject to liability for his debts, which premised the holding above so that if the husband may during life create an obligation which may be subject to satisfaction by the community after his death, such obligation may be satisfied out of community funds during his life. This would be a corollary to the husband's pre-1975 exclusive right of management and control.

■■■

Quicknotes

COMMUNITY PROPERTY In community property jurisdictions refers to all money or property acquired during the term of the marriage in which each spouse has an undivided one-half interest.

EXECUTION SALE A sheriff's sale of real property pursuant to a writ of execution on the property of a debtor.

TORT A legal wrong resulting in a breach of duty by the wrongdoer, causing damages as a result of the breach.

■■■

Marriage of Feldner

Cal. Ct. App., 40 Cal. App. 4th 617 (1995).

NATURE OF CASE: Marital dissolution proceeding.

FACT SUMMARY: The trial court judge declared a lawsuit filed against the husband to be a community obligation.

🏛 RULE OF LAW
The burden of proving intentional conduct of a spouse not benefiting the community falls on the aggrieved spouse.

FACTS: One of the issues in the Feldners' dissolution proceeding was the proper characterization of a lawsuit filed against William. The trial judge held that the lawsuit was a community obligation incurred during the marriage and declared each party equally obligated to any negative or positive result. Celena filed a motion for reconsideration to which she attached the written findings of a court-appointed referee to the effect that William breached the contract that was the subject of the suit in four ways. The family law judge denied the motion for reconsideration.

ISSUE: Does the burden of proving intentional conduct of a spouse not benefiting the community fall on the aggrieved spouse?

HOLDING AND DECISION: (Sills, J.) Yes. The burden of proving intentional conduct of a spouse not benefiting the community falls on the aggrieved spouse. Celena contends that because the potential liability was incurred by William's post-separation act of intentionally quitting his job, the resulting debt was his alone. Family Code § 903 provides that "in the case of a contract, a debt is incurred at the time the contract is made." Read together with § 910, the effect of § 903 is to characterize contract debts as community when the contract is made as distinct from performed during the marriage. Making Celena half responsible seems contrary to the basic rule that the marital community is not liable for post-separation debts. However, the statutory test, when combined with the possibility of credit and reimbursement for post-separation contributions, establishes a reasonable symmetry. The performance of a contract, however, is fundamentally different from the problem of determining its community or separate character. The classic solution to the problem created by a separation date during an extended period is to allow for reimbursement by the spouse who uses post-separation earnings to pay a preexisting community obligation. However, just because a spouse may have the right to request reimbursement does not mean the family law court has a duty to consider the possibility. Reimbursement is not automatic, but a combination of factors. Likewise, reimbursement to the community for losses caused by the separate conduct of one spouse also necessarily requires an affirmative showing. The burden of proving intentional

conduct of a spouse not benefiting the community falls on the aggrieved spouse. Here the trial court was correct in determining that the character of potential liability from the suit was community as the entire contract was made during the marriage. Second, William might have made a request for reimbursement from the community for the value of his post-separation services but did not, thereby waiving any right to the value of the post-separation services he performed. Likewise, Celena might have made a request for reimbursement of that potential liability represented by William's failure to perform post-separation services, but failed to do so. The court was not obligated to raise the issue for her. Affirmed.

▶ ANALYSIS

Another issue was the proper characterization of emotional distress damages sought in the lawsuit. The court concluded that since emotional distress damages are essentially tort damages and not recoverable in a contract action, their possible presence did not affect the community character of the contract damages.

━■

Quicknotes

BURDEN OF PROOF The duty of a party to introduce evidence to support a fact that is in dispute in an action.

COMMUNITY PROPERTY In community property jurisdictions refers to all money or property acquired during the term of the marriage in which each spouse has an undivided one-half interest.

DISSOLUTION PROCEEDING AND DECREE A proceeding and resulting decree to terminate a marriage.

SEPARATION When a husband and wife cease to cohabitate.

━■

American Olean Tile Co. Inc. v. Schultze

Promissory note creditor (P) v. Promissory note debtor (D)

Cal. Ct. App., 169 Cal. App. 3d 359 (1985).

NATURE OF CASE: Appeal from order dissolving prejudgment attachment of promissory note.

FACT SUMMARY: In American Olean Tile Company's (P) action against Horst and Irmgard Schulze (D) for default of payment of a promissory note, Irmgard (D) contended that when Horst (D) executed a note in American's (P) favor, Horst (D) was operating his business exclusively as his separate property, even though the execution occurred before the judgment of dissolution of Horst (D) and Irmgard's (D) marriage, and that Horst (D) was solely responsible for payment of the note.

🏛 RULE OF LAW
If, by execution of a marital settlement agreement, a community property business becomes the separate property of one of the spouses, a creditor seeking to enforce a business debt incurred thereafter will be restricted to satisfaction from the separate property of the debtor spouse.

FACTS: American Olean Tile Company (P) sued Horst and lrmgard Schultze (D), whose marriage had been dissolved, for nonpayment of a promissory note executed by Horst on May 6, 1981. The Schultzes (D) had separated on April 1, 1980, and on May 1, 1981, they executed a marital settlement agreement dividing their community property; it was incorporated by reference into the interlocutory judgment of dissolution of marriage filed June 19, 1981. Pursuant to the settlement agreement, Horst (D) received the community business as his separate property. Irmgard (D) received other property. Horst (D) failed to make any payments on the promissory note, and American (P) brought suit on the note. A default judgment was entered against Horst (D), and when Horst (D) could not be located for satisfaction of the judgment, Irmgard (D) was liable for the note since it was incurred and executed during her marriage to Horst (D). The court, however, denied American's (P) request for prejudgment attachment of the note, and American (P) appealed, contending that Irmgard (D) was responsible for payment of the note.

ISSUE: If, by execution of a marital settlement agreement, a community property business becomes the separate property of one of the spouses, will a creditor seeking to enforce a business debt incurred thereafter be restricted to satisfaction from the separate property of the debtor spouse?

HOLDING AND DECISION: (King, J.) Yes. If, by execution of a marital settlement agreement, a community property business becomes the separate property of one of the spouses, a creditor seeking to enforce a business

debt incurred thereafter will be restricted to satisfaction from the separate property of the debtor spouse. Here, the note was a separate obligation of Horst (D), having been incurred after the date of separation at a time when the business had become his separate property. Income earned and obligations incurred after separation in the operation of a separate property business are not community in nature, and American (P) as Horst's (D) creditor is not entitled to recover against former community assets transmuted into the separate property of Irmgard (D), the non-contracting spouse, since American (P) could have avoided the risk of unknown interspousal transfer by obtaining both spouses' signatures on the note. Affirmed.

► ANALYSIS

At dissolution, the community property must be divided equally between the spouses under Civil Code § 4800. Prior case law permitted a creditor to satisfy a debt out of any property that would have been liable for the debt prior to the division at dissolution. Civil Code § 5120.160 reversed the case law rule allowing a creditor to enforce a money judgment against former community property in the hands of a non-debtor spouse after dissolution.

■=■

Quicknotes

SEPARATE PROPERTY Property owned by one spouse prior to marriage, or any income derived therefrom, and any property received by one spouse pursuant to a gift, devise, bequest or descent.

■=■

Marriage of Braendle

Cal. Ct. App., 46 Cal. App. 4th 1037 (1996).

NATURE OF CASE: Marital dissolution proceeding.

FACT SUMMARY: American Overseas sought to enforce a judgment against community property held by the nondebtor spouse following the property division in a divorce proceeding.

> 🏛 **RULE OF LAW**
> Property received by a nondebtor spouse in a marital dissolution is not liable for a debt incurred by the person's spouse before or during marriage, and the person is not personally liable for the debt, unless the debt was assigned for payment by the person in the division of property.

FACTS: The Braendle's marriage was dissolved by a judgment and Ruediger was awarded the stock in American Overseas, valued at $1,438,651. Dina was awarded certain real and personal property and pension and bank accounts valued at less than the stock. To equalize the division, Ruediger was ordered to pay Dina $483,393. He was also ordered to turn over all the stock in the corporation to Dina's counsel to hold as security until the equalizing payments were made. Ruediger delivered the stock certificates and listed a debt to American Overseas of $58,000. The dissolution order did not assign the debt for payment. After the judgment was entered, American Overseas brought a breach of contract action against Ruediger alone. A judgment was entered plus attorney's fees and costs. American Overseas obtained a writ of execution and noticed its intention to go forward with a sheriff's sale. The court ruled that the security interest described in the judgment of dissolution had priority over American Overseas' judgment lien and that the certificates had been improperly transferred from the court to the sheriff. The court transferred ownership and possession of the stock to Dina. American Overseas appealed.

ISSUE: Is property received by a nondebtor spouse in a marital dissolution liable for a debt incurred by the person's spouse before or during marriage?

HOLDING AND DECISION: (Baron, J.) No. Property received by a nondebtor spouse in a marital dissolution is not liable for a debt incurred by the person's spouse before or during marriage, and the person is not personally liable for the debt, unless the debt was assigned for payment by the person in the division of property. The determinative issue is which party has a priority interest in the stock. While the parties were married, Family Code § 910 allowed Ruediger's creditors to go after community property to satisfy his debts regardless of whether one or both spouses are parties to the debt. Upon dissolution of the marriage and division of the community property, § 916 controlled the case. That section provides that "the property received by the

persons in the division is not liable for a debt incurred by the person's spouse before or during marriage, and the person is not personally liable for the debt, unless the debt was assigned for payment by the person in the division of property." If a money judgment is entered after the division, the property received by the married person in the division is not subject to the enforcement of the judgment and the judgment may not be enforced against the person, unless he or she is made a party to the judgment. The debt owed to American Overseas was not assigned to Dina in the division and she was not named as a party in the judgment after dissolution. Therefore, she is not personally liable on the loan, nor is any portion of the community property assigned to her reachable to satisfy the debt. The issue of whether Dina's interests take priority over American Overseas' judgment lien turns on the issue of whether Dina had a perfected security interest in the stock. Here possession of the stock certificates was transferred to the court clerk and constituted notice to the world in general. Thus, she had a perfected security interest in the stock at the time the court took possession of the certificates on her behalf. Affirmed.

▶ *ANALYSIS*

The statute at issue here reversed the former case law rule that a creditor may seek enforcement of a money judgment against former community property in the hands of a nondebtor spouse after dissolution.

■═■

Quicknotes

ASSIGNMENT OF RIGHTS The transfer of a party's interest or rights in property.

COMMUNITY PROPERTY In community property jurisdictions refers to all money or property acquired during the term of the marriage in which each spouse has an undivided one-half interest.

MARITAL DISSOLUTION Legal termination of the marital relationship.

PERFECTED SECURITY INTEREST A security interest that is safeguarded against other claims to the collateral; perfection is generally accomplished by legal steps necessary to give other creditors notice of the interest.

PROPERTY SETTLEMENT AGREEMENT An agreement entered into by spouses upon dissolution of the marriage that is either agreed to by the spouses and sanctioned by the court or is based on the court's division of the marital estate following the divorce proceeding.

■═■

Mejia v. Reed

Husband (D) v. Mistress (P)

Cal. Sup. Ct., 31 Cal. 4th 657 (2003).

NATURE OF CASE: Appeal of denial of summary judgment.

FACT SUMMARY: A husband and wife entered into a marital settlement agreement under which the husband transferred all of his interest in jointly held real estate to his wife. The husband's mistress claimed that the husband's intent in making the transfer was to prevent her from collecting child support and asked the court to put a lien on the property.

🏛 RULE OF LAW
The provisions of the Uniform Fraudulent Transfer Act apply to marital settlement agreements.

FACTS: Danilo Reed (D) had an affair with Rhina Mejia (P) that led to the birth of a child. Reed and his wife, Violeta, entered into a marital settlement agreement under which Danilo (D) transferred all of his interest in jointly held real estate to Violeta. He then quit practicing medicine and moved in with his mother. Mejia (P) claimed that the transfer's purpose was to prevent her from collecting child support and asked the court to put a lien on the property. She failed to provide direct evidence of intent to defraud, however. The trial court assumed that the Uniform Fraudulent Transfer Act applied to the marital settlement agreement, but entered summary judgment for Danilo (D) because there was no evidence presented of actual intent to defraud. The court of appeal reversed, finding that a transfer of real property under a marital settlement agreement could be found invalid under the Uniform Fraudulent Transfer Act, and that factual issues made summary judgment inappropriate.

ISSUE: Do the provisions of the Uniform Fraudulent Transfer Act apply to marital settlement agreements?

HOLDING AND DECISION: (Kennard, J.) Yes. The provisions of the Uniform Fraudulent Transfer Act apply to marital settlement agreements. While the language and legislative histories of the UFTA and the family law statutes do not provide guidance as to whether UFTA applies to marital settlement agreements, policy considerations, such as protecting creditors, underlie each statute and suggest that the UFTA applies to property transfers under marital settlement agreements. In light of the legislature's policy of protecting creditors, it is unlikely that the legislature intended to allow married couples the opportunity to defraud creditors by including a fraudulent transfer in a marital settlement agreement. And under the UFTA, even without actual fraudulent intent, a transfer may be fraudulent if the debtor does not receive reasonably equivalent value in exchange for the transfer, and the debtor was either insolvent at that time, or

became insolvent as a result. The court of appeals ruled correctly.

▌ ANALYSIS

Though this case is presented in the context of creditor protection, California marital agreements historically have been subject to several other public policy restraints. Agreements are unenforceable to the extent they "promote" dissolution, waive or limit child or spousal support, impinge on the court's exercise of jurisdiction to adjudicate child support or child custody, alter legal relations incident to marriage, or provide for fault-based penalties at marriage dissolution, among other things.

▪■▪

Quicknotes

SUMMARY JUDGMENT Judgment rendered by a court in response to a motion made by one of the parties, claiming that the lack of a question of material fact in respect to an issue warrants disposition of the issue without consideration by the jury.

▪■▪

Division of Community Property at Dissolution

Quick Reference Rules of Law

Marriage of Hufford

Husband (P) v. Ex-wife (D)

Cal. Ct. App., 152 Cal. App. 3d 825 (1984).

NATURE OF CASE: Appeal from denial of order to show spousal support.

FACT SUMMARY: In Guy Hufford's (P) action ordering a showing of cause for modification of spousal support against his ex-wife, Dorothy (D), Dorothy (D) contended that a stipulation and waiver of rights signed by Guy (P) at the time of dissolution which set the amount of spousal support Guy (P) had to pay Dorothy (D) was not modifiable.

RULE OF LAW
Although an agreement making spousal support nonmodifiable by the court is not contrary to public policy, the public interest is best served when support awards reflect changes in need or ability to pay.

FACTS: In March, 1978, Guy Hufford (P) and Dorothy Hufford (D) filed in court a signed written "stipulation" and waiver of rights covering spousal support, division of property, attorney fees and waiver. The agreement provided for Guy (P) to pay Dorothy (D) spousal support of $1,200 per month for the first two years after an entry of an interlocutory judgment of dissolution, and thereafter $600 per month until Dorothy (D) died or remarried. The agreement also provided that the parties could not alter the agreement except in a writing executed by both of them. An interlocutory decree of dissolution of marriage was entered ordering spousal support, but the decree did not in any way refer to the prior stipulation or contain provisions of the stipulation. In 1982, Guy (P) filed an order to show cause for modification of spousal support on alleged grounds of inability to pay because of lesser income and increased obligations. Dorothy (D) opposed the order, contending that the prior agreement setting the amount of spousal support which Guy (P) had to pay was not modifiable. The court denied Guy's (P) request for modification, and Guy (P) appealed.

ISSUE: Although an agreement making spousal support nonmodifiable by the court is not contrary to public policy, is the public interest best served when support awards reflect changes in need or ability to pay?

HOLDING AND DECISION: (Thompson, J.) Yes. Although an agreement making spousal support nonmodifiable by the court is not contrary to public policy, the public interest is best served when support awards reflect changes in need or ability to pay. Here, the agreement does not unequivocally exclude judicial modification and, therefore, is ambiguous on that issue. Any ambiguity, however, must be resolved in favor of the general statutory rule of modifiability as set forth in Civil Code § 4811. Section 4811 states the provisions of any agreement or order for the support of either party shall be subject to subsequent modification or revocation by court order except to the extent that any written agreement specifically provides to the contrary. Because the agreement here does not specifically exclude modification, the order denying Guy's (P) motion to show cause is reversed and remanded.

ANALYSIS

Property settlement agreements may be "incorporated" into a dissolution judgment. Incorporation can be accomplished by setting forth the agreement provisions in the judgment, or by reference to end clear identification of the agreement in the judgment. The fact of incorporation in and of itself has no legal significance and the legal effect turns on the intention of the parties—whether they intended merely to seek court approval of the agreement, or whether they intended the contract to become part of the judgment.

Quicknotes

INTERLOCUTORY JUDGMENT An order entered by the court determining an issue that does not resolve the disposition of the case, but is essential to a proper adjudication of the action.

SPOUSAL SUPPORT Payments made by one spouse to another in discharge of the spouse's duty pursuant to law, or in accordance with a written divorce or separation decree, in order to provide maintenance for the other spouse.

Gionis v. Superior Court

Wife (P) v. Husband (D)

Cal. Ct. App., 202 Cal. App. 3d 786 (1988).

NATURE OF CASE: An action seeking a writ of mandate to compel the Superior Court to change its order denying a motion to bifurcate a marital dissolution action.

FACT SUMMARY: In an action by Aissa Gionis (P) for dissolution of marriage, the trial court denied Thomas Gionis' (D) motion to bifurcate the issue of marital status from the issues of custody, support and property division.

RULE OF LAW
Only slight evidence is necessary to obtain bifurcation and resolution of marital status, while a spouse opposing bifurcation must present compelling reasons for denial.

FACTS: After a little over a year of marriage, Aissa Gionis (P) filed for dissolution of marriage from Thomas Gionis (D), requesting sole custody of their infant daughter, as well as child and spousal support. Thomas (D) moved to bifurcate the issue of marital status from the issues of custody, support, and property division, maintaining that reconciliation was impossible and the other issues would require a lengthy trial. Thomas (D) wanted his marital status resolved so he could make investments and obtain credit without having to seek quitclaim deeds from Aissa (P) or worry that a lender might rely on community rather than separate credit. Aissa's (P) opposition to the motion was only procedural, not substantive. The court denied the motion, and Thomas (D) filed a petition for a writ of mandate, contending the trial court abused its discretion by refusing to bifurcate the action.

ISSUE: Is only slight evidence necessary to obtain bifurcation and resolution of marital status?

HOLDING AND DECISION: (Wallin, J.) Yes. Only slight evidence is necessary to obtain bifurcation and resolution of marital status, while a spouse opposing bifurcation must present compelling reasons for denial. Severance of a personal relationship which the law has found to be unworkable and, as a result, injurious to the public welfare is not dependent upon final settlement of property disputes. The new Family Law Act, removing the issue of marital fault from domestic relations litigation, embodies a legislative intent that the dissolution of marriage should not be postponed merely because issues relating to property, support, attorney fees, or child custody are unready for decision. Courts have thus encouraged bifurcation of marital status from other issues. In light of the policies favoring bifurcation, the trial court was mistaken in its apparent belief that Thomas (D) was required to justify his request with a compelling showing of need. Absent a showing by Aissa (P) why

bifurcation should not be granted, Thomas' (D) declaration provided a proper basis for the motion. Writ granted, trial court's order reversed.

ANALYSIS

The concept of "divisible divorce" was first stated by the California Supreme Court in *Hull v. Superior Court*, 54 Cal. 2d 139 (1960). Two later cases, *In re Marriage of Fink*, 54 Cal. App. 3d 357 (1976), and *In re Marriage of Lusk*, 86 Cal. App. 3d 228 (1978), both upheld the granting of a bifurcation motion based on declarations strikingly similar to Thomas' (D). The philosophy of the Supreme Court decision in *Hull* was incorporated into the Family Law Act.

Quicknotes

BIFURCATION At trial, the consideration of issues separately.

MARITAL DISSOLUTION Legal termination of the marital relationship.

WRIT OF MANDATE The written order of a court directing a particular action.

Robinson v. Robinson

Husband (P) v. Wife (D)

Cal. Ct. App., 65 Cal. App. 2d 118, 150 P.2d 7 (1944).

NATURE OF CASE: Action to quiet title to real property.

FACT SUMMARY: In a divorce action, the court awarded Mrs. Robinson (D) a life interest in certain real property which was the separate property of Mr. Robinson (P).

🏛 RULE OF LAW
"The power of the court in disposing of the property of the parties in a divorce action is limited to their community property."

FACTS: On June 10, 1942, Mr. Robinson (P) and Mrs. Robinson (D) were awarded an interlocutory decree of divorce. Thereafter, the court in disposing of their property gave Mrs. Robinson (D) a life interest in certain real property (i.e., a dwelling house). This real property was Mr. Robinson's (P) separate property. Subsequently, Mr. Robinson (P) brought this action to quiet title to such real property in his name alone.

ISSUE: In a divorce action, can the court dispose of the separate property of the parties?

HOLDING AND DECISION: (Wood, J.) No. "The power of the court in disposing of the property of the parties in a divorce action is limited to their community property." As such, the court has no power to dispose of the separate property of either of the parties or to carve out a life estate therein. Here, there was no dispute about the ownership of the real property involved, i.e., it was the separate property of Mr. Robinson (P). Therefore, the divorce court had no power to award a life estate in such property to Mrs. Robinson (D). As such, Mr. Robinson (P) retains full and complete title to such property. Reversed.

▶ ANALYSIS

This case illustrates the general rule that the divorce court can dispose only of community property. However, the divorce court can determine which assets are separate and which are community. Furthermore, the court can consider the amount of the husband's separate property in determining his ability to pay child support or alimony. The court can, also, grant the wife a lien on her husband's separate property in order to secure child support or alimony payments. Note, too, that the court can direct either spouse to use his or her separate property to reimburse the community for any improper transfers of community property.

Quicknotes

COMMUNITY PROPERTY In community property jurisdictions, refers to all money or property acquired during the term of the marriage in which each spouse has an undivided one-half interest.

LIFE ESTATE An interest in land measured by the life of the tenant or a third party.

QUIET TITLE Equitable action to resolve conflicting claims to an interest in real property.

SEPARATE PROPERTY Property owned by one spouse prior to marriage, or any income derived therefrom, and any property received by one spouse pursuant to a gift, devise, bequest or descent.

■=■

Muckle v. Superior Court

Wife (P) v. Husband (D)

Cal. Ct. App., 102 Cal. App. 4th 218 (2002).

NATURE OF CASE: Motion to vacate order allowing personal jurisdiction.

FACT SUMMARY: Cassandra (P), a California resident, served Andrew (D), a Georgia resident, with dissolution papers. Andrew (D) moved to quash the service of summons for lack of personal jurisdiction.

🏛 RULE OF LAW
When determining whether the court has personal jurisdiction over an individual who is domiciled in another state, the court looks at the individual's contacts with the forum state at the time of the proceeding, not at past contacts, and at whether it would be reasonable to exercise jurisdiction.

FACTS: Andrew (D) and Cassandra (P) were married in Georgia and had no children together. During the marriage they lived in both Georgia and California. They lived in California for ten years prior to 1998. In 1998, while the couple was living in California, Andrew (D) took title to a home in Georgia in his name alone. The money used to purchase the Georgia property came from a workers' compensation payment made by a California employer. In December of 1998, Andrew (D), and then Cassandra (P), returned to Georgia to live in the house. In the spring of 2000, Cassandra (P) moved back to California and lived in a trailer that Andrew (D) had purchased for her. Cassandra (P) sold the trailer and then served dissolution papers on Andrew (D) in Georgia. Andrew (D) moved to quash service of summons for lack of personal jurisdiction. The trial court denied Andrew's (D) motion because it determined that Andrew (D) had the necessary minimum contacts with California. Andrew (D) moved to have the court vacate its order.

ISSUE: Can California exercise personal jurisdiction over Andrew (D)?

HOLDING AND DECISION: (Huffman, J.) No. Based on the contacts at the time of the proceeding, Andrew (D) does not have the necessary minimum contacts with California to justify it exercising personal jurisdiction. Even if minimum contacts were established it would be unreasonable to exercise personal jurisdiction. The court must have jurisdiction over the parties to adjudicate personal rights and obligations in a marital case. Personal jurisdiction can be exercised over a nonresident defendant when the defendant has sufficient minimum contacts with the forum state, such that the exercise of

jurisdiction would not offend traditional notions of fair play and substantial justice. The nonresident must have purposefully availed himself of the privilege of conducting activities within the forum state to invoke its benefits and protections, and a sufficient relationship must exist between the nonresident and the forum state such that it is fair to require him to appear locally to conduct a defense. The court looks at the contacts at the time of the proceeding, and not at whether past minimum contacts might suffice. In this case, at the time of the motion to quash, there was no evidence of any contacts by Andrew (D) with California at the time the dissolution action was filed by Cassandra (P); only past contacts with California by Andrew (D) were shown. The trial court took into consideration unsubstantiated alleged facts made by Cassandra (P) regarding Andrew's (D) continuing contacts with California after the matter was taken under submission. The record contains a lack of substantial evidence, however, of minimum contacts. Andrew's (D) contacts with California, therefore, were not substantial, continuous and systematic, nor did he purposeful direct any activities since 1998 toward California other than to provide shelter for Cassandra (P). Even if minimum contacts were established, however, it would still be unreasonable for the court to exercise personal jurisdiction over Andrew (D). Cassandra (P) is not a burden on the state and can pursue her action in Georgia. Andrew (D), on the other hand, has lived in Georgia for the past four years, he has a Georgia driver's license, he only owns property in Georgia, and it would be a financial burden for Andrew (D) to travel to California. Moreover, the parties married in Georgia and lived in Georgia about two years prior to separating. It would therefore be unreasonable and unfair to require Andrew (D) to come to California to litigate issues of spousal support and property rights. Reversed.

▶ ANALYSIS

When they have personal jurisdiction, California courts usually look to the domicile of the parties at the time the property was acquired when characterizing it as separate or community for the purposes of division and all property, wherever situated, acquired by a married person during the marriage, while domiciled in California, is community property.

■≡■

Continued on next page.

Quicknotes

FORUM STATE The state in which a court, or other location in which a legal remedy may be sought, is located.

MINIMUM CONTACTS The minimum degree of contact necessary in order to sustain a cause of action within a particular forum, consistent with the requirements of due process.

PERSONAL JURISDICTION The court's authority over a person or parties to a lawsuit.

Marriage of Andresen

Wife (P) v. Husband (D)

Cal. Ct. App., 28 Cal. App. 4th 873 (1994).

NATURE OF CASE: Marital dissolution proceeding.

FACT SUMMARY: Wife (P) filed a standard form petition for dissolution of marriage and simply listed those community property assets and debts to be divided; the court entered a default judgment against the husband (D).

🏛 RULE OF LAW
Due process is satisfied and sufficient notice given for § 580 purposes in marital dissolution actions by checking the appropriate box and inserting the information called for on the standard form dissolution petition which correspond or relate to the allegations made and the relief sought by the petitioner.

FACTS: Wife (P) filed a standard form petition for dissolution of the parties' marriage. She checked a box indicating that all assets and obligations were listed in the property declaration. In the property declaration she listed 10 separate items she considered to be community assets, as well as numerous creditors to whom she and her husband owed debts. She failed to attach specific values to the assets and debts, however, or to request that the court divide the community property in any particular manner. A default judgment was entered against the husband (D) and he moved to set aside the default judgment. The trial court denied the motion but ordered the judgment vacated because it gave relief to the wife (P) beyond the scope of the pleadings. Husband (D) appealed.

ISSUE: Is due process satisfied and sufficient notice given for § 580 purposes in marital dissolution actions by checking the appropriate box and inserting the information called for on the standard form dissolution petition which correspond or relate to the allegations made and the relief sought by the petitioner?

HOLDING AND DECISION: (DiBiaso, J.) Yes. Due process is satisfied and sufficient notice given for § 580 purposes in marital dissolution actions by checking the appropriate box and inserting the information called for on the standard form dissolution petition which correspond or relate to the allegations made and the relief sought by the petitioner. Husband (D) claimed the entry of default and default judgment is void because the petition did not allege the specific kind and amount of relief she obtained by means of the judgment. The general rule is that when the defendant has defaulted, the trial court may not grant relief to the plaintiff in excess of that which is demanded in the complaint. In *Marriage of Lippel*, 801 P.2d 1401 (1990), the Supreme Court held that the child support award violated the plain language of § 580 since

the petition did not request such relief. According to that decision, due process is satisfied and sufficient notice given for § 580 purposes in marital dissolution actions by checking the appropriate box and inserting the information called for on the standard form dissolution petition which correspond or relate to the allegations made and the relief sought by the petitioner. No greater specificity is needed. Since the wife (P) properly and fully completed the petition and its necessary attachments, the husband (D) was given adequate notice. If he wished to be heard on the subject of valuation and division of the listed items, he should have appeared. Affirmed.

▶ ANALYSIS

California Code of Civil Procedure § 580 was enacted to ensure defaulting parties adequate notice of the maximum judgment that may be asserted against them. Due process requires that a defendant have the right to be fully apprised of the relief being sought in order to make an informed decision regarding whether he should appear and defend himself.

Quicknotes

DEFAULT JUDGMENT A judgment entered against a defendant due to his failure to appear in a court or defend himself against the allegations of the opposing party.

DUE PROCESS The constitutional mandate requiring the courts to protect and enforce individuals' rights and liberties consistent with prevailing principles of fairness and justice and prohibiting the federal and state governments from such activities that deprive its citizens of life, liberty, or property interest.

KNOWLEDGE Having information or understanding of a fact.

Marriage of Stallworth

Husband (P) v. Wife (D)

Cal. Ct. App., 192 Cal. App. 3d 742 (1987).

NATURE OF CASE: Appeal from judgment of dissolution of marriage.

FACT SUMMARY: In William Stallworth's (P) action for dissolution against his wife, Carol (D), William (P) contended that the court's decision that Carol (D) and the Stallworths' son, Robert, be able to live in the family residence until Robert reached age 18 was in error and that the home should be sold and the community assets divided.

> ## 🏛 RULE OF LAW
> Under Civil Code § 4800.7, even if the evidence justifies a family home award to one of the spouses, the trial court must exercise its discretion in setting the duration of the award in accordance with the evidence on that issue.

FACTS: William (P) and Carol Stallworth (D) were married 14 1/2 years and had one son, Robert, age 10 at the time of this action. The Stallworths separated in 1983, and William (P) filed for dissolution in February 1984. The matter came to trial in 1985. At trial, the court allowed Carol (D) and Robert to live in the family residence until Robert reached the age of 18, at which time the home would be sold and the sale assets divided equally between the parties. William (P) appealed this distribution and contended that the home should be sold upon dissolution and the assets then divided.

ISSUE: Under Civil Code § 4800.7, even if the evidence justifies a family home award to one of the spouses, must the trial court exercise its discretion in setting the duration of the award in accordance with the evidence on that issue?

HOLDING AND DECISION: (King, J.) Yes. Under Civil Code § 4800.7, even if the evidence justifies a family home award to one of the spouses, the trial court must exercise its discretion in setting the duration of the award in accordance with the evidence on that issue. Given the extremely high cost of housing in urban areas of California, only the very wealthy are in a position to purchase a new home without receiving their share of a sizeable equity in an existing home. Thus, deferral of sale of the family home would not only interfere and perhaps preclude the spouse from obtaining suitable housing accommodations to be able to enjoy the frequent and continuing contact with his or her children which is the public policy of California, but may well preclude obtaining adequate housing for her or himself. The trial judge has broad discretion to defer the sale of the family home after weighing all factors. The problem here is that no evidence was presented, one way or the other, for the trial court to weigh.

This court expresses no opinion as to how the trial court should have exercised its discretion because of the lack of evidence in the record. Reversed and remanded.

CONCURRENCE AND DISSENT: (Haning, J.) The trial court found that Robert's condition and the financial condition of the parties required that the wife and child remain in the family residence until the circumstances changed even though the possible adverse consequences to William (P) were not presented to the trial court. The trial court's finding is supported by other evidence, however, and should be affirmed.

▶ ANALYSIS

Civil Code § 4800.7 provides express statutory recognition of the family home award as well as a standard for the modification of such awards. Prior case law and the original version of § 4800.7 authorized the use of the family home award only where there was a duty to support minor children. The sale of the family residence was usually deferred until the youngest child reached majority.

■═■

Quicknotes

COMMUNITY PROPERTY In community property jurisdictions refers to all money or property acquired during the term of the marriage in which each spouse has an undivided one-half interest.

■═■

Marriage of Tammen

Cal. Ct. App., 63 Cal. App. 3d 927 (1976).

NATURE OF CASE: Appeal from the division of community property in an interlocutory judgment of dissolution.

FACT SUMMARY: Mr. Tammen charged that the trial court had not effected an equal division of community property because the actual value of the promissory note his wife was ordered to execute was less than that of the offsetting community property she was awarded.

🏛 RULE OF LAW
Where a major item of community property not reasonably subject to division is awarded to one party, the other shall be compensated in some manner so as to maintain the required equal division of community property.

FACTS: The interlocutory judgment of dissolution awarded the family residence to Mrs. Tammen. In an attempt to equalize the division of community property, as required by statute, the judgment ordered Mrs. Tammen to execute and deliver to Mr. Tammen a promissory note for $19,820.80 bearing simple interest at 7%, secured by a second trust deed on the family residence. The note's principal, and all interest accruing thereon, was payable "upon the expiration of ten years from the date thereof, upon the wife's remarriage, the sale of said real property, voluntary refinancing by her, upon her ceasing to use or occupy the same as a family residence, or upon her death, whichever event shall first occur." Mr. Tammen appealed, contending the arrangement was inequitable and unfair in that the actual value of the note was far less than that of the offsetting $19,820.80 of community property taken by Mrs. Tammen.

ISSUE: If one party is awarded a major item of community property that is not reasonably subject to division, must the other party be compensated in some manner so as to maintain the required equal division of community property?

HOLDING AND DECISION: (Elkington, J.) Yes. According to Civil Code § 4800, the court may, where economic circumstances warrant, award any asset to one party on such conditions as it deems proper to effect a substantially equal division of the community property. However, if a major item of community property that is not reasonably subject to division is awarded to one party, it is clear that the other party must be compensated in some manner so as to maintain the required equal division. Such was not done in this case, since the actual value of the note is substantially less than its face value. Reversed and remanded.

▶ ANALYSIS

In re Marriage of Herrmann, 84 Cal. App. 3d 361 (1978), was one case in which the appellate court rejected the lower court's idea of using a promissory note to offset an award of the family residence to the wife. It ordered the lower court to put the residence into a tenancy in common that expressly provided for the division of the proceeds upon the happening of various contingencies such as sale of the house.

Quicknotes

COMMUNITY PROPERTY In community property jurisdictions refers to all money or property acquired during the term of the marriage in which each spouse has an undivided one-half interest.

INTERLOCUTORY JUDGMENT An order entered by the court determining an issue that does not resolve the disposition of the case, but is essential to a proper adjudication of the action.

PROMISSORY NOTE A written promise to tender a stated amount of money at a designated time and to a designated person.

Marriage of Eastis
Wife (P) v. Husband (D)

Cal. Ct. App., 47 Cal. App. 3d 459 (1975).

NATURE OF CASE: Action for dissolution of marriage.

FACT SUMMARY: In an action for dissolution of marriage brought by Mrs. Eastis (P), community obligations exceeded community assets.

RULE OF LAW
In an action for dissolution of marriage, "if there are no assets to divide, only obligations, or after the equal division of the assets there remain obligations to be disposed of, the court has the discretion to order the payment of such obligations in a manner that is just and equitable, depending upon the respective earning capacities of the spouses and other relevant factors."

FACTS: After granting Mrs. Eastis (P) dissolution of her marriage to Mr. Eastis (D), the divorce court divided the community property—i.e., assets totaling $5,250 and liabilities of $6,450. Mrs. Eastis (P) was awarded community assets valued at $3,500 and ordered to pay $1,000 in community obligations (i.e., leaving her net assets of $2,500). Mr. Eastis (D) was awarded community assets valued at $1,750 and ordered to pay $5,450 of community obligations (i.e., leaving a net deficit of $3,700). Subsequently, Mr. Eastis (D) appealed the division of community property on the ground that it was not equal.

ISSUE: In an action for dissolution of marriage, where community obligations exceed community assets, is the court required to divide both equally between the spouses?

HOLDING AND DECISION: (Gardner, J.) No. In an action for dissolution of marriage, "if there are no assets to divide, only obligations, or after the equal division of assets there remain obligations to be disposed of, the court has the discretion to order the payment of such obligations in a manner that is just and equitable, depending upon the respective earning capacities of the spouses and other relevant factors." This is true even though the Civil Code provides that "the court shall divide the community property equally" and the California Rules of Court define property as including "assets and obligations." "The definition of property as 'assets and obligations' cannot be tortured to mean simply 'obligations.'" Obligations by themselves are not property but the "complete antithesis of property." As such, obligations should not be considered property subject to equal division when they exceed assets. Here, since the obligations exceeded the assets, the divorce court had the discretion to divide such obligations unequally. However, the judgment must be reversed since the divorce court did not divide the community assets equally. Reversed and remanded.

ANALYSIS

Under the general rule, the divorce court must divide all community property equally. However, as this case points up, the court also has an inherent power to determine which spouse is to pay debts. Note that in *Mayberry v. Whittier*, 144 Cal. 322 (1904), the California Supreme Court stated that a husband's predissolution creditor must first attempt to reach that husband's property before pursuing former community property distributed to his wife upon dissolution.

Quicknotes

ASSET An item of real or personal property that is owned and has tangible value.

COMMUNITY PROPERTY In community property jurisdictions refers to all money or property acquired during the term of the marriage in which each spouse has an undivided one-half interest.

LIABILITY Any obligation or responsibility.

Marriage of Micalizio

Husband (P) v. Wife (D)

Cal. Ct. App., 199 Cal. App. 3d 662 (1988).

NATURE OF CASE: Appeal from the trial court's valuation of closely held stock in an action for marital dissolution.

FACT SUMMARY: After filing for dissolution of his marriage to Gerry Micalizio (D), Robert Micalizio (P) objected to the trial court's final valuation of stock he held in his employer's closely held corporation.

🏛 RULE OF LAW
A court faced with a valuation problem must consider each factor which might have a bearing on the value of the shares.

FACTS: Before and during his marriage to Gerry (D), Robert Micalizio (P) was employed by and held stock in the J.R. Norton Company, a closely held corporation. Before his marriage, Robert (P) financed a stock purchase by executing two promissory notes secured by a pledge of stock, which was issued in his name alone. A corporate buy-sell agreement restricted his ability to transfer or sell the stock to any third person. During the marriage, Gerry (D) wrote checks from a community account to make the principal payments on Robert's (P) promissory notes. After Robert (P) filed for dissolution, evidence showed the value of the stock to be approximately $13 a share. Norton's secretary-treasurer, Stevenson, testified that the value of the stock, assuming Norton liquidated all its assets, would be $25 per share. Finding that the community had contributed a total of 22.5% toward the purchase of the stock, the court also assigned it a value of $13.667 per share. After Gerry (D) filed an amended motion requesting a fair market rather than buy-out valuation, the court concluded that the "real value" of the stock was $25 per share, ordering Robert (P) to execute a promissory note to Gerry (D) to compensate her for her interest. Robert (P) appealed and remanded.

ISSUE: Must a court faced with a valuation problem consider each factor which might have a bearing on the value of the shares?

HOLDING AND DECISION: (Dabney, J.) Yes. A court faced with a valuation problem must consider each factor which might have a bearing on the value of the shares. The court did not consider that Robert (P) owned only a minority block of shares or that he was restricted both as to the price he could obtain for his shares and as to his ability to sell them. Those were factors which have a bearing on the value of the shares. When a trial court accepts an expert's ultimate conclusion without critical consideration of his reasoning, and it appears that the conclusion was based upon improper or unwarranted matters, then the judgment must be reversed for lack of substantial evidence. Here, Mr. Stevenson simply expressed an opinion on a hypothetical situation bearing no relation to the facts and was not asked to consider liquidation costs, contingent liabilities, or similar factors. The trial court is directed to consider whether the community stock should be divided in kind or, if that is not appropriate, to determine the value of the stock in light of the principles set forth in *In re Marriage of Hewitson*, 142 Cal. App. 3d 874 (1983). Reversed and remanded.

▶ ANALYSIS

Hewitson urged the trial court to use the factors listed in the Internal Revenue Service's Revenue Ruling 59-60 (1959)-1 Cum. Bull. 237, unless there is a statutory or decisional proscription against its use. Those factors include the nature and history of the business, the economic outlook in general and the outlook of the specific industry in particular, the book value of the stock and the financial condition of the business, the earning capacity of the company, the dividend-paying capacity, goodwill or other intangible value, sales of stock and the size of the block of stock to be valued, and the market price of similar stocks actively traded in a free and open market. The *Hewitson* court recognized that the value of closely held stock is a difficult legal problem.

■═■

Quicknotes

CLOSELY HELD CORPORATION A corporation whose voting shares are held by a closely knit group of shareholders or a single person.

■═■

Marriage of Harrington

Wife (P) v. Husband (D)

Cal. Ct. App., 6 Cal. App. 4th 1847 (1992).

NATURE OF CASE: Appeal from denial of motion to compel tax payments in marital dissolution action.

FACT SUMMARY: When Judith Harrington (P) failed to defer recognition of the capital gains tax on her share of the profit realized from the sale of the family residence during dissolution, she sought an order requiring Ronald Harrington (D) to pay one-half of the capital gains taxes then due.

🏛 RULE OF LAW
Each party alone is liable for his or her capital gains taxes after division of the community property.

FACTS: Six months after Judith Harrington (P) filed to dissolve her marriage to Ronald Harrington (D), they sold the family residence, realizing a profit of $480,000. They divided the profit equally, and Ronald (D), a lawyer, used part of his proceeds to purchase Judith's (P) community property interest in his law firm and to pay her for her waiver of spousal support. In court proceedings, Ronald (D) declared that he and Judith (P) had orally agreed that each of them alone would be liable for any capital gains income taxes resulting from their equal share in the profit. Ronald (D) successfully deferred capital gains tax on his share of the profit by acquiring a replacement residence for $251,250. Judith (P) purchased a condominium for $120,000 and invested $5,000 in improvements, deferring her capital gains tax on only $125,000 and incurring a tax of $52,000. She sought an order requiring Ronald (D) to pay half. Her motion was denied, and this appeal followed.

ISSUE: Is each party alone liable for his or her capital gains taxes after division of the community property?

HOLDING AND DECISION: (Gilbert, J.) Yes. Each party alone is liable for his or her capital gains taxes after division of the community property. Once the community property is divided equally, the court is not required to speculate about what either party may do with his or her share. The trial court was not required to account for the possibility that either spouse may or may not be able to postpone recognition of capital gains taxes by purchasing a replacement residence within two years. Neither was it required to retain jurisdiction into the indefinite future to consider apportionment of tax liabilities when any capital gains taxes become recognized. Because the trial court's order imposing tax liability upon each party for his or her share of the capital gain was proper as a matter of law, the court does not consider whether Ronald (D) and Judith (P) had a valid oral agreement to apportion tax liability. Affirmed.

▶ ANALYSIS

Civil Code § 4800(a) requires the trial court to distribute assets so that each party receives an equal share, after deduction of community liabilities. Whether either party could defer capital gains depends upon factors unrelated to the equal division of community property. These factors include individual income two years later, individual savings, receipt of gifts or inheritance, ability to borrow money, and other circumstances. Judith (P) claimed, albeit unsuccessfully, that burdening her with 100% of the tax penalized her for her inability to earn as much income as Ronald (D) and that she had acted responsibly by investing in a condominium she could afford, saving the remainder for her present support and future retirement.

Quicknotes

CAPITAL GAIN AND LOSS Gain or loss from the sale or exchange of a capital asset.

TAXABLE GAIN A recognition of increase in income that may be subject to income tax.

TAX ADJUSTMENT An increase or decrease in the amount of tax assigned to reflect the occurrence of events which affect the taxpayer's liability.

Marriage of Varner

Wife (P) v. Husband (D)

Cal. Ct. App., 55 Cal. App. 4th 128 (1997).

NATURE OF CASE: Appeal of order denying motion to set aside judgment of dissolution.

FACT SUMMARY: Kim (P) moved to have a judgment of dissolution, based on a stipulation between the parties, set aside because she claimed that at the time she signed the stipulation her husband, Stephen (D), had failed to disclose to her the extent or the value of the community property at issue.

RULE OF LAW
A judgment of dissolution, based on a stipulation of the parties dividing the community property, will be set aside when one party fails to disclose to the other party the extent or the value of the community property at the time that party signed the stipulation.

FACTS: In May 1992, Kim (P) filed an amended petition for dissolution in which she included a list of 32 items of community property assets that she wanted disposed of by the court. In May 1993, counsel for Kim (P) withdrew. In July 1993, the hearing for dissolution was held. The court denied Kim's (P) request to continue the matter because she did not have counsel. Stephen's (D) attorney argued that the experts Kim (P) had previously hired found the draft judgment to be a fair resolution and that it provided for an unequal division of community property and debts to Stephen's (D) disadvantage. Stephen (D) testified that Kim (P) would end up receiving a net value of $490,000 for their house. Stephen (D) went on to testify that the value of the four parcels of property that would be awarded to him had values of: $60,000 less the cost of sale, $45,000 and subject to tax liability, a $45,000 liability, and $200,000. Stephen (D) also testified that the totality of the various business entities in which he had an interest equaled about $0. He also valued his life insurance policies $0. According to Stephen (P), the total value of the assets to be allocated to Kim (P) was $544,830 and $281,000 for Stephen (D). The trial judge said that this would be a very good disposition of the case for Kim (P), if the figures were correct, and that if he were she, he would take the deal. A week later Kim (P) and Stephen (D) entered a signed settlement agreement, and the judgment of dissolution divided the community property pursuant to the stipulation. Stephen (D) was ordered to pay $6,000 per month as unallocated family support. Kim (P) was awarded nine items of property, and Stephen (D) was awarded twenty-one, including all the real property and assets related to the businesses of the parties. About six month later, Kim's (P) present attorney filed a motion to set aside the stipulation for judgment on the basis of mistake. I.Q. test results and psychological evaluations of Kim (P) were submitted to the court as well as business appraisals which valued two of the businesses at $1,060,000 and not $0. The fair market value of two of the other businesses came in at around $3,111,000 and not $0. Also submitted to the court was a document from an accountant that the wife had previously hired which stated that she had difficulty getting information from Stephen (D) which was necessary to complete her analysis. The motion was denied and Kim (P) appealed contending that Stephen (D) had failed to disclose to her the extent or the value of the community property at the time she signed the stipulation.

ISSUE: Should the judgment have been set aside?

HOLDING AND DECISION: (Ramirez, J.) Yes. The judgment should have been set aside because Stephen (D) had failed to disclose to Kim (P) the extent or the value of the community property at the time she signed the stipulation. A judgment may be set aside for mistake. Spouses have a fiduciary duty to one another. From the date of separation to the date of distribution of the assets of the community, each party to marriage dissolution is subject to the general rules governing the actions of persons occupying confidential relations with each other. Each spouse has a fiduciary obligation as to the accurate and complete disclosure of all assets and liabilities in which the party has, or may have, an interest or obligation and the disclosure of all current earnings, accumulations, and expenses. Based on the relationship between Kim (P) and Stephen (D) and the higher duty of disclosure to which they are held regarding the community property of the marriage, the mistake in the present case warrants the setting aside of the judgment. Stephen (D) breached his duty to provide an accurate and complete disclosure of all assets and liabilities of the parties at the time the negotiations of the stipulated judgment took place. The valuations of the property submitted by experts and the loan applications submitted to banks by Stephen (D) with valuations on them differ significantly from Stephen's (D) trial testimony regarding the valuations. Stephen's (D) lack of disclosure is also evidenced by the testimony of Kim's (P) accountant who stated that she was unable to get relevant information from him. Furthermore, although the stipulation may have been approved by Kim's (P) prior attorney and accountant, their approval was based on questionable information. Moreover, Kim (P) was not represented at trial. Stephen's (D) failure to fully disclose the values of the assets is grounds for setting aside the judgment. Reversed.

Continued on next page.

▶ *ANALYSIS*

The policy goals of ensuring a fair division of community property can be met only if there is a full disclosure of assets.

■▬■

Quicknotes

COMMUNITY PROPERTY In community property jurisdictions refers to all money or property acquired during the term of the marriage in which each spouse has an undivided one-half interest.

FIDUCIARY DUTY A legal obligation to act for the benefit of another, including subordinating one's personal interests to that of the other person.

STIPULATION An agreement by the parties regarding an issue before the court so as to avoid unnecessary expense and delay.

■▬■

Marriage of Kieturakis

Wife (P) v. Husband (D)

Cal. Ct. App., 138 Cal. App. 4th 56 (2006).

NATURE OF CASE: Appeal from order denying motion to set aside a marital settlement agreement.

FACT SUMMARY: The wife tried to undo a property division that was part of a marital settlement agreement reached in mediation, but refused to waive the mediation privilege to allow disclosure of what happened in mediation.

RULE OF LAW
The presumption of undue influence in marital transactions must yield to policies favoring mediation and finality of judgments.

FACTS: Anna (P) and Maciej (D) Kieturakis entered into a marital settlement agreement through mediation. Nearly two years later, Anna (P) sought to undo the property division on grounds of fraud, duress, and lack of disclosure. She refused to waive the mediation privilege to allow disclosure of what happened, however, in an attempt to prevent Maciej (D) from defending himself against her allegations. Maciej (D) had the burden of proof on those charges under the presumption of undue influence related to unequal marital transactions. To avoid that result, the trial court permitted the introduction of evidence from the mediation over Anna's (P) objection, and that evidence defeated Anna's (P) case. She appealed.

ISSUE: Must the presumption of undue influence in marital transactions yield to policies favoring mediation and finality of judgments?

HOLDING AND DECISION: (Reardon, J.) Yes. The presumption of undue influence in marital transactions must yield to policies favoring mediation and finality of judgments. Though the trial court correctly ruled that Maciej (D) should not have been put in a position of shouldering a burden of proof while being denied access to exonerating evidence, the way to avoid such a result was not to intrude upon the mediation, as the trial court did, but to remove the burden of proof from Maciej's (D) shoulders. While there is no dispute that the marital settlement agreement favored Maciej (D), and the spouse advantaged has the burden of dispelling the presumption of undue influence, the presumption of undue influence cannot be applied to the agreement and judgment in this case. First, it cannot be applied to marital settlement agreements reached through mediation, because mediators ensure voluntary participation and self-determination, and it would undermine the practice of mediating such agreements. Second, the presumption of undue influence should not apply where the influence is alleged with respect to a judgment that has been final for more than six months. In

such a case, the party seeking relief from the judgment must bear the burden of proof. Finally, the presumption of undue influence should not attach because the parties acknowledged in the agreement that no undue influence was exercised. Affirmed.

ANALYSIS

Mediation is an increasingly popular avenue toward marital settlement agreements, favored by parties and courts alike. For parties, they can expedite the process of dissolution and property division. And mediation lowers the burdens on court dockets. For those reasons, among other policy reasons, courts favor mediation and tend to protect it.

Quicknotes

BURDEN OF PROOF The duty of a party to introduce evidence to support a fact that is in dispute in an action.

MEDIATION A process of alternative dispute resolution engaged in before trial by the parties to a lawsuit either voluntarily or by court order in an attempt to resolve the case.

PRESUMPTION A rule of law requiring the court to presume certain facts to be true based on the existence of other facts, thereby shifting the burden of proof to the party against whom the presumption is asserted to rebut.

UNDUE INFLUENCE Improper persuasion that deprives an individual of freedom of choice.

Marriage of Rossi

Wife (P) v. Husband (D)

Cal. Ct. App., 90 Cal. App. 4th 34 (2001).

NATURE OF CASE: Appeal from a postjudgment property disposition order in a marital dissolution suit.

FACT SUMMARY: In a marital dissolution proceeding, Denise Rossi (P) fraudulently concealed her $1,336,000 lottery winnings, as a result of which the trial court, when the fraud became known, awarded 100 percent of the amount to her husband, Thomas (D).

> 🏛 **RULE OF LAW**
> In a marital dissolution proceeding, a spouse may be awarded 100 percent of any asset which the other spouse fails to disclose or transfers in breach of her marital fiduciary duties.

FACTS: In a marital dissolution proceeding, the trial court awarded all of the $1,336,000 lottery winnings concealed by wife, Denise Rossi (P), during the proceedings to ex-husband, Thomas Rossi (D). The trial court held that substantial evidence supported its findings that the concealment constituted fraud under California Civil Code § 3294 and came within the penalty provisions of California Family Code § 1101(h) which provided that a breach of fiduciary duties by a spouse may give rise to an award to the other spouse of 100 percent of any undisclosed asset. The trial court expressly found that Denise (P) intentionally failed to disclose her lottery winnings in the marital settlement agreement, the judgment, and her declaration of disclosure. Furthermore, she intentionally consulted with the Lottery Commission as to how to deprive Thomas (D) of a share of the prize, used her mother's address for all communications with the lottery officials, and did not disclose the winnings in the dissolution proceedings. Denise (P) appealed.

ISSUE: In a marital dissolution proceeding, may a spouse be awarded 100 percent of any asset which the other spouse fails to disclose or transfers in breach of her marital fiduciary duties?

HOLDING AND DECISION: (Epstein, J.) Yes. In a marital dissolution proceeding, a spouse may be awarded 100 percent of any asset which the other spouse fails to disclose or transfers in breach of her marital fiduciary duties. Here, the evidence established that Denise (P) filed for dissolution after learning that she had won a share of a substantial lottery jackpot; that she consulted the Lottery Commission personnel about ways in which she could avoid sharing the jackpot with her husband, Thomas (D); that she used her mother's address for all communications with the Lottery Commission to avoid notifying Thomas (D) of her winnings; and that she failed to disclose the winnings at any time during the dissolution proceedings despite her warranties in the marital settlement agreement and the judgment that all her assets had been disclosed. The family court expressly rejected her evidence that the winnings constituted a gift and, as such, were her separate property. The record supported the family court's conclusion that Denise (P) intentionally and fraudulently concealed the lottery winnings and that they were community property. Judgment is affirmed.

> ▶ **ANALYSIS**

In the *Rossi* case, the court noted that nothing in the language of the statute justified an exception to the penalty provision of Family Code § 1101(h) because of the supposed unclean hands of the spouse from whom the asset was concealed. Nor did any legislative history suggest such an exception. This undercut Denise's (P) primary argument on appeal that she was justified in concealing the lottery winnings because of Thomas's (D) behavior. The plain meaning of Family Code § 1101(h) disposed of her argument that there should be a "downward departure in any remedy against Denise" because, as she claimed, she was battered emotionally and physically by Thomas (D).

Quicknotes

FIDUCIARY DUTY A legal obligation to act for the benefit of another, including subordinating one's personal interests to that of the other person.

FRAUDULENT CONCEALMENT The concealing of a material fact that a party is under an obligation to disclose.

SEPARATE PROPERTY Property owned by one spouse prior to marriage, or any income derived therefrom, and any property received by one spouse pursuant to a gift, devise, bequest or descent.

WARRANTY An assurance by one party that another may rely on a certain representation of fact.

Henn v. Henn

Husband (P) v. Wife (D)

Cal. Sup. Ct., 26 Cal.3d 323, 605 P.2d 10 (1980).

NATURE OF CASE: Action seeking to have an asset declared community property and seeking its division.

FACT SUMMARY: In response to Mr. Henn's (P) motion to reduce her spousal support five years after her marriage was dissolved, Mrs. Henn (D) sought both a declaration that Mr. Henn's (P) military pension was community property and an order dividing it as such.

🏛 **RULE OF LAW**
Property which is not mentioned in the pleadings as community property is left unadjudicated by decree of divorce or dissolution, and is subject to future litigation, the parties being tenants in common meanwhile.

FACTS: In response to a motion filed by Mr. Henn (P), five years after dissolution, to reduce Mrs. Henn's (D) spousal support, Mrs. Henn (D) moved for a determination that a fully matured federal military retirement pension that Mr. Henn (P) had been receiving at the time of the interlocutory decree was community property, and that it should be divided as such. The pension had not been adjudicated or distributed in the dissolution. Mrs. Henn (D) had moved 2½ years earlier for an order to show cause why Mr. Henn's (P) retirement pension should not be divided as community property, such being in response to Mr. Henn's (P) motion to reduce spousal support. Her motion had been denied without opinion. After a judgment in favor of Mr. Henn (P), Mrs. Henn (D) appealed.

ISSUE: Is property that is not mentioned in the pleadings as community property left unadjudicated by decree of dissolution and thus subject to future litigation?

HOLDING AND DECISION: (Bird, J.) Yes. Under settled principles of California community property law, property which is not mentioned in the pleadings as community property is left unadjudicated by decree of divorce or dissolution and is thus subject to future litigation, the parties being tenants in common meanwhile. This rule applies to partial divisions of community property as well as divorces or dissolutions unaccompanied by any property adjudication whatsoever. There are no reported decisions holding that a community property asset left unmentioned in a prior judicial division of community property may be adjudicated in a motion to modify the prior decree. Thus, the denial of Mrs. Henn's (D) motion some 2½ years ago is no bar to her present action. Reversed.

▶ *ANALYSIS*

Prior to the Family Law Act, case law had set up an exception which specified that if the complaint had alleged there was no community property and a default judgment was entered, the decree was in fact adjudication as to this effect. However, in *Irwin v. Irwin*, 69 Cal.App.3d 317 (1977), the court held that in checking the box on a dissolution petition stating that "(t)here is no property subject to disposition by the court in this proceeding," the wife was merely reserving her right to have that issue resolved in a later proceeding and so the aforementioned exception did not apply.

■■■

Quicknotes

COMMUNITY PROPERTY In community property jurisdictions refers to all money or property acquired during the term of the marriage in which each spouse has an undivided one-half interest.

INTERLOCUTORY ORDER An order entered by the court determining an issue that does not resolve the disposition of the case, but is essential to a proper adjudication of the action.

TENANTS IN COMMON Two or more people holding an interest in property, each with equal right to its use and possession; interests may be partitioned, sold, conveyed, or devised.

■■■

Aloy v. Mash

Client (P) v. Attorney (D)

Cal. Sup. Ct., 38 Cal. 3d 413, 696 P.2d 656 (1985).

NATURE OF CASE: Appeal from summary judgment denying damages for legal malpractice.

FACT SUMMARY: In Aloy's (P) action against Mash (D), her former attorney in a dissolution action against Aloy's (P) husband, Aloy (P) contended that Mash (D) negligently failed to assert her community property interest in her husband's military retirement pension, which failure prevented her from receiving any share of his gross military retirement benefits.

🏛 RULE OF LAW
An attorney assumes an obligation to his client to undertake reasonable research in an effort to ascertain relevant legal principles and to make an informed decision as to a course of conduct based upon intelligent assessment of the problem.

FACTS: Aloy (P) employed Mash (D) in January 1971, to represent her in a dissolution action against her husband, Richard. Richard was on active military service and not receiving a pension although he was eligible to retire. Mash (D) failed to claim any community property interest in Richard's pension, and it was not put in issue in the dissolution action. The dissolution became final in December 1971, and Richard retired sometime between 1971 and 1980. In 1980 Aloy (P) filed an action against Mash (D), alleging that he negligently failed to assert her community property interest in Richard's pension, which prevented her from receiving any share of the pension benefits. Mash (D) moved for summary judgment on the ground that in 1971, the law regarding the character of federal military retirement pensions was unsettled, and that he had exercised informed judgment and was thus immune from a claim of professional negligence. The court granted Mash's (D) motion on the ground that no issue of triable fact existed, and Aloy (P) appealed.

ISSUE: Does an attorney assume an obligation to his client to undertake reasonable research in an effort to ascertain relevant legal principles and to make an informed decision as to a course of conduct based upon intelligent assessment of the problem?

HOLDING AND DECISION: (Kaus, J.) Yes. An attorney assumes an obligation to his client to undertake reasonable research in an effort to ascertain relevant legal principles and to make an informed decision as to a course of conduct based upon intelligent assessment of the problem. Here, Mash (D) relied on a single case, *French v. French* 17 Cal. 2d 775 (1941), for the proposition that a non-matured military pension was not subject to division upon dissolution. He thus never gave himself a chance to consider whether his client was entitled to a community share in monthly payments which, but for Richard's election not to retire, would have been vested pension payments. Mash (D) failed to act, on an incomplete reading of a single case, without appreciating the vital difference between a member of the armed forces who has not yet served long enough to be eligible to retire and one who has, but chooses to stay in the service. In sum, the record on which the motion for summary judgment was argued presented a trickle issue of negligence. Reversed and remanded.

DISSENT: (Reynoso, J.) With the exception of the majority opinion, there is no case which suggests that an attorney whose advice is correct may be held liable for malpractice. It is imperative that a lawyer remain free to choose one of a number of reasonable and legally supportable solutions to an otherwise unsettled legal question and advise the client accordingly without facing a malpractice suit.

▌ *ANALYSIS*

In *Aloy*, the court relied on the standard developed in *Smith v. Lewis* 13 Cal. 3d 349 (1975). Prior to *Smith*, attorneys in California were not liable for lack of knowledge as to the true state of the law where a doubtful point was involved. *Smith* modified that rule so that even with regard to an unsettled area of the law an attorney is obligated to undertake reasonable research in an effort to ascertain relevant legal principles and to make an informed decision.

Quicknotes

COMMUNITY PROPERTY In community property jurisdictions, refers to all money or property acquired during the term of the marriage in which each spouse has an undivided one-half interest.

SUMMARY JUDGMENT Judgment rendered by a court in response to a motion made by one of the parties, claiming that the lack of a question of material fact in respect to an issue warrants disposition of the issue without consideration by the jury.

VESTED INTEREST A present right to property, although the right to the possession of such property may not be enjoyed until a future date.

CHAPTER 7

Distribution of Community Property at Death

Quick Reference Rules of Law

Dawes v. Rich

Cal. Ct. App., 60 Cal. App. 4th 24 (1997).

NATURE OF CASE: Suit to rescind rent increases.

FACT SUMMARY: Tenants of a mobile home park owned by a company in which Dawes was a general partner sought to recover judgments entered against Dawes from the assets of certain trusts.

🏛 RULE OF LAW
Upon the death of a spouse, the marital community remains liable for debts incurred by either spouse before or during the marriage.

FACTS: Rancho Carlsbad Mobile Home Park was owned by Western Land & Development Company, a general partnership consisting of Dawes and Schwab. The tenants of the park commenced litigation against Western, Dawes and Schwab with respect to rent increases Western attempted to impose on the tenants. Prior to this time, Dawes and his wife transferred their community property to a revocable inter vivos trust. The trust instrument provided that upon the death of one of the spouses the property would pass into three separate trusts. Dorothy Dawes died in 1990 and the term of the trust became operative. Subsequently, judgments in the three actions were entered against Dawes. Dawes filed bankruptcy petitions and the tenants levied writs of execution on defendants and on David and Stuart Dawes as trustees of the B and C trusts. The trustees then filed a petition in probate court seeking a determination that the trust assets were not subject to execution on the tenants' judgment. The probate court entered judgment in favor of the trustees. The tenants appealed.

ISSUE: Upon the death of a spouse, does the marital community remain liable for debts incurred by either spouse before or during the marriage?

HOLDING AND DECISION: (Benke, J.) Yes. Upon the death of a spouse, the marital community remains liable for debts incurred by either spouse before or during the marriage. The tenants on appeal contend that the assets held in the B and C trusts are liable for the judgments entered against Dawes and the liability of the assets was asserted in a timely manner. In 1984 former Civil Code § 5120.160 was enacted, materially altering the continuance of liability of spouses for community debts incurred by former spouses. When a community estate is terminated by reason of death, however, community debts are treated differently. Under Probate Code § 11444, the surviving spouse, the personal representative or an interested party may petition the court for an allocation of debts between the surviving spouse and the deceased's estate and the personal representative and the surviving spouse may agree to an allocation. In the absence of such an agreement, the probate court is required to apportion the debt between the surviving spouse and the estate on the same basis it would be required to employ during marriage. When a deceased spouse's property is not subject to any administration but passes directly to the surviving spouse, the surviving spouse's liability for debts incurred by the deceased is governed by Probate Code § 13550 et seq. Under § 13550, the surviving spouse is personally liable in that case for the debts of the deceased chargeable against the property described in § 13551 to the extent provided in that section. Section 13551 provides that liability is not to exceed the fair market value of the community property and the decedent's separate property that passed to the survivor. Claims brought under this section must be brought within one year from the death of the deceased spouse. The problem posed here, the liability of a deceased spouse's estate for community debts incurred by a surviving spouse, are not addressed by statute. We agree with the tenants insofar as they argue the trustees did not receive Dorothy's share entirely free from liability. We find that any liability arising from the transfer of the community property upon the death of Dorothy was a personal liability subject to the time limitations set forth in former Code of Civil Procedure § 353(d). Because the levies of execution and declaratory relief action were not filed within those time limits, the probate court and trial court did not err in entering judgment in favor of the trustees. Affirmed.

▶ ANALYSIS

The rule prior to 1984 provided that one spouse who received community property following termination of the marriage was subject to liability for community debts incurred by the other spouse during the marriage whether such termination was due to death or divorce.

■■■

Quicknotes

BANKRUPTCY A legal proceeding whereby a debtor, who is unable to pay his debts as they become due, is relieved of his obligation to pay his creditors either by liquidation and distribution of his remaining assets or through reorganization and payment from future income.

COMMUNITY PROPERTY In community property jurisdictions refers to all money or property acquired during the term of the marriage in which each spouse has an undivided one-half interest.

INTER VIVOS TRUST Property that is held by one person for the benefit of another and which is created by an instrument that takes effect during the life of the grantor.

PROBATE The administration of a decedent's estate.

■■■

Collection Bureau of San Jose v. Rumsey

Collection agency (P) v. Husband of deceased debtor (D)

Cal. Sup. Ct., 24 Cal. 4th 301, 6 P.3d 713 (2000).

NATURE OF CASE: Appeal of statutory limitations determination in a collection action.

FACT SUMMARY: Collection (P) sued Rumsey (D) for medical bills incurred by his deceased wife. Rumsey (D) argued that a one-year, and not a four-year, statute of limitations applied to the suit.

🏛 RULE OF LAW
The one-year statutory limitations provision of the Probate Code exclusively controls an action to recover the medical expenses of a deceased debtor spouse from the surviving spouse.

FACTS: Collection (P) sued Rumsey (D) for recovery of $103,715.95 in medical bills incurred by Rumsey's wife, prior to her death, for the treatment of cancer. Technically, accounts receivables for medical expenses are open book accounts entitled to a four-year statute of limitations according to the Code of Civil Procedure. Collection (P) filed its action just before the expiration of the four-year period. However, the Code of Civil Procedure also specifies a one-year limitations period for surviving causes of action on the liability of decedents. The Probate Code states that the one-year limitations period of the Code of Civil Procedure is applicable to actions against the surviving spouse for debts remaining unpaid upon the death of the debtor spouse. Rumsey (D) thus asserted that Collection's (P) action was time barred. The trial court found the Probate Code provisions controlled, and barred Collection's (P) suit because it had not been filed within the one-year limitations period. Collection (P) appealed and the court of appeal reversed holding that although Collection's (P) suit was barred by the one-year statute of limitations period, an entirely separate and independent cause of action for recovery of the debt from the surviving spouse existed in the Family Code which makes a spouse personally liable for the other's debts incurred for the necessaries of life. It reasoned that Collection's (P) suit was, therefore, timely because it was filed within the four-year limitations period prescribed for open book accounts in the Code of Civil Procedure. Rumsey (D) appealed.

ISSUE: Which statute of limitations governs an action by a collection agency against a surviving spouse for recovery of the hospital and medical expense incurred by a deceased spouse?

HOLDING AND DECISION: (Baxter, J.) The one-year statutory limitations provision of the Probate Code exclusively controls an action to recover the medical expenses of a deceased debtor spouse from the surviving

spouse. The Probate Code makes a surviving spouse personally liable for the debts of the deceased spouse only to the extent such debts are chargeable against the community property of both spouses, and the separate property of the deceased spouse passes to the surviving spouse without formal probate administration. The Probate Code makes applicable to such actions the Code of Civil Procedure which states that an action may be commenced within one year after the date of death. The one-year statute of limitations was intended to apply in any action on a debt of the decedent regardless of whom the action was brought against. In this case, therefore, Rumsey (D) was personally liable for the debts left behind by his deceased spouse to the extent of his own share of the community property, and those portions of his deceased spouse's share of the community property and her separate property that passed to him without formal administration. Collection (P) had one year from the date of death of Rumsey's wife within which to file an action against her estate or Rumsey (D). Collection (P), however, waited more than a year in reliance on the Family Code's four-year statue of limitations. The Family Code's provisions of personal liability of the surviving spouse for debts incurred for the necessaries of life by a deceased's spouse, and its attending four-year statute of limitations, does not apply because it was the intent of the Legislature for the one-year statute of limitations to apply to a case such as Rumsey's (D). Such intent is evident in the plain language of the Probate Code, which states that the one-year limitations period of the Code of Civil Procedure is applicable to actions against the surviving spouse for any debt remaining unpaid upon the death of the debtor spouse. Furthermore, the Probate Code also controls because it is more specific on the issue as opposed to the Family Code. The Probate Code provisions specifically address the liability of a married person for the debts incurred by the other spouse upon the death of that spouse, whereas the Family Code merely addresses the general liability of a spouse for the debts the other spouse incurred during the marriage. The Probate Code also prescribes the limitations period for surviving causes of action on the liabilities of decedents, whereas the Family Code just sets forth a four-year limitations period generally applicable to all open book accounts. Furthermore, the Probate Code controls since it is a later enactment. In addition, the Family Code does not apply because it is directed towards the necessaries of life incurred during the marriage, not debts incurred after the community is terminated by death and the availability of the non-debtor spouse's separate property to satisfy those debts. Thus, if the provisions of the Family Code did apply, a creditor could

Continued on next page.

look to the surviving spouse's personal property for up to four years, but only to the rest of the property for one year. In addition, a conclusion that an action can be brought pursuant to the Family Code for up to four years against a surviving spouse to recover on a deceased spouse's debt for necessaries of life would be in conflict with the surviving spouse's right of reimbursement and the prescribed periods in which that right must be exercised. Although the Family Code makes a married person personally liable for any debts incurred by their spouse for the necessaries of life, that liability is derivative of the marital relationship. Reversed.

DISSENT: (Werdegar, J.) The four-year statue of limitations governed. It is the job of the Legislature, and not the court, to shorten the period within which creditors may sue a surviving spouse on obligations incurred for necessaries of life. Nothing in the Family Code suggests that such liability disappears when the spouse dies. Furthermore, the actions in the Probate Code and Family Code are independent. In addition, there is no basis for the majority's conclusion that the married person's right to reimbursement limits the creditor's right to satisfaction of the obligation. The majority also does not acknowledge the conditional nature of a married person's reimbursement right.

▌ *ANALYSIS*

The Legislative intent behind the Code of Civil Procedure was expeditious estate administration and security of title.

■══■

Quicknotes

STATUTE OF LIMITATIONS A law prescribing the period in which a legal action may be commenced.

■══■

Estate of Prager

Divisee of Estate (P) v. Wife of deceased (D)

Cal. Sup. Ct., 166 Cal. 450, 137 P. 37 (1913).

NATURE OF CASE: Appeal from a decree of distribution.

FACT SUMMARY: Mary Prager (D) (surviving widow) claimed her right to one-half of the community property, as well as the gifts to her in Charles Prager's will.

🏛 RULE OF LAW
A surviving widow may succeed to property bequeathed to her by will as well as one-half of the community property.

FACTS: Charles Prager died, leaving all of his real property situated in Los Angeles to his brother, nephews and nieces, and everything else to his wife Mary (D). Mary (D) claimed that she could take the residuary gift and one-half of the community assets bequeathed to others. Fannie Prager Cohn (devisee) (P) contended that by taking one-half of the community, Mary (D) was precluded from taking under the will as well.

ISSUE: Can a surviving widow take her one-half share of the community property even if she took property bequeathed to her by will from her husband?

HOLDING AND DECISION: (Sloss, J.) Yes. A surviving widow may succeed to property bequeathed to her by will, as well as one-half of the community property. Testator is presumed to understand that he could not devise more than one-half of the community property. He is also presumed not to have intended to bequeath that which would have vested in his spouse automatically. A surviving widow is forced to elect only whether to take according to the will or her statutory share where the testator demonstrates intent that the gift in the will is in lieu of her community property share. Since Charles Prager's will does not declare any of Mary's (D) gifts are in lieu of her share, she may take her community property share as well as her gifts. Judgment affirmed.

▶ ANALYSIS

The need to make an election arises only when one spouse bequeaths more than is actually his to give. For instance, in a case where an insurance policy names a wife as beneficiary but all of the community is left to others, the wife must elect whether to renounce her gift and take her statutory share, or to keep the gift and let the property be distributed as the husband directed. Of course, a spouse can give more than what is required by law. The crucial point is whether the testator indicated intent to leave a particular piece of property instead of that spouse's share.

Quicknotes

COMMUNITY PROPERTY In community property jurisdictions refers to all money or property acquired during the term of the marriage in which each spouse has an undivided one-half interest.

DEVISEE A person upon whom a gift of real or personal property is conferred by means of a testamentary instrument.

REAL PROPERTY Land, an interest in land, or anything attached to the land that is incapable of being removed.

TESTATOR One who executes a will.

Glossary

Common Latin Words and Phrases Encountered in the Law

A FORTIORI: Because one fact exists or has been proven, therefore a second fact that is related to the first fact must also exist.

A PRIORI: From the cause to the effect. A term of logic used to denote that when one generally accepted truth is shown to be a cause, another particular effect must necessarily follow.

AB INITIO: From the beginning; a condition which has existed throughout, as in a marriage which was void ab initio.

ACTUS REUS: The wrongful act; in criminal law, such action sufficient to trigger criminal liability.

AD VALOREM: According to value; an ad valorem tax is imposed upon an item located within the taxing jurisdiction calculated by the value of such item.

AMICUS CURIAE: Friend of the court. Its most common usage takes the form of an amicus curiae brief, filed by a person who is not a party to an action but is nonetheless allowed to offer an argument supporting his legal interests.

ARGUENDO: In arguing. A statement, possibly hypothetical, made for the purpose of argument, is one made arguendo.

BILL QUIA TIMET: A bill to quiet title (establish ownership) to real property.

BONA FIDE: True, honest, or genuine. May refer to a person's legal position based on good faith or lacking notice of fraud (such as a bona fide purchaser for value) or to the authenticity of a particular document (such as a bona fide last will and testament).

CAUSA MORTIS: With approaching death in mind. A gift causa mortis is a gift given by a party who feels certain that death is imminent.

CAVEAT EMPTOR: Let the buyer beware. This maxim is reflected in the rule of law that a buyer purchases at his own risk because it is his responsibility to examine, judge, test, and otherwise inspect what he is buying.

CERTIORARI: A writ of review. Petitions for review of a case by the United States Supreme Court are most often done by means of a writ of certiorari.

CONTRA: On the other hand. Opposite. Contrary to.

CORAM NOBIS: Before us; writs of error directed to the court that originally rendered the judgment.

CORAM VOBIS: Before you; writs of error directed by an appellate court to a lower court to correct a factual error.

CORPUS DELICTI: The body of the crime; the requisite elements of a crime amounting to objective proof that a crime has been committed.

CUM TESTAMENTO ANNEXO, ADMINISTRATOR (ADMINISTRATOR C.T.A.): With will annexed; an administrator c.t.a. settles an estate pursuant to a will in which he is not appointed.

DE BONIS NON, ADMINISTRATOR (ADMINISTRATOR D.B.N.): Of goods not administered; an administrator d.b.n. settles a partially settled estate.

DE FACTO: In fact; in reality; actually. Existing in fact but not officially approved or engendered.

DE JURE: By right; lawful. Describes a condition that is legitimate "as a matter of law," in contrast to the term "de facto," which connotes something existing in fact but not legally sanctioned or authorized. For example, de facto segregation refers to segregation brought about by housing patterns, etc., whereas de jure segregation refers to segregation created by law.

DE MINIMIS: Of minimal importance; insignificant; a trifle; not worth bothering about.

DE NOVO: Anew; a second time; afresh. A trial de novo is a new trial held at the appellate level as if the case originated there and the trial at a lower level had not taken place.

DICTA: Generally used as an abbreviated form of obiter dicta, a term describing those portions of a judicial opinion incidental or not necessary to resolution of the specific question before the court. Such nonessential statements and remarks are not considered to be binding precedent.

DUCES TECUM: Refers to a particular type of writ or subpoena requesting a party or organization to produce certain documents in their possession.

EN BANC: Full bench. Where a court sits with all justices present rather than the usual quorum.

EX PARTE: For one side or one party only. An ex parte proceeding is one undertaken for the benefit of only one party, without notice to, or an appearance by, an adverse party.

EX POST FACTO: After the fact. An ex post facto law is a law that retroactively changes the consequences of a prior act.

EX REL.: Abbreviated form of the term ex relatione, meaning upon relation or information. When the state brings an action in which it has no interest against an individual at the instigation of one who has a private interest in the matter.

FORUM NON CONVENIENS: Inconvenient forum. Although a court may have jurisdiction over the case, the action should be tried in a more conveniently located court, one to which parties and witnesses may more easily travel, for example.

GUARDIAN AD LITEM: A guardian of an infant as to litigation, appointed to represent the infant and pursue his/her rights.

HABEAS CORPUS: You have the body. The modern writ of habeas corpus is a writ directing that a person (body)

129

being detained (such as a prisoner) be brought before the court so that the legality of his detention can be judicially ascertained.

IN CAMERA: In private, in chambers. When a hearing is held before a judge in his chambers or when all spectators are excluded from the courtroom.

IN FORMA PAUPERIS: In the manner of a pauper. A party who proceeds in forma pauperis because of his poverty is one who is allowed to bring suit without liability for costs.

INFRA: Below, under. A word referring the reader to a later part of a book. (The opposite of supra.)

IN LOCO PARENTIS: In the place of a parent.

IN PARI DELICTO: Equally wrong; a court of equity will not grant requested relief to an applicant who is in pari delicto, or as much at fault in the transactions giving rise to the controversy as is the opponent of the applicant.

IN PARI MATERIA: On like subject matter or upon the same matter. Statutes relating to the same person or things are said to be in pari materia. It is a general rule of statutory construction that such statutes should be construed together, i.e., looked at as if they together constituted one law.

IN PERSONAM: Against the person. Jurisdiction over the person of an individual.

IN RE: In the matter of. Used to designate a proceeding involving an estate or other property.

IN REM: A term that signifies an action against the res, or thing. An action in rem is basically one that is taken directly against property, as distinguished from an action in personam, i.e., against the person.

INTER ALIA: Among other things. Used to show that the whole of a statement, pleading, list, statute, etc., has not been set forth in its entirety.

INTER PARTES: Between the parties. May refer to contracts, conveyances or other transactions having legal significance.

INTER VIVOS: Between the living. An inter vivos gift is a gift made by a living grantor, as distinguished from bequests contained in a will, which pass upon the death of the testator.

IPSO FACTO: By the mere fact itself.

JUS: Law or the entire body of law.

LEX LOCI: The law of the place; the notion that the rights of parties to a legal proceeding are governed by the law of the place where those rights arose.

MALUM IN SE: Evil or wrong in and of itself; inherently wrong. This term describes an act that is wrong by its very nature, as opposed to one which would not be wrong but for the fact that there is a specific legal prohibition against it (malum prohibitum).

MALUM PROHIBITUM: Wrong because prohibited, but not inherently evil. Used to describe something that is wrong because it is expressly forbidden by law but that is not in and of itself evil, e.g., speeding.

MANDAMUS: We command. A writ directing an official to take a certain action.

MENS REA: A guilty mind; a criminal intent. A term used to signify the mental state that accompanies a crime or other prohibited act. Some crimes require only a general mens rea (general intent to do the prohibited act), but others, like assault with intent to murder, require the existence of a specific mens rea.

MODUS OPERANDI: Method of operating; generally refers to the manner or style of a criminal in committing crimes, admissible in appropriate cases as evidence of the identity of a defendant.

NEXUS: A connection to.

NISI PRIUS: A court of first impression. A nisi prius court is one where issues of fact are tried before a judge or jury.

N.O.V. (NON OBSTANTE VEREDICTO): Notwithstanding the verdict. A judgment n.o.v. is a judgment given in favor of one party despite the fact that a verdict was returned in favor of the other party, the justification being that the verdict either had no reasonable support in fact or was contrary to law.

NUNC PRO TUNC: Now for then. This phrase refers to actions that may be taken and will then have full retroactive effect.

PENDENTE LITE: Pending the suit; pending litigation underway.

PER CAPITA: By head; beneficiaries of an estate, if they take in equal shares, take per capita.

PER CURIAM: By the court; signifies an opinion ostensibly written "by the whole court" and with no identified author.

PER SE: By itself, in itself; inherently.

PER STIRPES: By representation. Used primarily in the law of wills to describe the method of distribution where a person, generally because of death, is unable to take that which is left to him by the will of another, and therefore his heirs divide such property between them rather than take under the will individually.

PRIMA FACIE: On its face, at first sight. A prima facie case is one that is sufficient on its face, meaning that the evidence supporting it is adequate to establish the case until contradicted or overcome by other evidence.

PRO TANTO: For so much; as far as it goes. Often used in eminent domain cases when a property owner receives partial payment for his land without prejudice to his right to bring suit for the full amount he claims his land to be worth.

QUANTUM MERUIT: As much as he deserves. Refers to recovery based on the doctrine of unjust enrichment in those cases in which a party has rendered valuable services or furnished materials that were accepted and enjoyed by another under circumstances that would reasonably notify the recipient that the rendering party expected to be paid. In essence, the law implies a contract to pay the reasonable value of the services or materials furnished.

QUASI: Almost like; as if; nearly. This term is essentially used to signify that one subject or thing is almost analogous to another but that material differences between them do exist. For example, a quasi-criminal proceeding is one that is not strictly criminal but shares enough of the same characteristics to require some of the same safeguards (e.g., procedural due process must be followed in a parole hearing).

QUID PRO QUO: Something for something. In contract law, the consideration, something of value, passed between the parties to render the contract binding.

RES GESTAE: Things done; in evidence law, this principle justifies the admission of a statement that would otherwise be hearsay when it is made so closely to the event in question as to be said to be a part of it, or with such spontaneity as not to have the possibility of falsehood.

RES IPSA LOQUITUR: The thing speaks for itself. This doctrine gives rise to a rebuttable presumption of negligence when the instrumentality causing the injury was within the exclusive control of the defendant, and the injury was one that does not normally occur unless a person has been negligent.

RES JUDICATA: A matter adjudged. Doctrine which provides that once a court of competent jurisdiction has rendered a final judgment or decree on the merits, that judgment or decree is conclusive upon the parties to the case and prevents them from engaging in any other litigation on the points and issues determined therein.

RESPONDEAT SUPERIOR: Let the master reply. This doctrine holds the master liable for the wrongful acts of his servant (or the principal for his agent) in those cases in which the servant (or agent) was acting within the scope of his authority at the time of the injury.

STARE DECISIS: To stand by or adhere to that which has been decided. The common law doctrine of stare decisis attempts to give security and certainty to the law by following the policy that once a principle of law as applicable to a certain set of facts has been set forth in a decision, it forms a precedent which will subsequently be followed, even though a different decision might be made were it the first time the question had arisen. Of course, stare decisis is not an inviolable principle and is departed from in instances where there is good cause (e.g., considerations of public policy led the Supreme Court to disregard prior decisions sanctioning segregation).

SUPRA: Above. A word referring a reader to an earlier part of a book.

ULTRA VIRES: Beyond the power. This phrase is most commonly used to refer to actions taken by a corporation that are beyond the power or legal authority of the corporation.

Addendum of French Derivatives

IN PAIS: Not pursuant to legal proceedings.

CHATTEL: Tangible personal property.

CY PRES: Doctrine permitting courts to apply trust funds to purposes not expressed in the trust but necessary to carry out the settlor's intent.

PER AUTRE VIE: For another's life; during another's life. In property law, an estate may be granted that will terminate upon the death of someone other than the grantee.

PROFIT A PRENDRE: A license to remove minerals or other produce from land.

VOIR DIRE: Process of questioning jurors as to their predispositions about the case or parties to a proceeding in order to identify those jurors displaying bias or prejudice.

Casenote Legal Briefs